# THE POET'S CRAFT

Poetry is not like reasoning, a power to be exerted according to the determination of the will. A man cannot say, 'I will compose poetry'.

SHELLEY

That talk of inspiration is sheer nonsense; there is no such thing. It is a mere matter of craftsmanship.

WILLIAM MORRIS

Deux sortes de vers: les vers donnés et les vers calculés.

PAUL VALÉRY

# THE POET'S CRAFT

## A COURSE IN THE
## CRITICAL APPRECIATION OF POETRY

*based on the study of holograph manuscripts,*
*earlier and later versions of printed poems,*
*transpositions of prose into verse,*
*and contrasted translations*

BY

## A. F. SCOTT

WITH A SELECTION OF
UNSIGNED POEMS AND PASSAGES
FOR APPRECIATION

NEW YORK
DOVER PUBLICATIONS, INC.

Published in Canada by General Publishing
Company, Ltd., 30 Lesmill Road, Don Mills,
Toronto, Ontario.

Published in the United Kingdom by Constable
and Company, Ltd., 10 Orange Street, London,
W.C. 2.

This Dover edition, first published in 1967, is an
unabridged republication of the work first published by the Cambridge University Press in 1957.
A paper identifying the poems in Section V, formerly available separately, has been incorporated
into the present edition, where it occupies pages
219 through 222.

This edition is reprinted by permission of the
Cambridge University Press.

*Library of Congress Catalog Card Number: 66-20415*

Manufactured in the United States of America
Dover Publications, Inc.
180 Varick Street
New York, N.Y. 10014

# CONTENTS

v

## II. THE POET'S PRINTED REVISIONS

A selection of poems and passages of the first edition
compared with a revised, later edition

## III. THE POET'S RAW MATERIAL

Material adapted by the poet, presented for
comparison with the poetry

# IV. THE POET'S TRANSLATION

Selected translations of the same poems
for comparison

# CONTENTS

# PREFACE

Browning's Grammarian exclaimed:

> Show me their shaping,
> Theirs, who most studied man, the bard and sage.

This book tries in several different ways to present the 'shaping' of the poets by a close study of their use of language.

The first section consists of reproductions of manuscript poems; Section I many of these are of the original drafts, showing the corrections made as the poem was being composed. A study of these manuscripts gives an insight into the poet's mind and a personal contact not achieved from the printed page alone. We see, as it were, the hand moving across the page expressing thoughts and afterthoughts. We see a word struck out immediately after it was written down and another set in its place, following on at once with a second thought. Sometimes the correction denotes a change of mind; other corrections made above the line or in the margin are obviously not done immediately, but are later additions or substitutions.

It is interesting to note how the work of correction is often quite as inspired as 'the first onrush of words and ideas'. As we examine these manuscript poems we feel with C. M. Bowra that 'the poet must be his own critic and decide which are the right words among the many which come to him; he must exclude much that at first sight looks attractive, and adapt the outpourings of inspiration to the creative impulse which animates his poem'.

To these manuscript poems are added brief notes, and a literal transcription of the text.

The next section presents, for purposes of comparison, the first Section II published version of several well-known poems with the more widely accepted revised version. A brief history of the changes is given so that we may follow some of the poems over a period of years.

SECTION
III
The third section deals with the raw material used by the poet. As Sir Henry Newbolt says,

The more a writer struggles to invent the less he is likely to create. His true way is a different one; he finds his material among the accumulated stories of the race, whether ancient or modern; he sets to work to reject all that he judges unnecessary or unfit, to add all that is lacking; and finally, without effort, almost without consciousness of his power, he endows his work with his own personal quality in the act of making it serve his own purpose.

As we consider what Sir Thomas North received from Plutarch, and what Shakespeare received from North we see in action 'a kind of creative evolution'.

SECTION
IV
It has been said that the translation of a poem from one language into another is not the making of poetry but its destruction. There have been, however, many fine translations of poetry into English by poets such as Chapman, Dryden, Pope, Cowper, Bridges, and C. Day Lewis. Admittedly, the beauty of their productions depends upon their handling of English, and it is always different from the beauty of the original, because in poetry the meaning of words lies in their sound as much as in their sense.

In the fourth section translations of the same poem (or passage from a long poem) are set down for critical comparison, not as faithful renderings (for that the reader would obviously need an intimate knowledge of the original) but as examples of the poetic style of different poets using the same material. Turning from one poet to another we may appraise such a line as:

I who queen it through these courts of heaven

against

I who in high heaven move as a queen

and

I who through heaven its mistress move

all derived from Virgil's

Ast ego quae divum incedo regina.

SECTION
V
The last section contains a number of unsigned poems arranged according to subject, lending themselves to contrast and comparison.

Included also are some poems given in different versions for close analysis. Occasionally a poem and the material from which it is derived gives further opportunity for critical appreciation. Throughout, material is presented for a close analysis of words and language, leading to a fuller understanding of poetry and the poet's craft.

A. F. SCOTT

*27 April 1956*

## ACKNOWLEDGEMENTS

*Section I*

The following manuscripts are reproduced by permission of the British Museum: William Shakespeare: from *Sir Thomas More*; William Cowper: *The Halibut*; William Blake: *The Tyger*; William Wordsworth: from *The Waggoner*; S. T. Coleridge: *Lewti*; P. B. Shelley: from *The Death of Adonis*; T. L. Beddoes: *Dream Pedlary*; Lord Tennyson: *Milton, Alcaics*; Robert Browning: from *The Ring and the Book*; E. B. Browning: from *The Runaway Slave at Pilgrim's Point*; D. G. Rossetti: *Love's Compass*; Christina Rossetti: *Sleeping at Last*; A. C. Swinburne: from *Rococo*.

George Herbert: *Perfection* is reproduced by permission of Dr Williams's Library; John Milton: from *Lycidas* by permission of Trinity College Library, Cambridge; Thomas Gray: from *Elegy written in a Country Churchyard* by permission of Eton College Library; George Crabbe: *Jane Adair* by permission of the University Library, Cambridge; Lord Byron: *Oh! snatch'd away in Beauty's Bloom* by permission of Sir John Murray; John Keats: from *Ode to the Nightingale* by permission of the Syndics of the Fitzwilliam Museum, Cambridge; G. M. Hopkins: *The Starlight Night* by permission of Mr Gerard Hopkins, The Society of Jesus and The Bodleian Library, Oxford; Edward Thomas: *Adlestrop* by permission of Mrs Edward Thomas and the British Museum; Rupert Brooke: the first draft manuscript of *The Soldier* is reproduced by permission of the author's representatives and of Messrs Sidgwick and Jackson Ltd.; Wilfred Owen: *Anthem for Dead Youth* by permission of Messrs Chatto and Windus and the British Museum; Isaac Rosenberg: from *Moses* by permission of Messrs Chatto and Windus and the British Museum.

*Section IV*

F. L. Lucas: Homer, *Odyssey* XXIV, 1–14 is reproduced by permission of the Folio Society; Thomas Hardy: Catullus, *Ode* XXXI, from *Collected Poems of Thomas Hardy* (Macmillan) by permission of the publishers and the Trustees of the Hardy Estate; James Elroy Flecker: Virgil, *Aeneid* VI, 269–294 by permission of Messrs Secker and Warburg; Robert Bridges: Virgil, *Aeneid* VI, 269–294 from *Ibant Obscuri* (Clarendon Press) by permission of the publishers; Rolfe Humphries: Virgil, *Aeneid* VI, 269–294 by permission of Messrs Charles Scribner's Sons Ltd.; C. Day Lewis: Virgil, *Georgics* I, 311–334 by permission of Messrs Jonathan Cape Ltd.; G. S. Fraser: Horace, *Odes* I, v from

# ACKNOWLEDGEMENTS

*Voices from the Past* by James and Janet Maclean Todd (Phoenix House) by permission of the author; H. Rackham: Horace, *Odes* I, ix from *Greece and Rome* (Clarendon Press) by permission of the publishers; A. E. Housman: Horace, *Odes* IV, vii by permission of the Society of Authors as the Literary Representatives of the Trustees of the estate of the late A. E. Housman, and Messrs Jonathan Cape Ltd., publishers of A. E. Housman's *Collected Poems* (and Messrs Henry Holt and Co. Inc., New York); James Maclean Todd: Horace, *Odes* IV, vii from *Voices from the Past* by James and Janet Maclean Todd (Phoenix House) by permission of the author and publishers; Laurence Binyon: Dante, *Paradiso*, Canto XXXIII, 97–145 by permission of the Society of Authors and Mrs Cicely Binyon; Nevill Coghill: Chaucer, *Canterbury Tales, Nonne Preestes Tale*, 1–16 by permission of Penguin Books Ltd.

(In planning this section I found *Voices from the Past* by James and Janet Maclean Todd particularly helpful. A.F.S.)

## Section V

Robert Bridges: *Larks* from *The shorter Poems of Robert Bridges* (Clarendon Press) is reproduced by permission of the publishers; W. H. Davies: *Robin Redbreast* from *The Collected Poems of W. H. Davies* (Jonathan Cape) by permission of Mrs H. M. Davies and the publishers; Frank O'Connor: 'A hiding tuft, a greenbarked yewtree' by permission of Messrs A. D. Peters and W. B. Yeats's revised version of the same poem by permission of Mrs W. B. Yeats; Thomas Hardy: *In a Wood* from *Collected Poems of Thomas Hardy* (Macmillan) by permission of the publishers and the Trustees of the Hardy Estate; Sir John Squire: *There was an Indian* by permission of the author; Robert Frost: *Mowing* and *The Line Gang* from *Complete Poems of Robert Frost* (Jonathan Cape) by permission of the publishers; Edward Thomas: *Pewits* and *The Glory* by permission of Mrs Edward Thomas; C. Day Lewis: *Now the full-throated daffodils* from *Collected Poems* 1954 (Hogarth Press) by permission of the publishers; W. B. Yeats: *Her Praise* from *Collected Poems* (Macmillan) by permission of the publishers and of Mrs W. B. Yeats; A. E. Housman: *A Shropshire Lad* XXXI, XLIV and *Last Poems* XXVII by permission of the Society of Authors as the Literary Representative of the Trustees of the estate of the late A. E. Housman, and Messrs Jonathan Cape Ltd., publishers of A. E. Housman's *Collected Poems* (and Messrs Henry Holt and Co. Inc., New York); John Masefield: *On Malvern Hill* by permission of the Society of Authors, Dr John Masefield, O.M., and the Macmillan Company, New York; A. C. Benson: *The Hawk* from *The Poems of Arthur Christopher Benson* (John Lane, the Bodley Head Ltd.) by permission of the publishers; Walter de la Mare: *Song of the Mad Prince* by permission of the Society of Authors as the Literary Representative of the Trustees of the estate of the late Walter de la Mare, and Messrs Faber and Faber Ltd.; Sir A. Quiller-Couch: *Lord, in Thy Courts* from *Poems and Ballads* (Methuen) by permission of Messrs J. M. Dent & Sons; Emily Dickinson: *The Chariot* from *Poems by Emily Dickinson* (Little, Brown and Co., New York); Louis Macneice: *Prognosis* from *Collected Poems* (Faber and Faber Ltd.) by permission of the publishers; Louis Untermeyer: *To a Telegraph Pole* from *Burning Bush* by permission of Harcourt, Brace and Co., New York; G. M. Hopkins: *Inversnaid*, *Spring* and *The Windhover* from the collected poems of Gerard Manley Hopkins by permission of Oxford University Press.

# I

# THE POET'S
# MANUSCRIPT

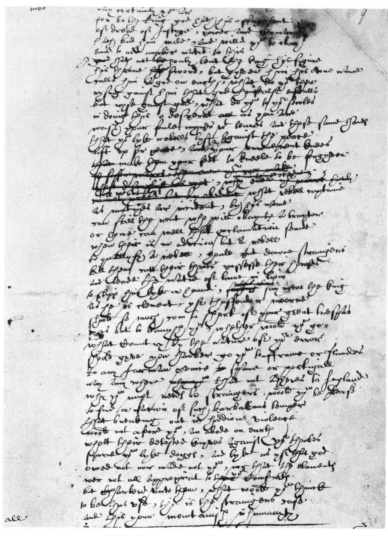

*MS. Harl. 7368 & 9, British Museum*

*moo*    *nay certainly yo^u ar*
*for to the king god hath his offyc lent*
*of dread of Juſtyce, power and Comaund*
*hath bid him rule, and willd yo^u to obay*
*and to add ampler māie to this*
*he ~~god~~ hath not ~~le~~ only lent the king his figure*
                  *&*
*his throne ~~his~~ ſword, but gyven him his owne name*
*calls him a god on earth, what do yo^u then,*
*ryſing gainſt him that god himſealf enſtalls*
*but ryſe gainſt god, what do yo^u to yo^r ſowles*
*in doing this o deſperat ~~ar~~ as you are·*
*waſh your foule mynds w^t teares and thoſe ſame hands*
*that yo^u lyke rebells lyſt againſt the peace*
*lift vp for peace, and your vnreuerent knees*
*~~that~~ make them your feet    to kneele to be forgyven*
*~~is ſafer warrs, then euer yo^u can make,~~*
                      *~~in in to yo^r obedienc~~*
*~~whoſe diſcipline is ryot; why even yo^r warrs hurly~~*
*tell me but this*
*~~cannot pceed but by obedienc~~ what rebell captaine*
*as muty^nes ar incident, by his name*
*can ſtill the rout who will obay ~~th~~ a traytor*
*or howe can well that pclamation ſounde*
*when their is no adicion but a rebell*
*to quallyſy a rebell, youle put downe ſtraingers*
*kill them cutt their throts poſſeſſe their howſes*
*and leade the matie of lawe in liom*
                  *~~alas alas~~*
*to ſlipp him lyke a hound; ~~ſayeng~~ ſay nowe the king*
*as he is clement,. yf thoffendor moorne*
*ſhoold ſo much com to ſhort of your great treſpas*
        *as but to banyſh yo^u, whether woold yo^u go·*
*what Country by the nature of yo^r error*
*ſhoold gyve you harber go yo^u to ffraunc or flanders*
*to any Jarman pvince, ~~to~~ ſpane or portigall*
*nay any where ~~why yo^u~~ that not adheres to Jngland*
*why yo^u muſt needs be ſtraingers, woold yo^u be pleaſd*
*to find a nation of ſuch barbarous temper*
*that breaking out in hiddious violence*
*woold not afoord yo^u, an abode on earth*
*whett their deteſted knyves againſt yo^r throtes*
*ſpurne yo^u lyke doggs, and lyke as yf that god*
*owed not nor made not yo^u, nor that the elaments*
               *yo^r*
*wer not all appropriat to ~~their~~ Comforts·*
*but Charterd vnto them, what woold yo^u thinck*
*to be thus vſd, this is the ſtraingers caſe*
*all*    *and this your momtaniſh inhumanyty*

3

The Church

Perfection The Elixer

Lord teach mee to referr
All things I doe to thee
That I not onely may not erre
But allso pleasing bee.

A man that looks on glass
On it may stay his ey;
Or if he pleaseth through it pass
And then the heaven espy.

If that doe ought for thee,
Marking thy St: for thine,
And noting this, this shafe & trifles,
These saith this fruit is mine:

A Servant of this perfect
Nothing can be so meane

The Church

A stroponter this plant,
Makes drudgery divine:
Who sweeps a roome as for thy Law,
Makes that, and th' action fine.

But these is another growth of gold:
Lasse his this they that doth
Sith on this Light is all things as tomb
And so this may they art.

This is ye famous stone
That turneth all to gold
For y & God doth touch & owne
Cannot for less be told.

4

*The Church*

Perfection <u>The Elixir</u>

Lord teach mee to referr
All things I doe to thee
That I not onely may not erre
But allso pleasing bee.

A man that looks on glafs
On it may stay his eye:
Or if he pleaseth through it pafs
And then the heav'en espy.

He that does ought for thee
Marketh yt deed for thine,
And when the Dvell shakes yt tree
Thou saist, this fruit is mine.

All may of thee pertake:
Nothing can be so ~~low~~ meane
Wth wth his tincture (for thy sake)
grow bright & cleane
Will not ~~~~

*The Church*

A servant wth this clause,
Makes drudgery divine.
                    room as
Who sweeps a ~~~~ for thy lawes,
Makes that, and th'action fine.

But these are high perfections:
Happy are they that age
Lett in the light to all their actions
And shew them as they are.

This is yr famous stone
That turneth all to gold
For yt wch God doth touch & owne
Can not for lefs be told.

5

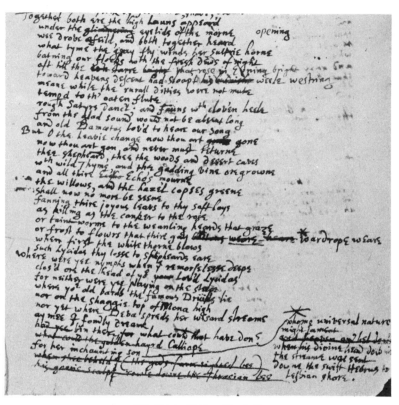

*MS. Trinity College, Cambridge*

Together both ere the high launs appear'd
under the ~~glimmering~~ eyelids of the morne    opening
wee drove afeild, and both together heard
what tyme the gray fly winds her sultrie horne
batning our flocks wth the fresh dews of night
oft till the ~~eah~~ starre ~~bright~~ that rose in Evning bright
toward heavens defcent had sloop't his ~~burnisht~~ weele westring
meane while the rurall ditties were not ~~mute~~
tempd to th' oaten flute
rough Satyrs danc't; and Fauns wth clov'en heele
from the glad sound would not be absent long
and old Dametas lov'd to heare our song.
But O the heavie change now thou art ~~gone~~ gone
now thou art gon, and never must returne
thee shepheard, thee the woods and desert caves
wth wild Thyme, and the gadding vine oregrowne
and all thire ~~Eccho~~ Echo's mourne
the willows, and the huzel copses greene
shall now no more be seene
fanning thire joyous leavs to thy soft lays
as killing as the canker to the rose
or taint-worme to the weanling heards that graze   ✳
or frost to flowrs that thire gay ~~blossoms weare weare~~ wardrope weare
when first the white thorne blows
such Lycidas thy losse to shepheards eare
Where were yee nymphs when yt remorfelesse deepe
clos'd ore the head of yoͬ ~~your~~ Lov'd Lycidas
for neither were yee playing on the steepe
where yoͬ old bards the famous Druids lie
nor on the shaggie top of Mona high
nor yet where Deva spreds her wisard streame
ay mee I fondly dreame
~~had yee~~ bin there for what could that have don?
~~what could the golden haird~~ Calliope
for her inchaunting son
~~when shee beheld (the gods farr sighted bee)~~
~~his goorie scalpe rowle downe the Thracian lee~~

whome universal nature
might lament
~~and heaven and hel dony~~
when his divine head downe
the streame was sent
downe the swift Hebrus to the
Lefbian shore.

7

*MS. Eton College*

Oft as the Woodlark piped her farewell Song
With whistful Eyes pursue the setting Sun
    spreading  nodding
Oft at the Foot of yonder hoary Beech
That wreathes its old fantastic Roots so high.
His listlefs Length at Noontide would he stretch,
And pore upon the Brook that babbles by.
 With Gestures quaint now smileing as in Scorn,
    wayward fancies ~~loved~~ would be
Mutt'ring his fond Conceits he ~~wont to~~ rove:
 drooping,
Now woeful wan, ~~he droop'd~~, as one forlorn
Or crazed with Care, or crofs'd in hopelefs Love.
 One Morn we mifs'd him on th'æcustomd Hill,
 Along the   near
By the Heath-~~side~~, & at his fav'rite Tree.
Another came, nor yet beside the Rill,
   by
Nor up the Lawn, nor at the Wood was he.
~~There scatter'd oft, the earliest~~
Then next with Dirges meet in sad Array
  by
Slow thro the Church-way Path we saw him born
Approach & read, for thou can'st read the Lay
 Graved carved    yon
Wrote on the Stone beneath that ancient Thorn
      Year
There scatter'd oft the earliest of yᵗ ~~Spring~~
    Showers of
By Hands unseen are frequent Vi'lets found.
 Redbreast
The Robin loves to build & warble there,
And little Footsteps lightly print the Ground. `

9

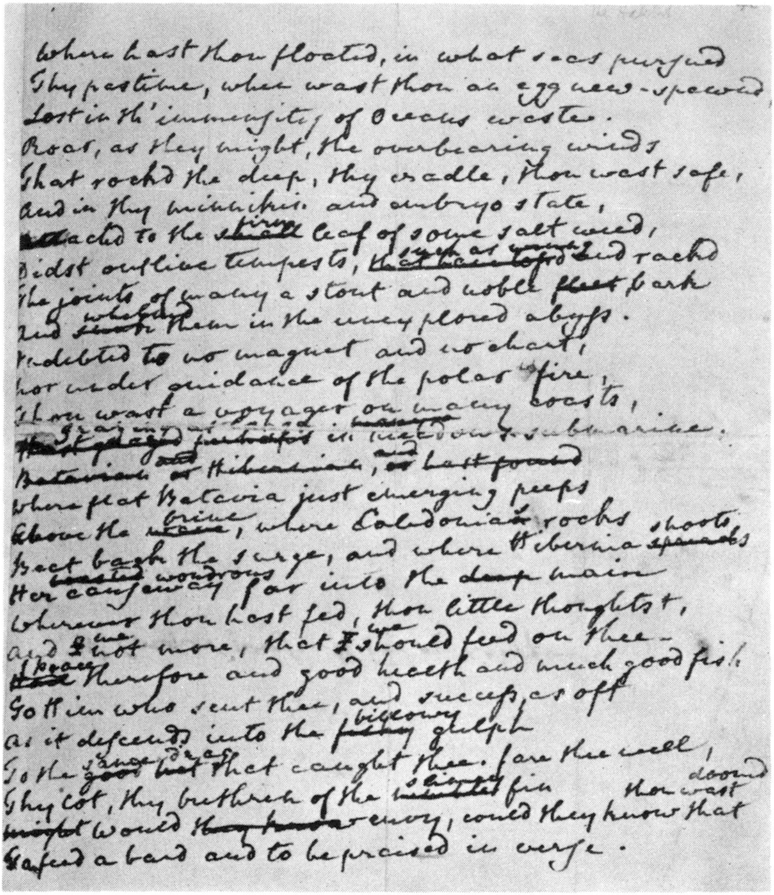

*MS. Add. 37059 f. 45, British Museum*

*Where hast thou floated, in what seas purfued*
*Thy pastime, where wast thou an egg new-spawnd,*
*Lost in th'immenfity of Oceans waste.*
*Roar, as they might, the overbearing winds*
*That rockd the deep, thy cradle, thou wast safe,*
*And in thy minnikin and embryo state,*
      *firm*
*Attachd to the ~~small~~ leaf of some salt weed,*
           *such as wrung*
*Didst outlive tempests, ~~that have tofsd~~ and rackd*
*The joints of many a stout and noble ~~fleet~~ bark*
    *whelmd*
*And ~~sunk~~ them in the unexplored abyfs*
*Indebted to no magnet and no chart,*
*Nor under guidance of the polar fire,*
*Thou wast a voyager on many coasts,*
    *Grazing at large*   ~~many a~~
~~Hast grazed~~ ~~perhaps~~ *in meadows submarine,*
   ~~and~~      ~~and~~
~~Batavian or Hibernian, or hast found~~
*Where flat Batavia just emerging peeps*
    *brine*
*Above the ~~wave~~, where Caledonian^s rocks*
              *shoots*
*Beat back the surge, and where Hibernia ~~spreads~~*
   ~~boasted~~ *wondrous*
*Her caufeway far into the ~~deep~~ main*
*Wherever thou hast fed, thou little thoughtst,*
  *we*         *we*
*And ~~I~~ not more, that ~~I~~ should feed on thee*
    *Peace*
~~Have~~ *therefore and good health and much good fish*
*To Him who sent thee, and succefs, as oft*
      *billowy*
*As it defcends into the ~~fishy~~ gulph*
    *same drag*
*To the ~~good boat~~ that caught thee, fare thee well,*
        *slimey*
*Thy lot, thy brethren of the ~~nimble~~ fin*     *doomd*
                            *thou wast*
~~Might~~ *Would ~~they know~~ envy, could they know that*
*To feed a bard and to be praised in verfe.*

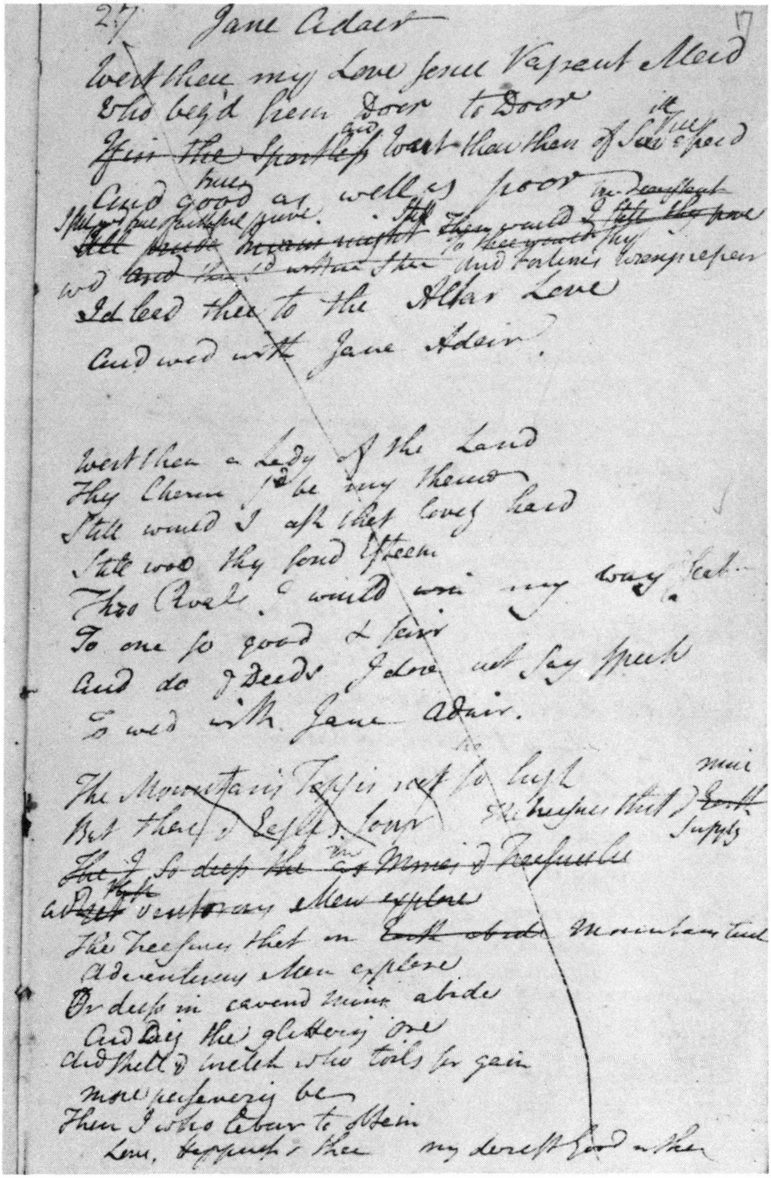


*MS. Cambridge University Library*

27|    *Jane Adair* |

*Wert thou my Love some Vagrant Maid*
*Who beg'd from Door to Door*       ill
                    and                Vice
~~If in the spotless~~ *wert thou then of* ~~Six~~ *afraid*
        true
*And good as well as poor*
*I still wd true & faithful prove*        Still    tru. constant.
~~All pride In vain might~~   ~~Then would I still thy prove~~
                                   To ~~thee would thy~~
wd   ~~And then I with me share~~   *And Fortunes wrongs repair*
~~Id lead thee to the Altar Love~~
*And wed with Jane Adair.*

*Wert thou a Lady of the Land*
*Thy Charm s*ᵈ *be my theme*
*Still would I ask that lovely hand*
*Still woo thy fond Esteem*
*Thro Perils I would win my way*
*To one so good & fair*
*And do ∂ Deeds I dare not say speak*
*To wed with Jane Adair*

                        too
*The Mountain Too is not so high*        mine
*But there ∂ Eagles soar the treasures that ∂* ~~Earth~~
            in                     supply
~~The I so deep the as Mines & Treasures lie~~
    ~~Hope~~
*And* ~~Yet venturous Men explore~~
*The Treasures that in* ~~Earth abide~~ *Mountains tied*
*Adventurous Men explore*
*Or deep in cavernd Mine abide*
    *And Dig the glittering Ore*
*And shall ∂ wretch who toils for gain*
    *More persevering be*
*Than I who labour to obtain*
    *Love, Happiness & thee*        my dearest Good in thee

13

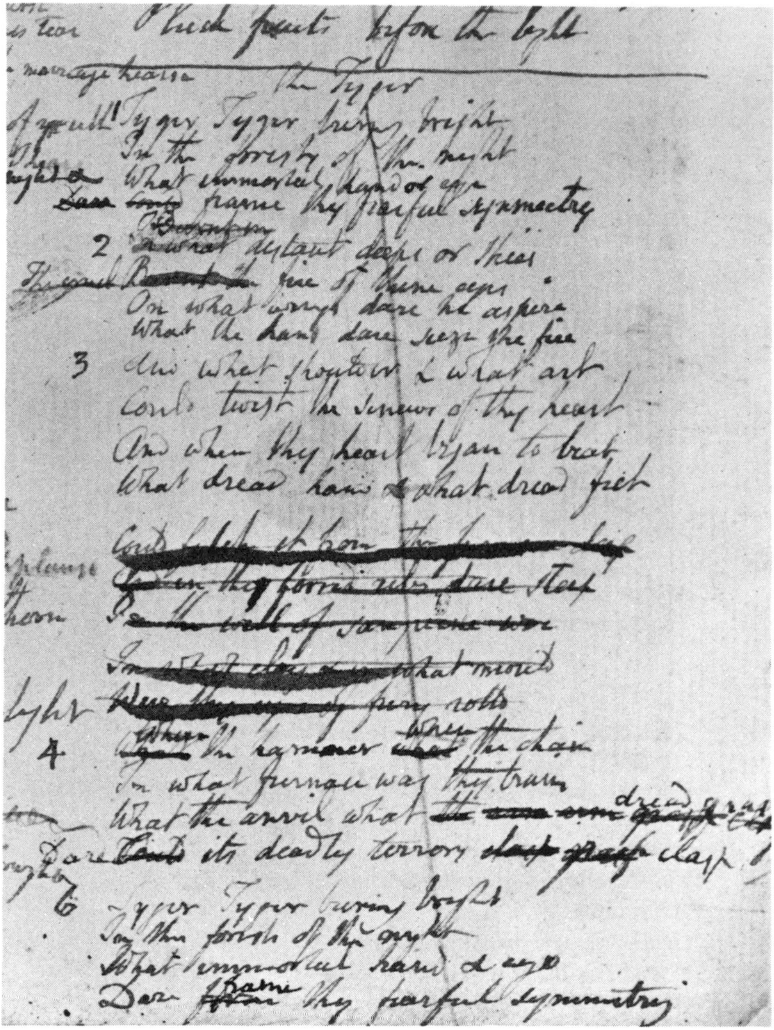

Pluck fruits before the light

The Tyger

Tyger Tyger burning bright
In the forests of the night
What immortal hand or eye
frame thy fearful symmetry

2 distant deeps or skies
the fire of thine eyes
On what wings dare he aspire
What the hand dare seize the fire

3 And what shoulder & what art
Could twist the sinews of thy heart
And when thy heart began to beat
What dread hand & what dread feet

4 In what furnace was thy brain
What the anvil what dread grasp
Dare its deadly terrors clasp

6 Tyger Tyger burning bright
In the forests of the night
What immortal hand & eye
Dare frame thy fearful symmetry

*Rossetti MS., British Museum*

The *Tyger*

1   *Tyger Tyger burning bright*
*In the forests of the night*
*What immortal hand or eye*
~~*Dare*~~  ~~*Could*~~ *frame thy fearful symmetry*

     *Burnt in*
2   ~~*In what*~~ *distant deeps or skies*
~~*The cruel Burnt the*~~ *fire of thine eyes*
*On what wings dare he aspire*
*What the hand dare sieze the fire*

3   *And what shoulder & what art*
*Could twist the sinews of thy heart*
*And when thy heart began to beat*
*What dread hand & what dread feet*

   ~~*Could fetch it from the furnace deep*~~
   ~~*And in thy horrid ribs dare steep*~~
   ~~*In the well of sanguine woe*~~
   ~~*In what clay & in what mould*~~
   ~~*Were thy eyes of fury rolld*~~

   *Where*      *where*
4   ~~*What*~~ *the hammer* ~~*what*~~ *the chain*
*In what furnace was thy brain*
             *dread grasp*
*What the anvil what* ~~*the arm arm grasp clasp*~~
*Dare*  ~~*Could*~~ *its deadly terrors* ~~*clasp grasp*~~ *clasp*

6   *Tyger Tyger burning bright*
*In the forests of the night*
*What immortal hand & eye*
     *frame*
*Dare* ~~*form*~~ *thy fearful symmetry*

15

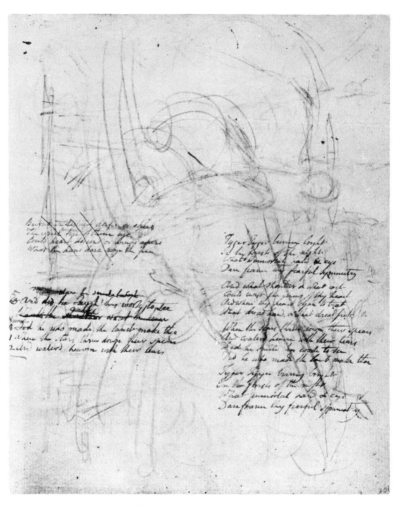

*Rossetti MS. , British Museum*

Burnt in distant deeps or skies
The cruel fire of thine eye,
Could heart descend or wings aspire
What the hand dare seize the fire

dare he ~~smile laugh~~
5 3 And ~~did he laugh~~ his work to see
~~ankle~~
~~What the shoulder what the knee~~
Dare
4 ~~Did~~ he who made the lamb make thee
1 When the stars threw down their spears
2 And waterd heaven with their tears

Tyger Tyger burning bright
In the forests of the night
What Immortal hand & eye
Dare frame thy fearful symmetry

And what shoulder & what art
Could twist the sinews of thy heart
And when thy heart began to beat
What dread hand & what dread feet

When the stars threw down their spears
And waterd heaven with their tears
Did he smile his work to see
Did he who made the lamb make thee

Tyger Tyger burning bright
In the forests of the night
What immortal hand & eye
Dare frame thy fearful symmetry

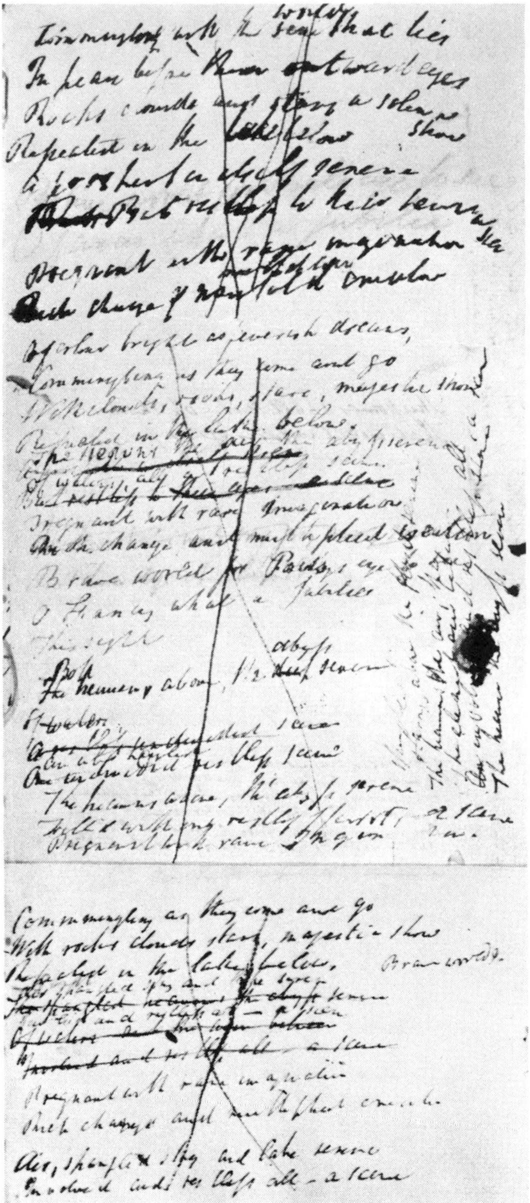

*MS. Ashley 4637, British Museum*

world
Commingling with the scene that lies
In peace before their outward eyes
Rocks clouds and stars a solemn
show
Repeated in the lake below
A prospect in itself serene
Brave world for Poet's eye to see
~~But~~ But restless to their heaven
O fancy what a jubilee          a scene
Pregnant with rare imagination
multiplied
Rich change of manifold creation

Of colour bright as feverish dreams,
Commingling as they come and go
With clouds, rocks, stars, majestic show
Repeated in the lake below
The heav'ns the air the abyfs serene
A pros~~pect in itself serene~~
Of waters all a restlefs scene
Bu~~t restlefs to their eyes a scene~~
Pregnant with rare Imagination
Rich change and multiplied creation
Brave world for Poet's eye to see
O Fancy what a Jubilee
This sight
Both                    abyfs
The heaven above the ~~deep~~ serene
Of ~~waters,~~
A ~~restlefs undivided~~ scene
An ab spangled
An undivided restlefs scene
The heavens above, th'abyfs serene
Fill'd with my restlefs spirit, a scene
Pregnant with rare Imagination.
Commingling as they come and go
With rocks clouds stars, majestic show
Repeated in the lake below,
Earth                              Brave world &
Air spangled sky and lake serene
~~The spangled heavens, the abyfs serene~~
Involv'd and restlefs all — a scene
~~Of waters and the air between~~
~~Involved and restlefs all — a scene~~
Pregnant with rare imagination
Rich change and multiplied creation
Air, spangled sky and lake serene
Involved and restlefs all — a scene

spangled
starry, above the abyfs serene
The heavens the air, that
The element all between
all, a scene
~~An~~ involved and restlefs scene
The heavens the abyfs serene

19

The ~~Bounti-~~ *Circassian's* Love-chaunt.

High o'er the ~~river~~ *rocks* at night I rov'd 2.
To forget the form, I lov'd.
Image of ~~Mira!~~ *Lewti!* from my mind
Depart! for ~~Mira~~ *Lewti* is not kind!

Bright was the Moon: the Moon's bright beam
Speckled with many a moving shade,
Danc'd upon Tamaha's stream;
But brightlier on the Rock it play'd,
The Rock, half-shelter'd from my view
By pendent boughs of tressy Yew!
True to Love, but false to Rest,
My fancy whisper'd in my breast —
So shines my ~~Mira's~~ *Lewti's* forehead fair
Gleaming thro' her sable hair.
Image of ~~Mira~~ *Lewti*! from my mind
Depart! for ~~Mira~~ *Lewti* is not kind.

I saw a cloud of whitest hue;
Onward to the Moon it pass'd!
Still brighter and more bright it grew
With floating colours not a few,
Till it reach'd the moon at last

The ~~Wild Indian's~~ Circaſsian's Love-chaunt.

rocks
High o'er the ~~silver~~ at night I rov'd
To forget the form, I lov'd.
                    Lewti!
Image of ~~Cora~~ from my mind
                    Lewti
Depart! for ~~Cora~~ is not kind!

Bright was the Moon: the Moon's bright beam
Speckled with many a moving Shade,
Danc'd upon Tamaha's stream;
But brightlier on the Rock it play'd,
The Rock, half-shelter'd from my view
By pendent boughs of treſsy Yew!
True to Love, but false to Rest,
My fancy whisper'd in my breast —
                    Lewti's
So shines my ~~Cora's~~ forehead fair
Gleaming thro' her sable hair.
                    Lewti
Image of ~~Cora!~~ from my mind
                    Lewti
Depart! for ~~Cora~~ is not kind.

I saw a cloud of whitest hue;
Onward to the Moon it paſs'd!
Still brighter and more bright it grew
With floating colours not a few,
Till it reach'd the Moon at last.

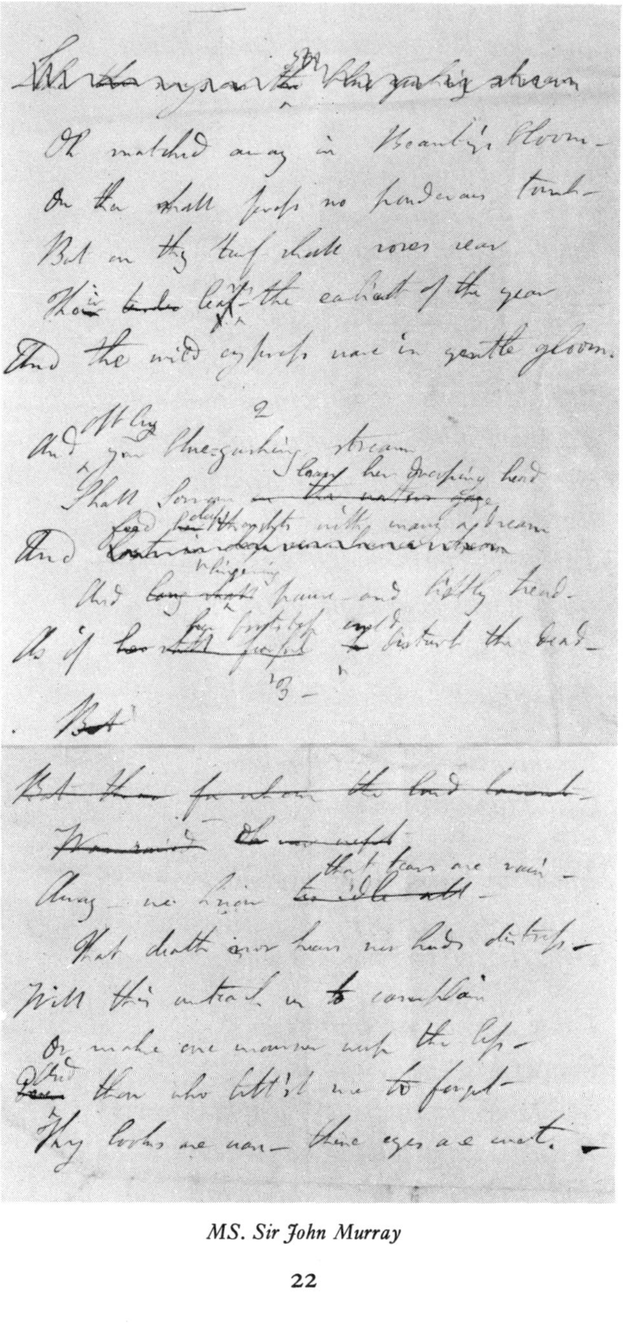

*cyan*
~~Like the rays on the blue gushing stream~~
Oh snatched away in Beauty's bloom —
On thee shall prefs no ponderous tomb —
But on thy turf shall roses rear
   *ir*      *ves*
Their ~~tender~~ leaf — the earliest of the year
And the wild cyprefs wave in gentle gloom.


2

   *oft by*
And yon blue-gushing stream
              *lean her drooping head*
Shall Sorrow ~~on the waters gaze~~
    *deep*
feed ~~her~~ thoughts    with many a dream
And ~~lost in deep remembrance dream~~
    *& lingering*
And ~~long shall~~ pause — and lightly tread —
    *her footstep could*
As if ~~her still fearful to~~ disturb the dead —


3 —

~~But~~
~~But thou for whom the loud lament~~
~~Was rais'd — Oh ever wept~~
            *that tears are vain —*
Away — we know ~~tis idle all —~~
That death nor hears nor heeds distrefs —
Will this unteach us to complain
Or make one mourner weep the lefs —
   *And*
~~Even~~ thou who tell'st me to forget
Thy looks are wan — thine eyes are wet. —

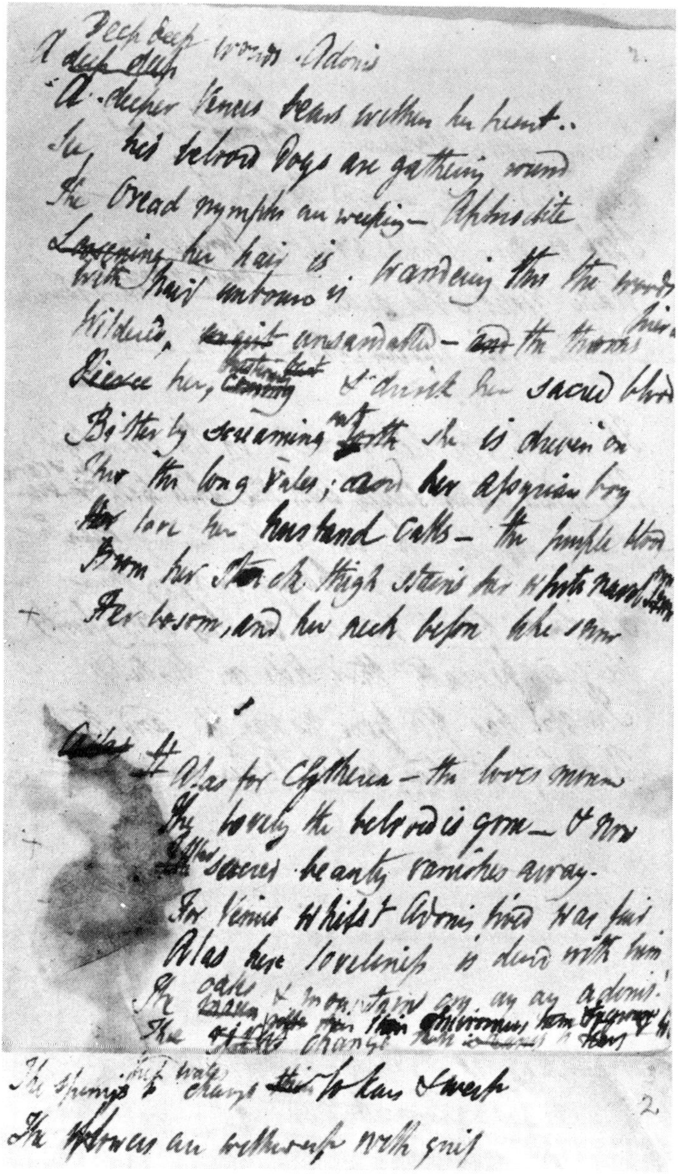


*MS. Ashley 5031, British Museum*

Deep deep
A ~~deep deep~~ wounds Adonis
  A deeper Venus bears within her heart.
  See, his beloved Dogs are gathering round
  The Oread nymphs are weeping — Aphrodite
  ~~Loosening her hair is~~
    With hair unbound is  wandering thro the woods
                            pierce
    Wildered, ~~ungirt~~ unsandalled ~~and~~ the thorns
        hastening ~~feet~~
  ~~Pierce~~ her, ~~coming~~    & drink her sacred blood
         out
  Bitterly screaming ~~forth~~ she is driven on
  Thro the long vales; and her Aſsyrian boy
  Her love her husband calls — the purple blood
                      now
  From her struck thigh stains her white navel ~~snow~~
  Her bosom, and her neck before like snow

~~Alas If~~
    Alas for Cytherea — the loves mourn
    The lovely the beloved is gone — & now
      Her
    ~~The~~ sacred beauty vanishes away.
    For Venus whilst Adonis lived was fair
    Alas her lovelineſs is dead with him
        oaks
    The ~~moun~~ and mountains cry, ay ay Adonis!
      ~~rills their~~ their murmurs tears & groans
                              we
    The ~~rivers~~ change   their ~~streams~~ to   ~~tears~~
      springs
        their waters
    The springs ʌ    change ~~their~~ to tears & weep
    The flowers are withered up with grief

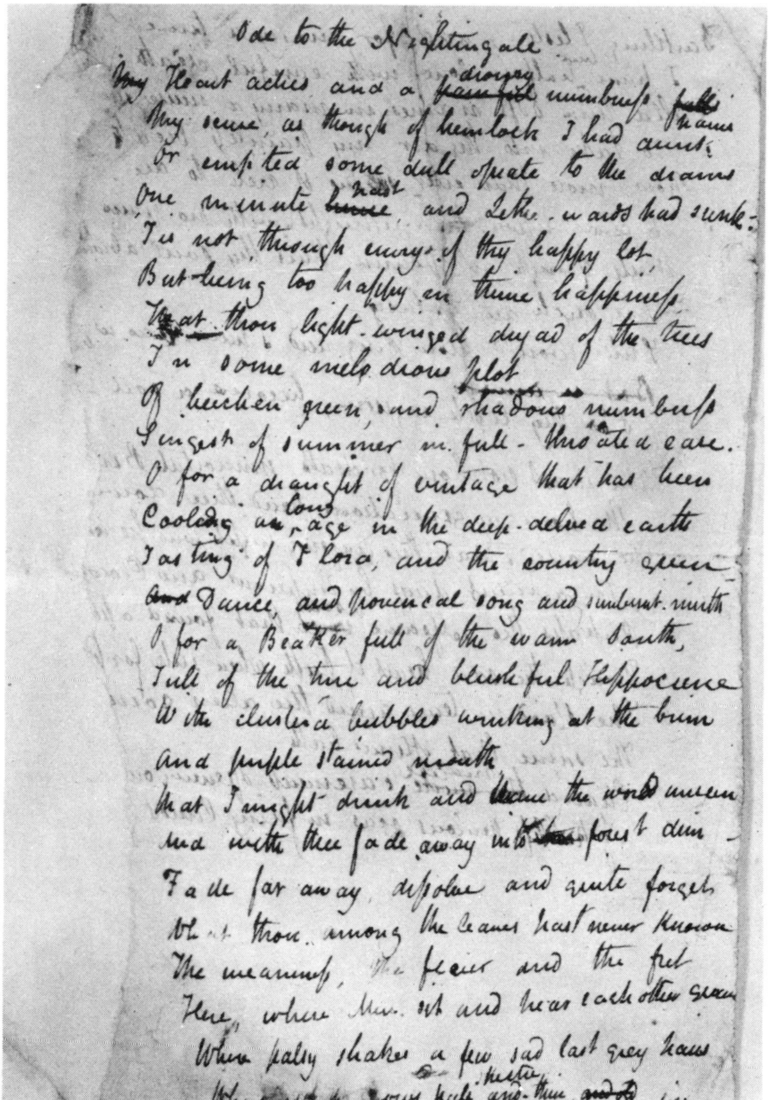

MS. Fitzwilliam Museum, Cambridge

*Ode to the Nightingale*

         *drowsy*
~~My~~ *Heart aches and a ~~painful~~ numbnefs ~~falls~~*
                  *pains*
*My sense, as though of hemlock I had drunk*
*Or emptied some dull opiate to the drains*
         *past*
*One minute ~~hence~~ and Lethe-wards had sunk:*
*'Tis not through envy of thy happy lot,*
*But being too happy in thine happinefs,*
*That thou light-winged dryad of the trees*
*In some melodious plot*
*Of beechen green, and shadows numberlefs*
*Singest of summer in full-throated ease.*
*O for a draught of vintage that has been*
         *long*
*Cool~~ing~~ an age in the deep-delved earth*
*Tasting of Flora, and the country green*
*~~And~~ Dance, and provencal song and sunburnt mirth*
*O for a Beaker full of the warm South,*
*Full of the true and blushful Hippocrene*
*With cluster'd bubbles winking at the brim*
*And purple stained mouth,*
*That I might drink and leave the world unseen*
*And with thee fade away into the forest dim —*
*Fade far away, difsolve and quite forget*
*What thou among the leaves hast never known*
*The wearinefs, the fever and the fret*
*Here, where Men sit and hear each other groan*
*Where palsy shakes a few sad last grey hairs*
               *spectre*
*Where youth grows pale and —thin ~~and old~~*
                 *and dies*

*Song*

If there were dreams to sell
What wd you buy?
Some cost a passing bell
Some a light sigh
That shakes from Life's fresh crown
Only a roseleaf down.
If there were dreams to sell — Merry and sad to tell
What would you buy? and the criers rung the bell

A cottage lone & still
With bowers nigh
Shadowy, my woes to still
Until I die.
Such pearl from Life's fresh crown
Fain would I shake me down
If there were dreams to believe at will
This would I buy — This would not heal my ill
But there were dreams to sell
Ill didst thou buy
Life is a dream they tell;
Waking, to die.
Dreaming a dream to prize.
Is wishing ghosts to rise —
And if I had the spell,
What ghost raised I?
If there were ghosts to raise
What shall I call,
Out of hell's murky haze,
Heavens blue pall?
Raise my the loved longlost boy
To lead me to his joy.
There are no ghosts to raise — out of death lead no ways
Vain is the call
Knowst thou not ghosts to sue?
No love thou hast
Else lie as I will do — Thus are the ghosts to sue
And breathe thy last Thus are all dreams
Scent of Life's fresh crown. Ever to last
Fall like a roseleaf down.

*MS. 39674 f. 9b, British Museum*

28

*Song*  *If there were dreams to sell*
      *What wd you buy?*
    *Some cost a passing bell*
      *Some a light sigh*
    *That shakes from life's fresh crown*
      *Only a roseleaf down.*
        *If there were dreams to sell*  *Merry and sad to tell*
        *What would you buy?*  *And the crier rung the bell*

    *A cottage lone & still*
      *With bowers nigh*
    *Shadowy, my woes to still*
      *Until I die*
    *Such pearl from life's fresh crown*
      *Fain would I shake me down*
        *If there Were dreams to have at will*
        *This would I buy*  *This would not please me ill*
                                      *best heal my*

    *But there were dreams to sell*
      *Ill didst thou buy*
    *Life is a dream they tell:*
      *Waking, to die*
    *Dreaming a dream to prize*
      *Is wishing ghosts to rise —*
        *And if I had the spell,*  *To raise call the ghosts up well*
        *What ghost raised I?*

    *If there were ghosts to raise*
      *What shall I call*
    *Out of hell's murky haze*
        *Heavens blue pall?*

          *my*
    *Raise the loved longlost boy*
      *To lead me to his joy.*
      *There are no ghosts to raise*
        *Vain is the call*  *Out of death lead no ways*
      *Knowst thou not ghosts to sue?*
        *No love thou hast*
    *Else lie as I will do*      *Thus are the ghosts to woo*
      *And breathe thy last*  *Thus are all dreams*
    *So out of life's fresh crown*              *made true*
      *Fall like a rose leaf down.*  *Ever to last*

Milton

## Alcaics

—

O mighty-mouth'd inventor of harmonies,
O skill'd [Equal] to sing of Time or Eternity,
    God-gifted organ-voice of England,
        Milton, a name to resound for ages,
Whose Titan angels, Gabriel, Abdiel,
Starr'd from Jehovah's gorgeous armouries,
    Tower, as the deep-domed empyrean
        Rings to the roar of an angel onset—
Me rather all that bowery loneliness,
Those brooks of Eden mazily murmuring,
    And bloom profuse & cedar arches
        Charm, as a wanderer out in ocean,
Where some refulgent sunset of India
Streams o'er a rich ambrosial ocean isle,
    And crimson-hued the stately palmwoods
        Whisper in odorous heights of ever.

Not to be read as a dactyl, but as a trochee by
long syllable, for the line is meant to be read
slowly.

MS. 37515 (a), British Museum

30

2

*Milton*

—

*Alcaics*

—

O mighty-mouth'd inventor of harmonies,
  ~~Equal~~ to sing of Time or Eternity,
O skill'd
        God-gifted organ-voice of England,
            Milton, a name to resound for ages,
Whose Titan Angels, Gabriel, Abdiel,
    r'd
Star**s** from Jehovah's gorgeous armouries,
        Tower, as the deep-domed empyrëan
            Rings to the roar of an angel onset —
Me rather all that bowery loneliness,
Those brooks of Eden mazily murmuring,
        And bloom profuse & cedar arches
            Charm, as a wanderer out in ocean,
Where some refulgent sunset of India

   ~~Dies~~
~~Streams~~ o'er a rich ambrosial ŏcean isle,
   ~~Dies~~
( Streams / And crimson-hued the stately palmwoods
            Whisper in odorous heights of ~~Eden~~.
                        even.

˘Not to be read as a dactyl, but as a trochee &
long syllable, for the line is meant to be read
slowly.

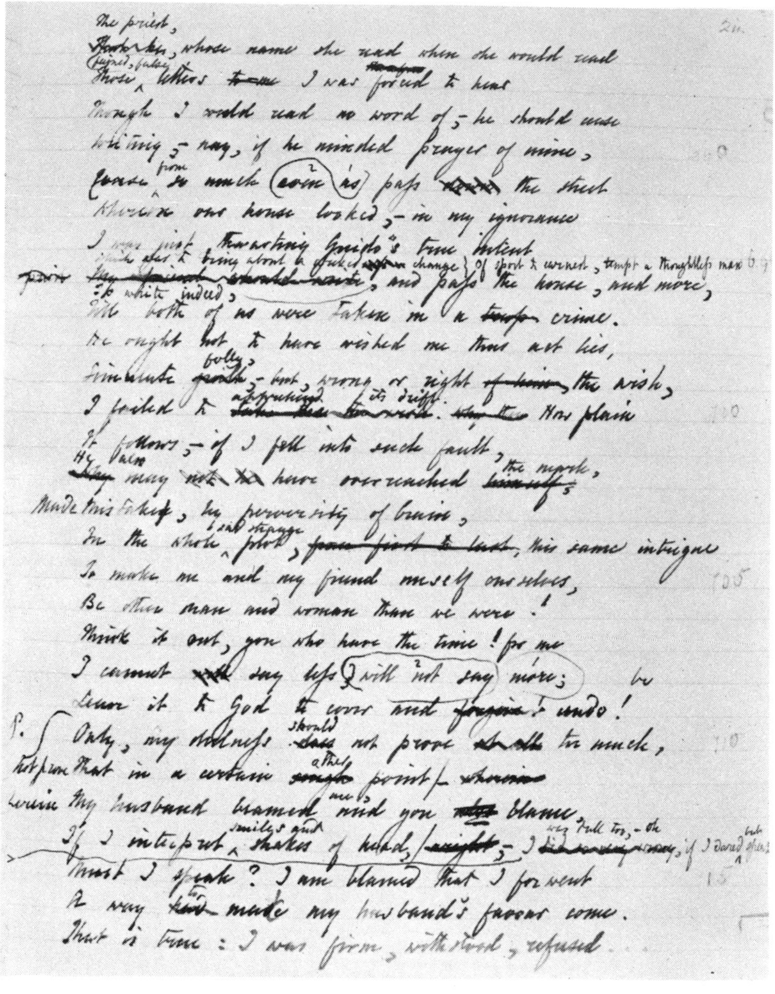

MS. Add. 43486, British Museum

The priest,
~~How has~~, whose name she read when she would read
(feigned, false)          ~~therefore~~
Those ⌃ ~~letters to me~~ I was forced to hear
Though I could read no word of, — he should cease
Writing, — nay, if he minded prayer of mine,
　　from
Cease ⌃ so much (even as pass down the street
Whereon our house looked, — in my ignorance
I was just thwarting Guido's true intent
Which was to bring about a wicked change (Of sport to earnest, tempt a thoughtless man
priest. ~~My friend should write~~, and pass the house, and more,
To write indeed,
Till both of us were taken in a ~~temp~~ crime.
He ought not to have wished me thus act lies,
　　　folly,
Simulate ~~guilt~~, — but, wrong or right ~~of him~~, the wish,
　　　apprehend its drift.
I failed to ~~take this the wish. Why then~~ How plain
It follows, — if I fell into such fault,
He also　　　　　　　　　　　　the mark,
~~Why~~ may not he have over reached ~~himself~~
Made Mistaken, by perversity of brain,
　　　sad strange
In the whole ⌃ plot, ~~from first to last~~, this same intrigue
To make me and my friend unself ourselves,
Be other man and woman than we were!
Think it out, you who have the time! for me
I cannot will say less, (I will not say more;)　　be
Leave it to God to cover and ~~forgive~~'s undo!
　　　should
P.　　　　Only, my dulness ~~does~~ not prove ~~at all~~ too much,
　　　　　　　other
not prove　That in a certain ~~single~~ point| — ~~wherein~~
　　　　　　me,
wherein　My husband blamed ⌃ and you ~~who~~ blame
　　　smiles and　　　　　was dull too, — oh　　　but
If I interpret ⌃ shakes of head, | ~~aright, I did so very wrong~~, If I dared ⌃ speak
Must I speak? I am blamed that I forwent
　　　to
A way ~~had~~ make my husband's favour come.
That is true: I was firm, withstood, refused...

33

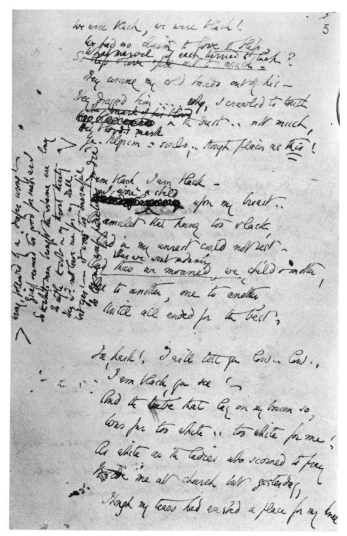

*MS. Ashley 2517, British Museum*

We were black, we were black!
  We had no claim to love & bliſs
What marvel, if each turned to lack?
~~So bliſs & love fill out to wrack~~
  They wrung my cold hands out of his —
They dragged him....why, I crawled to touch
  ~~The mark of his blood~~
~~His blood mark~~ in the dust..not much
  His blood's mark
Ye Pilgrim-souls,..though plain as this!

I am black, I am black —
  I wore a child
~~A child bearing~~ upon my breast..
An amulet that hung too slack
  And in my unrest could not rest —
    Thus we went moaning
And thus <u>we moaned, we</u>, child & mother,
One to another, one to another,
  Until all ended for the best,

For hark! I will tell you low.. low..
  I am black, you see, —
And the babe that lay on my bosom so,
  Was far too white:.too white for me;
As white as the ladies who scorned to pray
Beside me at church but yesterday,
  Though my tears had washed a place for my knee

*Wrongs, followed by a deeper wrong! —*
*Grief seemed too good for such as I*
*So the white men brought the shame ere long*
*To stifle the sob in my throat thereby*
*They wᵈ not leave me for my dull*
*Wet eyes! — it was too merciful*
*To let me weep pure tears & die!*

35

*Love's Comp***

Sometimes thou seemest not as thyself alone,
But as the meaning of all things that are;
A breathless wonder, shadowing forth afar
Some heavenly solstice hushed & halcyon;
Whose unstirred lips are music's visible tone;
Whose eyes the sun-gate of the soul unbar,
Being of its furthest fires oracular;—
The cloud-heart of all life's Noon & moon.

Even such Love is; and is not thy name Love?
Yea, by thy hand the Love-god rends apart
All gathering clouds of Night's ambiguous art;
Flings them far down, & sets thine eyes above;
And simply, as some gage of flower or glove,
Stakes with a smile the world against thy heart.

*MS. Add. 34813.3, British Museum*

## CHRISTINA ROSSETTI

Sleeping at last, the trouble & tumult over,
Sleeping at last, the struggle & horror past,
Cold & white out of sight of friend & of lover
Sleeping at last.

No more a tired heart downcast or overcast,
No more pangs that wring & shifting fears that hover,
Sleeping at last in a dreamless sleep locked fast.

Fast asleep. Singing birds in their leafy cover
Cannot wake her, nor shake her the gusty blast.
Under the purple thyme & the purple clover
Sleeping at last.

*MS. Add. 34813, British Museum*

*Love's ~~Secret~~*
*~~Beauty's~~ Compaſs (H. of L.)*

     *thou*       *thyself*
*Sometimes ~~you~~ seemst not as ~~yourself~~ alone,*
   *But as the meaning of all things that are;*
   *A breathleſs wonder, shadowing forth afar*
*Some heavenly solstice hushed & halcyon;*
*Whose ~~still~~ unstirred lips are music's visible tone;*
       *~~down gate~~ sun-gate*
  *Whose eyes the ~~silence~~ of the soul unbar,*
     *with of the its*
  *Being ~~made of~~ ∧ furthest fires oracular; —*
       *life*
*The evident heart of all ~~things~~ sown & mown.*

*Even such Love is;*
*~~Is Love not there~~; and is not thy name Love?*
   *Yea, by thy hand the Love-god rends apart*
   *All gathering clouds of Night's ambiguous art;*
*Flings them far down, & sets thine eyes above;*
*And simply, as some gage of flower or glove,*
   *Stakes with a smile the world against thy heart.*


'SLEEPING AT LAST'

*Sleeping at last, the trouble & tumult over,*
*Sleeping at last, the struggle & horror past,*
*Cold & white out of sight of friend & of lover*
*Sleeping at last.*

   *a*
*No more ~~of~~ tired heart downcast or overcast,*
*No more pangs that wring, or shifting fears that hover,*
*Sleeping at last in a dreamleſs sleep locked fast.*
*Fast asleep. Singing birds in their leafy cover*
*Cannot wake her, nor shake her the gusty blast.*
*Under the purple thyme & the purple clover*
*Sleeping at last.*

        *over*

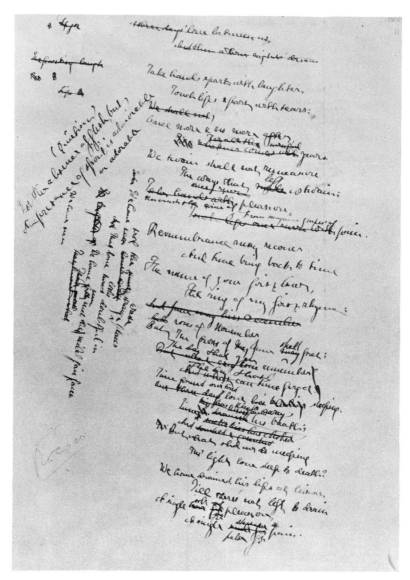

*MS. Ashley A 1851, British Museum*

~~Three days' love between us~~
~~And then a three nights' dream~~
Take hands & part with laughter,
   Touch lips & part with tears;
~~We shall not~~
Once more & no more after,
   ~~For all the mournful~~
~~YYY~~ ~~Whatever comes with~~ years
We twain shall not remeasure
                        left
   The ways that ~~made~~ us twain;
~~once more~~
~~Take hands with~~ pleasure
Nor crush the wine of
                  From sanguine grapes of
   ~~Touch lips once more with~~ pain
Remembrance may recover
   And time bring back to time
The name of your first lover,
   The ring of my first rhyme;
~~And June may kiss December~~
~~And~~ roses of November
                        shall
But the frost of ~~May~~ June ~~may~~ fret;
   The day that you
~~But what can love~~ remember
   The day that I
~~And what can time~~ forget
Time found our tired
~~Our three days~~ love ~~lies bleeding~~ sleeping
                  kissed & away,
      ~~kiss fierce~~   ~~kissed such~~
~~Time~~      draws   his breath;
      ~~sucks kiss had choked~~
And ~~touched & quenched~~
~~Ev~~ But what shd we do weeping
   Tho' light love sleep to death?
We have drained his lips at leisure,
   Till there's not left to drain
            sob of
A single ~~tear for~~ pleasure
            for
      ~~shiver~~ &
A single ~~smile for~~ pain.
      pulse for

Marginal annotations (left):

If you
The parting laugh
Lips &

(Question)
Not the absence of flesh but
the presence of spirit is admirable
   or adorable

We have seen

The ~~laughter of~~ We have ~~not~~ such the veiled fair faces
~~That know what~~

~~Take~~ We have seen ~~faces~~

~~And~~ That love ~~turns~~ doubtful in

trod the ~~dusty~~ strange places

We have ~~seen~~

looks

waste

Rococo

39

The Starlight Night — Sonnet

Look at the stars! look, look up at the skies!
O look at all the fire-folk sitting in the air!
The bright boroughs, the quivering citadels there!
Look, the elf-rings; look at the out round earded eyes!
The grey lawns cold where quaking gold-dew lies!
Wind-beat whitebeam, airy abeles all on flare!
Flake-doves sent floating out at a farmyard scare! —
Ah well! It is a purchase and a prize.

Rall.
Buy then! Bid then! — what? — Prayer, patience,
alms, vows. —
Look, look — a May-mess, like on orchard boughs!
Look — March-bloom, like on mealed-with-yel-
low sallows!
These are the barn, indeed: within doors house
the shocks. This pale and parcelled hides the
spouse
Christ and the mother of Christ and all His
Hallows.

Feb. 24

x The dim woods quick with diamond wells; the elf-eyes!
ξ The diamond wells through dim woods quick, the elf-eyes!

† The shocks. This day-shot paling hides the spouse
The shocks. This pierced-well paling hides the spouse
The shocks, this 'piece-bright'

the bright, boroughs, the silver citadels there;
the diamond wells quick in dim woods; the elf eyes;
through dim woods, the elf eyes;
The grey lawns, cold where jaunting gold & dew lies
The grey lawns cold jaunting there gold dew lies
the grey lawns cold, jaunting where gold dew lies;

*MS. The Bodleian Library, Oxford*

40

*The Starlight Night — Sonnet*

*Look at the stars! look, look up at the skies!*
*O*
*~~Lo~~ look at all the fire-folk sitting in the air!*
*The bright boroughs, the quivering citadels there!*
*~~* Look, the elf-rings; look at the out round eager-eyes!~~*
*where*
*The grey lawns cold ~~qua~~ quaking gold-dew lies!*

*Wind-beat whitebeam, airy abeles all on flare!*
*Flake-doves sent floating out at a farmyard*
*scare! —*
*Ah well! It is a purchase and a prize.*
*Rall.*
*Buy then! Bid then! — what? — Prayer, patience,*
*alms, vows. —*
*Look, look — a May-mess, like on orchard boughs!*
*Look — March-bloom, like on mealed-with-yel-*
*low sallows!*
*These are the barn, indeed: within doors house*
*†The shocks. This pale and parclose hides the*
*spouse*
*Christ and the Mother of Christ and all His*
*Hallows.*
*Feb, 24*

*\*{ The dim woods quick with diamond wells; the elf-eyes!*
*{ The diamond wells through dim woods quick, the elf-eyes!*

*† The shocks. This day-shot paling hides the Spouse*
*The shocks. This pierced — well paling hides the spouse*
*The shocks. This piece-bright — — — —*


*The bright boroughs, the silver citadels there;*
*in*
*The diamond wells quick ~~in~~ dim woods; the elf eyes;*
*~~down dim woods~~*
*through dim woods; the elf eyes;*
*The grey lawns cold where jaunt~~ed~~ing gold ~~its~~ dew lies*
*there*
*{ The grey lawns cold jaunting, ~~for~~ gold dew lies;*
*{ The grey lawns cold, jaunting where gold dew lies;*

Adlestrop

Yes, I remember Adlestrop —
At least the name. One afternoon
Of heat ~~the express train~~ drew up there
~~Against its custom~~: It was June.

Yes, I remember Adlestrop —
The name, because One afternoon
Of heat, the express train drew up there
~~Against its custom~~
Unwontedly. It was late June.

The steam hissed. Someone cleared his throat.
No one left & no one came
On the bare platform. What I saw
Was Adlestrop, only the name,

And, willows, willow-herb & grass,
And meadowsweet. The hay cocks dry
Were not less still & lonely fair
Than the high clouds ~~that~~ in the sky.

And all that minute a blackbird sang
Close by, and round him, mistier,
Farther & farther, all the birds
Of Oxfordshire & Gloucestershire.

*MS. 44990. 641f, British Museum*

42

*Adlestrop*

*Yes, I remember Adlestrop —*
*At least the name. One afternoon*
  *the express train*
*Of heat ~~the train slowed down~~ drew up there*
 *Against its custom It's was June.*
*~~There unexpectedly.~~*

*Yes, I remember Adlestrop —*
 *The name, because*
*~~At least the name.~~ One afternoon*
*Of heat, the express train drew up there*
*~~Against its custom~~*
*Unwontedly. It was late June.*

*The steam hissed. Someone cleared his throat.*
*No one left & no one came*
*On the bare platform. What I saw*
*Was Adlestrop, only the name,*

*And, willows, willow herb & grass,*
*And meadowsweet. The haycocks dry*
*Were not less still & lonely fair*
*Than the high cloudlets ~~tiers~~ in the sky*

*And all that minute a blackbird sang*
*Close by, and round him, mistier,*
*Farther & farther, all the birds*
*Of Oxfordshire & Gloucestershire.*

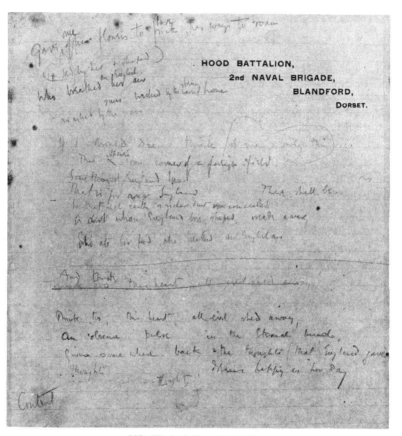

*MS. King's College, Cambridge*

once      *love*
*Gave, of her flowers to pick, her ways to roam*

*(& fed by her & shaped)*
*an English*
*Who breathed her air*    HOOD BATTALION,
*streams*  2nd NAVAL BRIGADE,
*washed by the waves of home*  BLANDFORD,
*rivers*            DORSET
*washed by the rivers*

*If I should die think of me only this*
*there's*
*That ~~in~~ some corner of a foreign field*
~~*Something of England lies*~~      (*is*)
*That is for ever England*    There shall be
*In that rich earth a richer dust ~~ton~~ concealed*
*A dust whom England bore, shaped, made aware,*
*Gav*
*Who ate her food, who breathed an English air*

*And think*
~~*Think too, this heart, all evil shed away,*~~
*Think, too, this heart, all evil shed away,*
*An 'obscure pulse in the Eternal mind,*
*Gives some where back the thoughts (that England gave.)*
*Thoughts*        *dreams happy as her day*
*thought,*
*Content*

45

*MS. Add. 43721, British Museum*

*Anthem for Dead Youth*

    passing
What ~~minute~~ bells for these who die so fast?
     ( ~~solemn~~      the
— Only the ( monstrous anger of ~~our~~ guns.
   blind insolence    iron
Let the ~~majestic insults~~ of ~~their~~ ~~iron~~ mouths
     requiem
  Be as the ~~priest-words~~ of their ~~burials~~ —
  Learn     organs for the old    requiem
~~Of~~ choristers and holy music, _none;_
  Nor any voice of mourning, save the wail
And the     hiss.   lonely
~~The~~ long-~~drawn~~ ~~wail~~ of ~~high-far~~-sailing shells.
         to light
  What candles may we hold ~~for~~ these lost? ~~souls?~~
—Not in the hands of boys, but in their eyes
   shine the ~~tapers~~    the holy ~~tapers~~.. candles
Shall ʌ many ~~candles; shine; and Love will light them.~~
   ~~holy~~ flames: to
And Women's wide-spread~~ed~~ arms shall be their wreaths,
  And pallor of girls' cheeks shall be their palls.
         ~~mortal~~
  Their flowers, the tenderness of ~~all men's~~ minds
         ~~comrades'~~
         rough mens

   each slow
And ~~every~~ Dusk, a drawing-down of blinds.

       First ~~Draught~~ Draft
      (With Sassoon's amendments.)

He is ~~beautiful~~
~~His~~
Moses is ~~ine~~ ~~experienced~~
His ~~love~~ of pleasure his pleasure in
~~Ferocious~~ in + the earnestness of self mastery
~~Already~~ bring himself & us to ruin
We ~~will~~ suffer more
— They suspect him already

Old Hebrew to himself. His youth is flattered at
Moses kind speech to him
To the young Hel. ~~I am broken &~~ ~~grey~~, have seen much in my time
And all this gay grotesque of childish ~~ruin~~
~~along~~ past ~~itself~~, half blind ~~I~~ grumble at I only grumble
I am not blind or deaf enough for peace
I have seen splendid fools
Into a prophets
So many crazed shadows puffed away.
And contrions cheats with such an
They'd make a bonfire of themselves for ~~form~~
Mouthed the ~~queres~~ in the public
This ~~prime~~ lives pleasure, his pleasure in
His wild ~~flesh is his in~~ Ferocious + this will ~~preshion~~
Egypt ~~To~~ ~~trust in~~ Egypt ~~Short~~ ~~with terror~~
~~his abroad~~ follows him

Mouthed in the square
to ~~road~~ in the
public eye

*He is ~~hurtful~~*
*~~His f~~*
*Moses is ~~inexperienced~~*
*His love of pleasure his pleasure in*
*mastery*
*Ferocious in the earnestness of self*
*~~Abnegation~~ bring himself & us to ruin*
*~~Will~~*
*only*
*We will suffer more*
*~~They suspect him already~~*
*Old Hebrew to himself. His youth is flattered at*
*His                         Moses kind speech to him*
*am broken &    have*
*To the young Heb    I ~~have grown~~ grey & seen much*
*in my time*
*And all this gay grotesque of*
*Long                    childish man*
*~~Ive past, it all & all I grumbled at~~*
*half blind half deaf I only*
*grumble*
*now*
*I am not blind or deaf enough for peace*
*young*
*I have seen splendid fools*
*cheat themselves*
*Into a prophets frenzy, I have seen*
*So many crazed shadows puffed away*
*And concious cheats with such an*
*ich for fame*
*~~Mouthed in the squares~~     Theyed make a bonfire of themselves*
*~~broad in the~~            in the public eye*
*~~public eye~~        Mouthed the squares    ~~rather~~*
*to be*
*in the public eye,*
*~~Moses~~ loves pleasure, his pleasure in*
*This prince                    mastery*
*& ~~his will~~*
*Ferocious & ~~tenacious~~*
*His wild flesh is his ruin              unsafe & ~~fall~~*
*~~of~~*
*~~To those~~ at play      shot with terror*
*Trust in    Eypt suspects him now*
*~~Egyptian~~ woman*
*Heres Abinoah follows him about*

49

# II

# THE POET'S
# PRINTED REVISIONS

# 1

Bid me but live, and I will live
 Thy Votary to be:
Or bid me love, and I will give
 A loving heart to thee.

A heart as soft, a heart as kind,
 A heart as soundly free,
As in the world thou canst not find,
 That heart Ile give to thee.

Bid that heart stay, and it shall stay,
 And honour thy Decree:
Or bid it languish quite away,
 And it shall do't so for thee.

Bid me to weep, and I will weep,
 While I have eyes to see:
Or having none, yet I will keep
 A heart to weep for thee.

Thou art my life, my love, my heart,
 The very eye of me:
And hast command of every part,
 To live and die for thee.

This song by Robert Herrick was set to music by Henry Lawes, and appeared in a music-book *Select Musicall Ayres and Dialogues*, published by John Playford in 1652.

It also appears in the *Hesperides*, published in 1648, under the title *TO ANTHEA, who may command him any thing*. We know that many of Herrick's songs in Playford's music-books were based upon manuscript versions which are really early drafts of the poems. So we may be fairly certain that the Hesperides version is the correct and final text, and the one given above a reprint of one of these earlier drafts.

Here is the *Hesperides* text of this well-known poem for purposes of comparison. One must remark on the more arresting opening; the reader may consider the variant readings himself, and decide upon the fifth stanza, which does not appear in the song-book.

### TO ANTHEA, *who may command him any thing*

1. Bid me to live, and I will live
   Thy Protestant to be:
   Or bid me love, and I will give
   A loving heart to thee.

2. A heart as soft, a heart as kind,
   A heart as sound and free,
   As in the whole world thou canst find,
   That heart Ile give to thee.

3. Bid that heart stay, and it will stay,
   To honour thy Decree:
   Or bid it languish quite away,
   And't shall doe so for thee.

4. Bid me to weep, and I will weep,
   While I have eyes to see:
   And having none, yet I will keep
   A heart to weep for thee.

5. Bid me despaire, and Ile despaire,
   Under that *Cypresse* tree:
   Or bid me die, and I will dare
   E'en Death, to die for thee.

6. Thou art my life, my love, my heart,
   The very eyes of me:
   And hast command of every part,
   To live and die for thee.

## 2

Goldsmith's most famous poem, *The Deserted Village*, was enthusiastically received when it first appeared in May, 1770. The pictures in which it excels are the result of the poet's accurate observation. He was storing his mind with descriptions many years before the poem was written. Occasionally, he expressed himself in a rough draft, or in a letter, and made use of the passage in a modified form in his greater work. Here is his description of an Author's Bedchamber. It comes from a letter written to his brother, the Rev. Henry Goldsmith, in 1759, which Goldsmith begins:

Your last letter, I repeat it, was too short: you should have given me your opinion of the design of the heroicomical poem which I sent you: you remember I intended to introduce the hero of the poem, as lying in a paltry alehouse. You may take the following specimen of the manner, which I flatter myself is quite original. The room in which he lies, may be described somewhat in this way:

> The window, patch'd with paper, lent a ray,
> That feebly shew'd the state in which he lay.
> The sanded floor, that grits beneath the tread:
> The humid wall with paltry pictures spread;
> The game of goose was there expos'd to view
> And the twelve rules the royal martyr drew:
> The seasons, fram'd with listing, found a place,
> And Prussia's monarch shew'd his lamp-black face.
> The morn was cold; he views with keen desire,
> A rusty grate unconscious of a fire.
> An unpaid reck'ning on the frieze was scor'd,
> And five crack'd tea-cups dress'd the chimney board.

These lines appear, with a few alterations, in Letter XXX of *The Citizen of the World*, published in 1762. They are read aloud at a club of authors by a poet in 'shabby finery', who asserts that he had composed them the day before, and explains his design in these words: 'The poem begins with the description of an author's bedchamber: the picture was sketched in my own apartment; for you must know, gentlemen, that I am myself the hero.' Then putting himself into the attitude of an orator, with all the emphasis of voice and action, he proceeds:

'Where the Red Lion flaring o'er the way,
Invites each passing stranger that can pay;
Where Calvert's butt, and Parson's black champagne,
Regale the drabs and bloods of Drury-Lane;
There in a lonely room, from bailiffs snug,
The Muse found Scroggen stretch'd beneath a rug;
A window patch'd with paper lent a ray,
That dimly show'd the state in which he lay;
The sanded floor that grits beneath the tread;
The humid wall with paltry pictures spread:
The royal game of goose was there in view,
And the twelve rules the royal martyr drew;
The seasons, fram'd with listing, found a place,
And brave prince William show'd his lamp-black face:
The morn was cold, he views with keen desire
The rusty grate unconscious of a fire;
With beer and milk arrears the frieze was scor'd,
And five crack'd teacups dress'd the chimney board;
A nightcap deck'd his brows instead of bay,
A cap by night—a stocking all the day!'

From this second version Goldsmith adapted his description of the inn parlour in *The Deserted Village*:

Low lies that house where nut-brown draughts inspir'd,
Where grey-beard mirth and smiling toil retir'd,
Where village statesmen talk'd with looks profound,
And news much older than their ale went round.
Imagination fondly stoops to trace
The parlour splendours of that festive place;
The white-wash'd wall, the nicely-sanded floor,
The varnish'd clock that click'd behind the door;
The chest contriv'd a double debt to pay,
A bed by night, a chest of drawers by day;

> The pictures plac'd for ornament and use,
> The twelve good rules, the royal game of goose;
> The hearth, except when winter chill'd the day,
> With aspen boughs, and flowers, and fennel, gay;
> While broken tea-cups, wisely kept for show,
> Rang'd o'er the chimney, glisten'd in a row.

One may almost trace the changes in Goldsmith's fortunes by comparing these three versions. When he submitted to his brother Henry a sample of a heroi-comic poem describing a Grub Street writer lying in a 'paltry alehouse', he was himself living miserably in the squalor of Green Arbour Court, Old Bailey. Soon, however, his fortunes began to mend. He published his periodical *The Bee*, contributed to various magazines, and was employed by John Newbery, the publisher. He made the acquaintance of Garrick and Johnson, and was one of the original members of 'The Club'.

The second version of the poem first appeared in Newbery's *Public Ledger* in one of the series of 'Chinese Letters', subsequently published as *The Citizen of the World*. The scene has now become the Red Lion in Drury Lane. The poem is changed slightly to suit the occasion—the description of the proceedings of the club of authors, most of whom do not wish to hear the first book of an heroic poem read by one of their number. In spite of this the poet holds forth, and when he reaches the last line he cries, 'there is a description for you; Rabelais's bedchamber is but a fool to it.'

> A cap by night—a stocking all the day!

There is sound, and sense, and truth, and nature in the trifling compass of ten little syllables.'

This line has its parallel in the adapted version in *The Deserted Village*, where a piece of furniture pays a double debt—

> A bed by night, a chest of drawers by day.

Once again Goldsmith's circumstances have changed, and produced their changes in the poem. He is no longer a Grub Street writer. Unharassed by poverty, he casts his mind back to Sweet Auburn. Distance adds its own charm to the scene. The village inn has no windows 'patch'd with paper', or 'humid walls', or empty grate. Instead we have

> The parlour splendours of that festive place,

shown further in 'the white-wash'd wall' and 'the varnish'd clock'. But certain accessories are retained: 'the sanded floor', the 'twelve good rules', the pictures, no longer paltry, but 'plac'd for ornament and use', the tea-cups, now broken, are 'wisely kept for show'. The hearth is filled with 'aspen boughs and flowers, and fennel gay'. This inn parlour is a pleasant place; but it derives from the description of a 'paltry ale-house' written twelve years before.

## 3

The poplars are fell'd and adieu to the shade
And the whispering sound of the cool colonnade,
Their winds play no longer and sing in the leaves,
Nor Ouse in its bosom their image receives.

Twelve years had elaps'd since I last took a view
Of my favourite field and the bank where they grew,
When behold on their sides in the grass they were laid,
And I sat on the trees under which I had stray'd.

The blackbird has sought out another retreat
Where the hazels afford him a screen from the heat,
And the scene where his notes have oft charm'd me before,
Shall resound with his sweet-flowing ditty no more.

My fugitive years are all hast'ning away,
And I must alas! lie as lowly as they,
With a turf on my breast, and a stone at my head,
Ere another such grove rises up in its stead.

The change both my heart and my fancy employs,
I reflect on the frailty of man, and his joys;
Short-lived as we are, yet our pleasures, we see,
Have a still shorter date, and die sooner than we.

William Cowper wrote *The Poplar-Field* in 1784, and it was published, as above, in *The Gentleman's Magazine* in January of the following year. As a result of some friendly criticism, the poem was considerably altered, and was afterwards published in 1800 in this revised version:

> The poplars are fell'd farewell to the shade
> And the whispering sound of the cool colonnade,
> The winds play no longer, and sing in the leaves,
> Nor Ouse on his bosom their image receives.
>
> Twelve years have elaps'd since I first took a view
> Of my favourite field and the bank where they grew,
> And now in the grass behold they are laid,
> And the tree is my seat that once lent me a shade.
>
> The blackbird has fled to another retreat
> Where the hazels afford him a screen from the heat,
> And the scene where his melody charm'd me before,
> Resounds with his sweet-flowing ditty no more.
>
> My fugitive years are all hasting away,
> And I must ere long lie as lowly as they,
> With a turf on my breast, and a stone at my head,
> Ere another such grove shall arise in its stead.
>
> 'Tis a sight to engage me, if any thing can,
> To muse on the perishing pleasures of man;
> Though his life be a dream, his enjoyments, I see,
> Have a being less durable even than he.

The reader may consider why the changes were made, and whether the poem in its revised form is an improvement or not.

# 4

We all know Wordsworth's poem *The Daffodils*, which makes the sparkling scene live for us again. Anyone would imagine it to be the spontaneous description of a memorable occasion. But the immediate account of that April scene was written in Dorothy Wordsworth's *Journal*, in unstudied prose, which you may consider to be as lovely as her brother's lyric. They were returning together from Eusemere to Dove Cottage.

When we were in the woods beyond Gowbarrow Park we saw a few daffodils close to the water-side. We fancied that the lake had floated the seeds ashore, and that the little colony had so sprung up. But as we went along there were more and yet more: and at last, under the boughs of the trees, we saw that there was a long belt of them along the shore, about the breadth of a country turnpike road. I never saw daffodils so beautiful. They grew among the mossy stones about and about them; some rested their heads upon these stones as on a pillow for weariness; and the rest tossed and reeled and danced, and seemed as if they verily laughed with the wind, that blew upon them over the lake: they looked so gay, ever glancing, ever changing. This wind blew directly over the lake to them. There was here and there a little knot, and a few stragglers a few yards higher up, but they were so few as not to disturb the simplicity, unity and life of that one busy highway.

This was written on 15 April 1802. It was two years later that Wordsworth recorded the incident in verse. He may have 'recollected the scene in tranquillity', or he may have read the description in his sister's *Journal* and thus recalled the walk back to Grasmere, and 'the long belt' of daffodils, by the water-side. The poem was not published till 1807, and then not as we know it today. It had three verses.

> I wandered lonely as a cloud
> That floats on high o'er vales and hills,
> When all at once I saw a crowd,
> A host, of dancing daffodils;

Beside the lake, beneath the trees,
Fluttering and dancing in the breeze.

The waves beside them danced; but they
Out-did the sparkling waves in glee:
A poet could not but be gay,
In such a laughing company:
I gazed—and gazed—but little thought
What wealth the show to me had brought:

For oft when on my couch I lie
In vacant or in pensive mood,
They flash upon that inward eye
Which is the bliss of solitude;
And then my heart with pleasure fills,
And dances with the daffodils.

The two lines:

They flash upon that inward eye
Which is the bliss of solitude;

were by Mrs Wordsworth. They were said by Wordsworth to be 'the two best lines in the poem'.

He revised the poem, making two alterations; the word 'golden' was substituted for 'dancing' in line 4, and 'jocund' for 'laughing' in line 10. He wrote another stanza, which was placed second in the version published in 1815, the version which was to become so universally known.

I wandered lonely as a cloud
That floats on high o'er vales and hills,
When all at once I saw a crowd,
A host, of golden daffodils;
Beside the lake, beneath the trees
Fluttering and dancing in the breeze.

Continuous as the stars that shine
And twinkle on the milky way,
They stretched in never-ending line
Along the margin of a bay:
Ten thousand saw I at a glance,
Tossing their heads in sprightly dance.

The waves beside them danced; but they
Out-did the sparkling waves in glee:
A poet could not but be gay,
In such a jocund company:
I gazed—and gazed—but little thought
What wealth the show to me had brought:

For oft, when on my couch I lie
In vacant or in pensive mood,
They flash upon that inward eye
Which is the bliss of solitude;
And then my heart with pleasure fills,
And dances with the daffodils.

This, I think we shall agree, is an improvement. Wordsworth has suggested the landscape, bare and austere, by comparing his own loneliness with that of a cloud floating over vales and hills. We are merely told of the lake and trees. The daffodils provide the gay company amid this winter scene. They are the heralds, telling of the invasion of Spring, bursting upon the poet like an army. The very economy of epithets makes the word 'golden' enhance the pictorial effect still more, giving that warmth of colour which makes the scene leap to the eye. 'Dancing daffodils' as the original version had it, though pleasant in sound, would weaken the last line—

Fluttering and dancing in the breeze.

The second stanza adds much to the poem. We can already see the daffodils as a host, by the water-side, underneath the trees. This presents that unforgettable picture of the 'long belt of them along the shore, about the breadth of a country turnpike road'. The comparison with the stars on the milky way is happy and appropriate; it enlarges the imagination, giving radiance as well as number. It connects the great sweep of the stars with the arresting line of flowers, and combines the crystal freshness with twinkling movement. The eye follows the 'tossing heads' along that far margin. If the poem were without this stanza we should lose the spaciousness of the scene, the completeness of the picture.

The word 'laughing' in line 10 of the first version reminds us of Dorothy's description; the change to 'jocund' suggests that the flowers expressed their joy completely in the sparkling movement of the dance. Sound, even of laughter, does not intrude upon the scene. The final effect of the poem is one of joyful motion, which can fill the heart with pleasure.

When we consider how the poem was composed, we can say that three people had a hand in it. And even this delightful lyric, spontaneous as it may appear, was not written with that immediacy which one so often associates with poetic creation.

# 5

*The Ancient Mariner*, Coleridge's finest poem, was first planned, and in part composed, during a memorable walk begun on the afternoon of 13 November 1797. Dorothy Wordsworth gave him continual encouragement during the early months of 1798; and on 23 March he brought the poem to her at last completed.

It was published in the volume of *Lyrical Ballads* in the following September by Joseph Cottle at Bristol. It is entitled *The Rime of the Ancyent Marinere, in Seven Parts*, and is the first poem in the original octavo edition.

Here is a literal reprint of Part III from the first edition:

### III

I saw a something in the Sky
No bigger than my fist;
At first it seem'd a little speck
And then it seem'd a mist:
It mov'd and mov'd, and took at last
A certain shape, I wist.

A speck, a mist, a shape, I wist!
And still it ner'd and ner'd;
And, an it dodg'd a water-sprite,
It plung'd and tack'd and veer'd.

With throat unslack'd, with black lips bak'd
  Ne could we laugh, ne wail:
Then while thro' drouth all dumb they stood
I bit my arm and suck'd the blood
  And cry'd, A sail! a sail!

With throat unslack'd, with black lips bak'd
  Agape they hear'd me call:
Gramercy! they for joy did grin
And all at once their breath drew in
  As they were drinking all.

She doth not tack from side to side—
  Hither to work us weal
Withouten wind, withouten tide
  She steddies with upright keel.

The western wave was all a flame,
  The day was well nigh done!
Almost upon the western wave
  Rested the broad bright Sun;
When that strange shape drove suddenly
  Betwixt us and the Sun.

And strait the Sun was fleck'd with bars
  (Heaven's mother send us grace)
As if thro' a dungeon grate he peer'd
  With broad and burning face.

Alas! (thought I, and my heart beat loud)
  How fast she neres and neres!
Are those *her* Sails that glance in the Sun
  Like restless gossameres?

Are these *her* naked ribs, which fleck'd
  The sun that did behind them peer?
And are these two all, all the crew,
  That woman and her fleshless Pheere?

*His* bones were black with many a crack,
  All black and bare, I ween;

Jet-black and bare, save where with rust
Of mouldy damps and charnel crust
  They're patch'd with purple and green.

*Her* lips are red, *her* looks are free,
  *Her* locks are yellow as gold:
Her skin is as white as leprosy,
And she is far liker Death than he;
  Her flesh makes the still air cold.

The naked Hulk alongside came
  And the Twain were playing dice;
'The Game is done! I've won, I've won!'
  Quoth she, and whistled thrice.

A gust of wind sterte up behind
  And whistled thro' his bones;
Thro' the holes of his eyes and the hole of his mouth
  Half-whistles and half-groans.

With never a whisper in the Sea
  Off darts the Spectre-ship;
While clombe above the Eastern bar
The horned Moon, with one bright Star
  Almost atween the tips.

One after one by the horned Moon
  (Listen, O Stranger! to me)
Each turn'd his face with a ghastly pang
  And curs'd me with his ee.

Four times fifty living men,
  With never a sigh or groan,
With heavy thump, a lifeless lump
  They dropp'd down one by one.

Their souls did from their bodies fly,—
  They fled to bliss or woe;
And every soul it pass'd me by,
  Like the whiz of my Cross-bow.

The text was revised in 1800, 1802, 1805, and 1817. Here is the same passage in the final version, as given in 1817 in *Sibylline Leaves*:

### III

There passed a weary time. Each throat
Was parched, and glazed each eye.
A weary time! a weary time!
How glazed each weary eye,
When looking westward, I beheld
A something in the sky.

At first it seemed a little speck,
And then it seemed a mist;
It moved and moved, and took at last
A certain shape, I wist.

A speck, a mist, a shape, I wist!
And still it neared and neared:
As if it dodged a water-sprite,
It plunged and tacked and veered.

With throats unslaked, with black lips baked,
We could nor laugh nor wail;
Through utter drought all dumb we stood!
I bit my arm, I sucked the blood,
And cried, A sail! a sail!

With throats unslaked, with black lips baked,
Agape they heard me call:
Gramercy! they for joy did grin,
And all at once their breath drew in,
As they were drinking all.

See! see! (I cried) she tacks no more!
Hither to work us weal;
Without a breeze, without a tide,
She steadies with upright keel!

The western wave was all a-flame.
The day was well nigh done!
Almost upon the western wave
Rested the broad bright Sun;

When that strange shape drove suddenly
Betwixt us and the Sun.

And straight the Sun was flecked with bars,
(Heaven's Mother send us grace!)
As if through a dungeon-grate he peered
With broad and burning face.

Alas! (thought I, and my heart beat loud)
How fast she nears and nears!
Are those *her* sails that glance in the Sun,
Like restless gossameres?

Are those *her* ribs through which the Sun
Did peer, as through a grate?
And is that Woman all her crew?
Is that a DEATH? and are there two?
Is DEATH that woman's mate?

*Her* lips were red, *her* looks were free,
Her locks were as yellow as gold:
Her skin was as white as leprosy,
The Night-mare LIFE-IN-DEATH was she,
Who thicks man's blood with cold.

The naked hulk alongside came,
And the twain were casting dice;
'The game is done! I've won! I've won!'
Quoth she, and whistles thrice.

The Sun's rim dips; the stars rush out:
At one stride comes the dark;
With far-heard whisper, o'er the sea,
Off shot the spectre-bark.

We listened and looked sideways up!
Fear at my heart, as at a cup,
My life-blood seemed to sip!
The stars were dim, and thick the night,
The steersman's face by his lamp gleamed white;
From the sails the dew did drip—
Till clomb above the eastern bar
The horned Moon, with one bright star
Within the nether tip.

One after one, by the star-dogged Moon,
Too quick for groan or sigh,
Each turned his face with a ghastly pang
And cursed me with his eye.

Four times fifty living men,
(And I heard nor sigh nor groan)
With heavy thump, a lifeless lump,
They dropped down one by one.

The souls did from their bodies fly,—
They fled to bliss or woe!
And every soul, it passed me by,
Like the whizz of my cross-bow!

Why did Coleridge make so many corrections in the subsequent editions of *The Ancient Mariner?* It is worth our consideration, in regard to craftsmanship, because every correction, and omission, improved the poem. Had he been quite satisfied that the poem which he brought to Dorothy Wordsworth was the final form which his inspiration could take, we should have a much less perfect poem than we have today. Some of the finest lines have been built up from unimpressive lines in the 1798 version. It has been said that the Romantic poets were not sound critics of their own work. This is not true of Coleridge in respect of *The Ancient Mariner.* When the poem was adversely received, he scrupulously revised it, and the results of that revision can be judged by comparing the two versions of Section III given above.

The severe handling which the poem received was due very largely to Southey. No doubt the quarrel over pantisocracy still rankled, and Southey took the opportunity to show his feelings when the *Lyrical Ballads* appeared. A few days after their publication, he wrote to William Taylor of Norwich:

Have you seen a volume of *Lyrical Ballads?* They are by Coleridge and Wordsworth, but their names are not affixed. Coleridge's *Ballad of the Ancyent Marinere* is, I think, the clumsiest attempt at German sublimity I ever saw. Many of the others are very fine;

and some I shall re-read upon the same principle that led me through Trissino, whenever I am afraid of writing like a child or an old woman.

About the same time as this letter, his review of the *Lyrical Ballads* was published in the *Critical Review* of October 1798. In this he says:

In a very different style of poetry is the *Rime of the Ancient Mariner*; a ballad (says the advertisement) 'professedly written in imitation of the *style*, as well as the spirit of the elder poets'. We are tolerably conversant with the early English poets; and can discover no resemblance whatever, except in antiquated spelling and a few obsolete words. This piece appears to us perfectly original in style as well as in story. Many of the stanzas are laboriously beautiful; but in connection they are absurd or unintelligible....We do not sufficiently understand the story to analyse it. It is a Dutch attempt at German sublimity. Genius has here been employed in producing a poem of little merit.

It is obvious that the reviewers of the first edition of the *Lyrical Ballads* took their line of attack from Southey's article, especially in regard to Coleridge's poem. One critic says, of the *Ancient Mariner*, 'We are not pleased with it; in our opinion it has more of the extravagance of a mad German poet, than of the simplicity of our ancient ballad writers....'

We find even Wordsworth writing to Cottle in 1799:

From what I can gather it seems that the *Ancient Mariner* has, on the whole, been an injury to the volume. I mean that the old words and the strangeness of it have deterred readers from going on. If the volume should come to a second edition, I would put in its place some little things which would be more likely to suit the common taste.

It is not surprising that Coleridge set about revising the poem. The tone of the reviewers underwent a gradual change; though critics still persisted in fault finding, they remarked on the beauties of the poem also. The *British Critic*, in October 1799, remarks that the beginning and the end 'are striking and well-conducted', but the middle part is 'confused' and 'not quite intelligible'. The language is criticized as incorrect, and in places 'nonsensical'; 'but the ancient style is well imitated, while the antiquated words are so very few, that the latter might with advantage be entirely removed without detriment to the effect of the Poem.'

Coleridge profited from all these comments, for the final version of the poem is free from many of the original archaisms; he also diminished much of the grotesqueness, the realism, and horror, and reduced some of the iteration of the 1798 version. This careful revision greatly enriched the poem, which remains one of the finest examples in our literature of poetic imagination combined with supreme craftsmanship in words.

# 6

Keats's most ambitious poetic undertaking was *Hyperion*, which he began in the autumn of the year 1818. The subject had been long in his mind, but due to many anxieties he worked at it by fits and starts then, and throughout the early part of the following year. In September 1819, he wrote to his friend Reynolds giving his reasons for discontinuing the poem as follows:

'There were too many Miltonic inversions in it—Miltonic verse cannot be written but in an artful, or rather, artist's humour. I wish to give myself up to other sensations. English ought to be kept up.'

Here is a passage from the poem:

> Meanwhile in other realms big tears were shed,
> More sorrow like to this, and such like woe,
> Too huge for mortal tongue or pen of scribe:
> The Titans fierce, self-hid, or prison-bound,
> Groan'd for the old allegiance once more,
> And listen'd in sharp pain for Saturn's voice.
> But one of the whole mammoth-brood still kept
> His sov'reignty, and rule, and majesty;—

Blazing Hyperion on his orbed fire
Still sat, still snuff'd the incense, teeming up
From man to the sun's God; yet unsecure:
For as among us mortals omens drear
Fright and perplex, so also shuddered he—
Not at dog's howl, or gloom-bird's hated screech,
Or the familiar visiting of one
Upon the first toll of his passing-bell,
Or prophesyings of the midnight lamp;
But horrors, portion'd to a giant nerve,
Oft made Hyperion ache. His palace bright
Bastion'd with pyramids of glowing gold,
And touch'd with shade of bronzed obelisks,
Glar'd a blood-red through all its thousand courts,
Arches, and domes, and fiery galleries;
And all its curtains of Aurorian clouds
Flush'd angerly: while sometimes eagle's wings,
Unseen before by Gods or wondering men,
Darken'd the place; and neighing steeds were heard,
Not heard before by Gods or wondering men.
Also, when he would taste the spicy wreaths
Of incense, breath'd aloft from sacred hills,
Instead of sweets, his ample palate took
Savour of poisonous brass and metal sick.

In November and December of 1819 Keats made an attempt to reconstruct the poem, calling it *The Fall of Hyperion*. We know that he considered the diction of *Hyperion* laboured and artificial. However, as many of the changes he made were unhappily for the worse, it was thought for many years that *The Fall of Hyperion* was in fact the first version of the poem. Internal evidence has shown conclusively that *The Fall of Hyperion* was not a first draft but a recast attempted by the poet because he was dissatisfied with the poem as it stood. The relation of the two poems is of vital interest in the study of Keats's poetic art. It is profitable to consider parallel passages side by side, and to find reasons for the omissions and alterations made in revising the piece. The former passage appears as follows in *The Fall of Hyperion*:

In melancholy realms big tears are shed,
More sorrow like to this, and such like woe,
Too huge for mortal tongue, or pen of scribe.
The Titans fierce, self hid or prison bound,
Groan for the old allegiance once more,
Listening in their doom for Saturn's voice.
But one of our whole eagle-brood still keeps
His sov'reignty, and rule, and majesty;
Blazing Hyperion on his orbed fire
Still sits, still snuffs the incense teeming up
From Man to the Sun's God: yet unsecure.
For as upon the earth dire prodigies
Fright and perplex, so also shudders he:
Nor at dog's howl or gloom-bird's Even screech,
Or the familiar visitings of one
Upon the first toll of his passing bell:
But horrors, portioned to a giant nerve,
Make great Hyperion ache. His palace bright,
Bastion'd with pyramids of glowing gold,
And touch'd with shade of bronzed obelisks,
Glares a blood-red thro' all the thousand courts,
Arches, and domes, and fiery galleries:
And all its curtains of Aurorian clouds
Flush angerly; when he would taste the wreaths
Of incense breathed aloft from sacred hills,
Instead of sweets, his ample palate takes
Savour of poisonous brass and metals sick.

# 7

In 1833 Tennyson published a volume of poems which included *The Lotos-Eaters*. It was reviewed by Lockhart in the *Quarterly Review*, April 1833. He did not spare the poet, hailing him as 'another and a brighter star of that galaxy or *milky way* of poetry of which the lamented Keats was the harbinger...'. He quotes some fourteen lines from the concluding passage of *The Lotos-Eaters*, and says, 'Our readers will, we think, agree that this is admirably characteristic, and that the singers of this song must have made pretty free with the intoxicating fruit. How they got home you must read in Homer: Mr Tennyson—himself, we presume, a dreamy lotus-eater, a delicious lotus-eater—leaves them in full song.'

Here is the passage in the original version of 1833 which produced this comment:

### The Lotos-Eaters

We have had enough of motion,
Weariness and wild alarm,
Tossing on the tossing ocean,
Where the tusked sea-horse walloweth
In a stripe of grass-green calm,
At noon tide beneath the lee;
And the monstrous narwhale swalloweth
His foam-fountains in the sea.
Long enough the wine-dark wave our weary bark did carry.
This is lovelier and sweeter,
Men of Ithaca, this is meeter,
In the hollow rosy vale to tarry,
Like a dreamy Lotos-eater, a delirious Lotos-eater!
We will eat the Lotos, sweet
As the yellow honeycomb,
In the valley some, and some
On the ancient heights divine;
And no more roam,
On the loud hoar foam,
To the melancholy home
At the limit of the brine,
The little isle of Ithaca, beneath the day's decline.
We'll lift no more the shattered oar,
No more unfurl the straining sail;
With the blissful Lotos-eaters pale
We will abide in the golden vale
Of the Lotos-land till the Lotos fail;
We will not wander more.
Hark! how sweet the horned ewes bleat
On the solitary steeps,

And the merry lizard leaps,
And the foam-white waters pour;
And the dark pine weeps,
And the lithe vine creeps,
And the heavy melon sleeps
On the level of the shore:
Oh! islanders of Ithaca, we will not wander more.
Surely, surely slumber is more sweet than toil, the shore
Than labour in the ocean, and rowing with the oar,
Oh! islanders of Ithaca, we will return no more.

It is significant that almost every line with which the critic found fault was either omitted or re-written in future editions of Tennyson's works. Lockhart's pleasantries were certainly justified in regard to *The Lotos-Eaters*. The last part of the Choric Song was considerably altered, and Tennyson produced some of his happiest revisions. Here is the version of 1853 for purposes of comparison:

The Lotos blooms below the barren peak:
The Lotos blows by every winding creek:
All day the wind breathes low with mellower tone:
Thro' every hollow cave and alley lone
Round and round the spicy downs the yellow Lotos-dust is blown.
We have had enough of action, and of motion we,
Roll'd to starboard, roll'd to larboard, when the surge was seething
free,
Where the wallowing monster spouted his foam-fountains in the sea.
Let us swear an oath, and keep it with an equal mind,
In the hollow Lotos-land to live and lie reclined
On the hills like Gods together, careless of mankind.
For they lie beside their nectar, and the bolts are hurl'd
Far below them in the valleys, and the clouds are lightly curl'd
Round their golden houses, girdled with the gleaming world:
Where they smile in secret, looking over wasted lands,
Blight and famine, plague and earthquake, roaring deeps and fiery
sands,
Clanging fights, and flaming towns, and sinking ships, and praying
hands.

But they smile, they find a music centred in a doleful song
Steaming up, a lamentation and an ancient tale of wrong,
Like a tale of little meaning tho' the words are strong;
Chanted from an ill-used race of men that cleave the soil,
Sow the seed, and reap the harvest with enduring toil,
Storing yearly little dues of wheat, and wine and oil;
Till they perish and they suffer—some, 'tis whisper'd—down in hell
Suffer endless anguish, others in Elysian valleys dwell,
Resting weary limbs at last on beds of asphodel.
Surely, surely, slumber is more sweet than toil, the shore
Than labour in the deep mid-ocean, wind and wave and oar;
Oh rest ye, brother mariners, we will not wander more.

# 8

Rossetti's *The Blessed Damozel* provides another interesting illus-
tration of the way in which a poem may be composed only after
much 'labour of the file'. This intensely individual lyric was written
when the poet was nineteen years of age. It was first published in
the Pre-Raphaelite periodical *The Germ*, in 1850. The poem was
frequently revised in the effort to attain that perfect expression
which was Rossetti's constant aim.

The final version of the poem is generally accepted as that of
1870. These lines in the first stanza:

> Her eyes were deeper than the depth
> Of waters stilled at even;

were originally:

> Her blue grave eyes were deeper much
> Than a deep water even.

and passed through an intermediate stage in the *Oxford and Cambridge Magazine*:

> Her eyes knew more of rest and shade
> Than waters stilled at even.

The seventh stanza was the most altered. When first published
it ran:

> Heard hardly, some of her new friends
> Playing at holy games,
> Spake, gentle-mouthed among themselves
> Their virginal new names
> And the souls mounting up to God
> Went by her like thin flames.

In the *Oxford and Cambridge Magazine* this was changed:

> She scarcely heard her sweet new friends
> Playing at holy games,
> Softly they spake among themselves
> Their virginal chaste names
> And the souls mounting up to God
> Went by her like thin flames.

This is how it reads in the 1870 version:

> Heard hardly, some of her new friends
> Amid their loving games
> Spake evermore among themselves
> Their virginal chaste names;
> And the souls mounting up to God
> Went by her like thin flames.

Two other examples will suffice to show how this delicate, archaic,
imaginative poem was fastidiously revised to its final form.
Stanza eight appears in *The Germ* as follows:

> And still she bowed herself and stooped
> Into the vast waste calm,
> Till her bosom's pressure must have made
> The bar she leaned on warm.
> And the lilies lay as if asleep
> Along her bended arm.

The first four lines were revised in the *Oxford and Cambridge
Magazine*:

> And still she bowed above the vast
> Waste sea of worlds that swam,
> Until her bosom must have made
> The bar she leaned on warm.

This is how the stanza finally appeared:

> And still she bowed herself and stooped
> Out of the circling charm;
> Until her bosom must have made
> The bar she leaned on warm,
> And the lilies lay as if asleep
> Along her bended arm.

In the next stanza changes are made which once again improve the poem. In *The Germ* the stanza reads:

> From the fixt lull of heaven she saw
> Time, like a pulse, shake fierce
> Through all the worlds. Her gaze still strove,
> In that steep gulf, to pierce
> The swarm: and then she spake as when
> The stars sang in their spheres.

This is its final form:

> From the fixed place of Heaven she saw
> Time like a pulse shake fierce
> Through all the worlds. Her gaze still strove
> Within the gulf to pierce
> Its path; and now she spoke as when
> The stars sang in their spheres.

Rossetti spared no pains; only four verses in the whole poem remained unaltered since 1848 when it was first composed. Even in 1881 we find him hesitating between 'she *cast* her arms along the golden barriers', and 'she *laid* her arms...', and in the last four words of the poem considering whether to say 'I *heard* her tears' or 'I *felt* her tears'.

Such patient labour as this shows that he was as deliberate an artist as Herrick or Keats or Tennyson, combining fastidious workmanship and lyrical inspiration.

# III

# THE POET'S RAW MATERIAL

# 1

From Sir Thomas North's *Translation of Plutarch's 'Lives of the Noble Grecians and Romans'*.

Therefore when she was sent unto by divers letters, both from *Antonius* himself, and also from his friends, she made so light of it, and mocked *Antonius* so much, that she disdained to set forward otherwise, but to take her barge in the river of *Cydnus*; the poop whereof was of gold, the sails of purple, and the oars of silver, which kept stroke in rowing after the sound of the musicke of flutes, howboys, citherns, viols, and such other instruments as they played upon in the barge. And now for the person of herself: she was laid under a pavilion of cloth of gold of tissue, apparelled and attired like the goddess *Venus* commonly drawn in picture: and hard by her, on either hand of her, pretty fair boys apparelled as Painters do set forth god *Cupid*, with little fans in their hands, with the which they fanned wind upon her. Her Ladies and Gentlewomen also, the fairest of them were apparelled like the Nymphs *Nereids* (which are the mermaids of the waters) and like the *Graces*, some steering the helm, others tending the tackle and ropes of the barge, out of the which there came a wonderful passing sweet savour of perfumes, that perfumed the wharf's side, pestered with innumerable multitudes of people. Some of them followed the barge all along the river-side: others also ran out of the city to see her coming in. So that in the end there ran such multitudes of people one after another to see her, that *Antonius* was left post alone in the market-place in his Imperial seat to give audience: and there went a rumour in the people's mouths, that the goddess *Venus* was come to play with the god *Bacchus*, for the general good of all Asia.

From Shakespeare's *Antony and Cleopatra* (Act II, scene ii).

> The barge she sat in, like a burnish'd throne,
> Burn'd on the water: the poop was beaten gold;
> Purple the sails, and so perfumed that
> The winds were love-sick with them; the oars were silver,

Which to the tune of flutes kept stroke, and made
The water which they beat to follow faster,
As amorous of their strokes. For her own person,
It beggar'd all description: she did lie
In her pavilion—cloth-of-gold of tissue—
O'er-picturing that of Venus where we see
The fancy outwork nature: on each side her
Stood pretty dimpled boys, like smiling Cupids,
With divers-coloured fans, whose wind did seem
To glow the delicate cheeks which they did cool,
And what they undid did.

Her gentlewomen, like the Nereides,
So many mermaids, tended her i' the eyes,
And made their bends adornings: at the helm
A seeming mermaid steers: the silken tackle
Swell with the touches of those flower-soft hands,
That yarely frame the office. From the barge
A strange invisible perfume hits the sense
Of the adjacent wharfs. The city cast
Her people out upon her; and Antony,
Enthroned i' the market-place, did sit alone,
Whistling to the air; which, but for vacancy,
Had gone to gaze on Cleopatra too,
And made a gap in nature.

# 2

From Sir Thomas North's *Translation of Plutarch's 'Lives of the Noble Grecians and Romans'*.

The Senate being afeard of their departure, did send unto them certain of the pleasantest old men, and the most acceptable to the people among them. Of these Menenius Agrippa was he, who was sent for chief man of the message from the Senate. He, after many good persuasions and gentle requests made to the people, on the behalf of the Senate: knit up his oration in the end, with a notable tale, in this manner. That on a time all the members of man's body did rebel against the belly, complaining of it, that it only remained in the midst of the body, without doing anything, neither did bear any labour to the maintenance of the rest: whereas all other parts and members did labour painfully, and were very careful to satisfy the appetites and desires of the body. And so the belly, all this notwithstanding laughed at their folly, and said: It is true, I first receive all meats that nourish man's body; but afterwards I send it again to the nourishment of other parts of the same. Even so (quoth he) O you, my maisters, and citizens of Rome: the reason is alike between the Senate and you. For matters being well digested, and their counsels thoroughly examined, touching the benefit of the commonwealth: the Senators are cause of the common commodity that cometh unto every one of you.

From Shakespeare's *Coriolanus* (Act I, scene i).

*Menenius.* Either you must
Confess yourselves wondrous malicious,
Or be accus'd of folly.  I shall tell you
A pretty tale: it may be you have heard it;
But, since it serves my purpose, I will venture
To stale't a little more.
   *First Citizen.* Well, I'll hear it, sir: yet you must not think to
fob-off our disgrace with a tale: but, an't please you deliver.
   *Menenius.* There was a time when all the body's members
Rebell'd against the belly; thus accus'd it:—
That only like a gulf it did remain
I' the midst o' the body, idle and unactive,
Still cupboarding the viand, never bearing
Like labour with the rest; where th'other instruments
Did see and hear, devise, instruct, walk, feel,
And, mutually participate, did minister
Unto the appetite and affection common
Of the whole body. The belly answer'd,—
   *First Citizen.* Well, sir, what answer made the belly?
   *Menenius.* Sir, I shall tell you.—With a kind of smile,
Which ne'er came from the lungs, but even thus—
For, look you, I may make the belly smile

As well as speak—it tauntingly replied
To the discontented members, the mutinous parts
That envied his receipt; even so most fitly
As you malign our senators for that
They are not such as you.
    *First Citizen.*        Your belly's answer? What!
The kingly-crowned head, the vigilant eye,
The counsellor heart, the arm our soldier,
Our steed the leg, the tongue our trumpeter,
With other muniments and petty helps
In this our fabric, if that they—
    *Menenius.*        What then?—
'Fore me, this fellow speaks!—what then? what then?
    *First Citizen.* Should by the cormorant belly be restrain'd,
Who is the sink o' the body,—
    *Menenius.*        Well, what then?
    *First Citizen.* The former agents, if they did complain,
What could the belly answer?
    *Menenius.*        I will tell you;
If you'll bestow a small—of what you have little—
Patience awhile, you'll hear the belly's answer.
    *First Citizen.* Y'are long about it.
    *Menenius.*        Note me this, good friend;
Your most grave belly was deliberate,
Not rash like his accusers, and thus answer'd:
'True is it, my incorporate friends,' quoth he,
'That I receive the general food at first,
Which you do live upon; and fit it is,
Because I am the store-house and the shop
Of the whole body: but, if you do remember,
I send it through the rivers of your blood,
Even to the court, the heart,—to the seat o' the brain;
And, through the cranks and offices of man,
The strongest nerves and small inferior veins
From me receive that natural competency
Whereby they live: and though that all at once,
You, my good friends,'—this says the belly, mark me,—
    *First Citizen.* Ay, sir; well, well.
    *Menenius.*        'Though all at once can not

See what I do deliver out to each,
Yet I can make my audit up, that all
From me do back receive the flour of all
And leave me but the bran.'—What say you to't?
  *First Citizen.* It was an answer: how apply you this?
  *Menenius.* The senators of Rome are this good belly,
And you the mutinous members: for examine
Their counsels and their cares; digest things rightly
Touching the weal o' the common; you shall find,
No public benefit which you receive
But it proceeds or comes from them to you,
And no way from yourselves.

## 3

From Arthur Golding's *Translation of Ovid's 'Metamorphoses'* VII.

Ye Airs and Winds: ye Elves of Hills, of Brooks, of Woods alone,
Of standing Lakes, and of the Night approach ye everyone.
Through help of whom (the crooked banks much wondering at the
    thing)
I have compelled streams to run clean backward to their spring.
By charms I make the calm seas rough, and make the rough seas
    plain.
And cover all the sky with clouds and chase them hence again.
By charms I raise and lay the winds, and burst the Vipers jaw.
And from the bowels of the earth both stones and trees do draw.
Whole Woods and Forests I remove: I make the mountains shake,
And even the earth itself to groan and fearfully to quake.
I call up dead men from their graves and thee, O lightsome Moon
I darken oft, though beaten brass abate thy peril soon.
Our Sorcery dims the Morning fair, and darks the Sun at noon.

From Shakespeare's *The Tempest* (Act v, scene i).

    Ye elves of hills, brooks, standing lakes, and groves,
    And ye that on the sands with printless foot
    Do chase the ebbing Neptune, and do fly him
    When he comes back; you demi-puppets that

By moonshine do the green sour ringlets make,
Whereof the ewe not bites; and you whose pastime
Is to make midnight mushrooms, that rejoice
To hear the solemn curfew; by whose aid—
Weak masters though ye be—I have bedimm'd
The noontide sun, call'd forth the mutinous winds,
And 'twixt the green sea and the azur'd vault
Set roaring war: to the dread rattling thunder
Have I given fire, and rifted Jove's stout oak
With his own bolt; the strong-bas'd promontory
Have I made shake, and by the spurs pluck'd up
The pine and cedar; graves at my command
Have wak'd their sleepers, op'd, and let them forth
By my so potent art.

# 4

From Holinshed's *Chronicles*.

For the space of six months together, after this heinous murder thus committed, there appeared no sun by day nor moon by night in any part of the realm, but still was the sky covered with continual clouds, and sometimes such outrageous winds arose, with lightnings and tempests, that the people were in great fear of present destruction. . . .

Monstrous sights also that were seen within the Scottish kingdom that year were these: horses in Lothian, being of singular beauty and swiftness, did eat their own flesh, and would in no wise taste any other meat. There was a sparrowhawk also strangled by an owl. Neither was it any less wonder that the sun, as before is said, was continually covered with clouds for six months space. But all men understood that the abominable murder of King Duffe was the cause hereof.

From Shakespeare's *Macbeth* (Act II, scene iv).

*Old Man.* Threescore and ten I can remember well:
Within the volume of which time I have seen

Hours dreadful and things strange; but this sore night
Hath trifled former knowings.
    *Ross.*               Ha, good father,
Thou seest, the heavens, as troubled with man's act,
Threatens his bloody stage: by th' clock 'tis day,
And yet dark night strangles the travelling lamp:
Is't night's predominance, or the day's shame,
That darkness does the face of earth entomb,
When living light should kiss it?
    *Old Man.*           'Tis unnatural,
Even like the deed that's done. On Tuesday last,
A falcon, towering in her pride of place,
Was by a mousing owl hawk'd at and kill'd.
    *Ross.* And Duncan's horses—a thing most strange and certain,—
Beauteous and swift, the minions of their race,
Turn'd wild in nature, broke their stalls, flung out,
Contending 'gainst obedience, as they would make
War with mankind.
    *Old Man.*    'Tis said they eat each other.
    *Ross.* They did so,—to th' amazement of mine eyes,
That look'd upon 't.

# 5

From the *Decameron* of Boccaccio, the Fifth Story on the Fourth
Day.

And so, saddest of women, knowing that she might not bewail him
there, she would gladly, if she could, have carried away the body
and given it more honourable sepulture elsewhere; but as she might
not do so, she took a knife, and, as best she could, severed the head
from the trunk, and wrapped it in a napkin and laid it in the lap of
her maid; and having covered the rest of the corpse with earth, she
left the spot, having been seen by none, and went home. There she
shut herself up in her room with the head, and kissed it a thousand
times in every part, and wept long and bitterly over it, till she had

bathed it in her tears. She then wrapped it in a piece of fine cloth, and set it in a large and beautiful pot of the sort in which marjoram or basil is planted, and covered it with earth, and therein planted some roots of the goodliest basil of Salerno, and drenched them only with her tears, or water perfumed with roses or orange-blossoms. And 'twas her wont ever to sit beside this pot, and, all her soul one yearning, to pore upon it, as that which enshrined her Lorenzo, and when long time she had so done, she would bend over it, and weep a great while, until the basil was quite bathed in her tears.

Fostered with such constant, unremitting care, and nourished by the richness given to the soil by the decaying head that lay therein, the basil burgeoned out in exceeding great beauty and fragrance. And, the girl persevering ever in this way of life, the neighbours from time to time took note of it, and when her brothers marvelled to see her beauty ruined, and her eyes as it were evanished from her head, they told them of it, saying: 'We have observed that such is her daily wont.'

From Keats's *Isabella; or, The Pot of Basil.*

### L

With duller steel than the Persean sword
They cut away no formless monster's head,
But one, whose gentleness did well accord
With death, as life. The ancient harps have said,
Love never dies, but lives, immortal Lord:
If Love impersonate was ever dead,
Pale Isabella kiss'd it, and low moan'd.
'Twas love; cold,—dead indeed, but not dethroned.

### LI

In anxious secrecy they took it home,
And then the prize was all to Isabel:
She calm'd its wild hair with a golden comb,
And all around each eye's sepulchral cell
Pointed each fringed lash; the smeared loam
With tears, as chilly as a dripping well,
She drench'd away:—and still she comb'd, and kept
Sighing all day—and still she kiss'd, and wept.

### LII

Then in a silken scarf,—sweet with the dews
Of precious flowers pluck'd in Araby,
And divine liquids come with odorous ooze
Through the cold serpent-pipe refreshfully,—
She wrapped it up; and for its tomb did choose
A garden-pot, wherein she laid it by,
And cover'd it with mould, and o'er it set
Sweet Basil, which her tears kept ever wet.

### LIII

And she forgot the stars, the moon, and sun,
And she forgot the blue above the trees,
And she forgot the dells where waters run,
And she forgot the chilly autumn breeze;
She had no knowledge when the day was done,
And the new morn she saw not: but in peace
Hung over her sweet Basil evermore,
And moisten'd it with tears unto the core.

### LIV

And so she ever fed it with thin tears,
Whence thick, and green, and beautiful it grew,
So that it smelt more balmy than its peers
Of Basil-tufts in Florence; for it drew
Nurture besides, and life, from human fears,
From the fast mouldering head there shut from view:
So that the jewel safely casketed,
Came forth, and in perfumed leafits spread.

\*    \*    \*    \*    \*

### LVIII

And, furthermore, her brethren wonder'd much
Why she sat drooping by the Basil green;
And why it flourish'd, as by magic touch;
Greatly they wonder'd what the thing might mean:
They could not surely give belief, that such
A very nothing would have power to wean
Her from her own fair youth, and pleasures gay,
And even remembrance of her love's delay.

# 6

Tennyson went to Sir Thomas Malory's *Le Morte d'Arthur* for his blank verse *Morte D'Arthur*. It is interesting to compare the two. Here is an extract from *Le Morte d'Arthur* as printed by Caxton in 1485, but with the spelling modernized, and with the addition of quotation marks and paragraphing.

'Therefore,' said Arthur unto Sir Bedivere, 'take thou Excalibur my good sword, and go with it to yonder water side, and when thou comest there I charge thee throw my sword in that water, and come again and tell me what thou there seest.'

'My lord,' said Bedivere, 'your commandment shall be done, and lightly bring you word again.'

So Sir Bedivere departed, and by the way he beheld that noble sword, that the pommel and the haft was all of precious stones; and then he said to himself: 'If I throw this rich sword in the water, thereof shall never come good, but harm and loss.' And then Sir Bedivere hid Excalibur under a tree.

And so, as soon as he might, he came again unto the king, and said he had been at the water, and had thrown the sword in the water.

'What saw thou there?' said the king.

'Sir,' he said, 'I saw nothing but waves and winds.'

'That is untruly said of thee,' said the king, 'therefore go thou lightly again, and do my commandment; as thou art to me lief and dear, spare not but throw it in.'

Then Sir Bedivere returned again, and took the sword in his hand: and then him thought sin and shame to throw away that noble sword, and so efte he hid the sword, and returned again, and told to the king that he had been at the water, and done his commandment.

'What saw thou there?' said the king.

'Sir,' he said, 'I saw nothing but the waters wappe and waves wanne.'

'Ah, traitor untrue,' said King Arthur, 'now hast thou betrayed me twice. Who would have weened that, thou that hast been to me so lief and dear? and thou art named a noble knight, and would betray me for the richness of the sword. But now go again lightly, for thy long tarrying putteth me in great jeopardy of my life, for I have taken cold. And but if thou do now as I bid thee, if ever I may see thee, I shall slay thee with mine own hands; for thou wouldst for my rich sword see me dead.'

Then Sir Bedivere departed, and went to the sword, and lightly took it up, and went to the water side; and there he bound the girdle about the hilts, and then he threw the sword as far into the water as he might; and there came an arm and an hand above the water and met it, and caught it, and so shook it thrice and brandished, and then vanished away the hand with the sword in the water.

So Sir Bedivere came again to the king, and told him what he saw. 'Alas,' said the king, 'help me hence, for I dread me I have tarried over long.'

Then Sir Bedivere took the king upon his back, and so went with him to that water side. And when they were at the water side, even fast by the bank hoved a little barge with many fair ladies in it, and among them all was a queen, and all they had black hoods, and all they wept and shrieked when they saw King Arthur.

'Now put me into the barge', said the king.

And so he did softly. And there received him three queens with great mourning; and so they set them down, and in one of their laps King Arthur laid his head.

And then that queen said: 'Ah, dear brother, why have ye tarried so long from me? alas, this wound on your head hath caught overmuch cold.'

And so then they rowed from the land, and Sir Bedivere beheld all those ladies go from him.

Then Sir Bedivere cried: 'Ah, my lord Arthur, what shall become of me, now ye go from me and leave me here alone among mine enemies?'

'Comfort thyself,' said the king, 'and do as well as thou mayest, for in me is no trust for to trust in. For I will into the vale of Avilion to heal me of my grievous wound: and if thou hear nevermore of me, pray for my soul.'

But ever the queens and ladies wept and shrieked, that it was pity to hear. And as soon as Sir Bedivere had lost the sight of the barge, he wept and wailed, and so took the forest.

Tennyson's *Morte D'Arthur* was published in 1842 and subsequently incorporated in *The Passing of Arthur*, one of the *Idylls of the King*.

> Then spake King Arthur to Sir Bedivere:
> 'Thou therefore take my brand Excalibur,
> Which was my pride: for thou rememberest how
> In those old days, one summer noon, an arm
> Rose up from out the bosom of the lake,
> Clothed in white samite, mystic, wonderful,
> Holding the sword—and how I row'd across
> And took it, and have worn it, like a king:
> And wheresoever I am sung or told
> In aftertime, this also shall be known:
> But now delay not: take Excalibur,
> And fling him far into the middle mere:
> Watch what thou seest, and lightly bring me word.'
>     To him replied the bold Sir Bedivere:
> 'It is not meet, Sir King, to leave thee thus,
> Aidless, alone, and smitten thro' the helm
> A little thing may harm a wounded man.
> Yet I thy hest will all perform at full,
> Watch what I see, and lightly bring thee word.'
>     So saying, from the ruin'd shrine he stept
> And in the moon athwart the place of tombs,
> Where lay the mighty bones of ancient men,
> Old knights, and over them the sea-wind sang
> Shrill, chill, with flakes of foam. He, stepping down
> By zig-zag paths, and juts of pointed rock,
> Came on the shining levels of the lake.
>     There drew he forth the brand Excalibur,
> And o'er him drawing it, the winter moon,
> Brightening the skirts of a long cloud, ran forth
> And sparkled keen with frost against the hilt:
> For all the haft twinkled with diamond studs
> Myriads of topaz-lights, and jacinth-work
> Of subtlest jewellery. He gazed so long
> That both his eyes were dazzled, as he stood,
> This way and that dividing the swift mind,

In act to throw: but at the last it seem'd
Better to leave Excalibur conceal'd
There in the many-knotted waterflags,
That whistled stiff and dry about the marge.
So strode he back slow to the wounded king.
   Then spake King Arthur to Sir Bedivere:
'Hast thou perform'd my mission which I gave?
What is it thou hast seen? or what hast heard?'
   And answer made the bold Sir Bedivere:
'I heard the ripple washing in the reeds,
And the wild water lapping on the crag.'
   To whom replied King Arthur, faint and pale:
'Thou hast betrayed thy nature and thy name,
Not rendering true answer, as beseem'd
Thy fealty, not like a noble knight:
For surer sign had followed, either hand,
Or voice, or else a motion of the mere.
This is a shameful thing for men to lie.
Yet now, I charge thee, quickly go again
As thou art lief and dear, and do the thing
I bad thee, watch, and lightly bring me word.'
   Then went Sir Bedivere the second time
Across the ridge, and paced beside the mere,
Counting the dewy pebbles, fix'd in thought;
But when he saw the wonder of the hilt,
How curiously and strangely chased, he smote
His palms together, and he cried aloud.
   'And if indeed I cast the brand away,
Surely a precious thing, one worthy note,
Should thus be lost for ever from the earth
Which might have pleased the eyes of many men.'
What good should follow this, if this were done?
What harm, undone? deep harm to disobey,
Seeing obedience is the bond of rule.
Were it well to obey then, if a king demand
An act unprofitable, against himself?
The King is sick, and knows not what he does.
What record, or what relic of my lord
Should be to aftertime, but empty breath

And rumours of a doubt? but were this kept,
Stored in some treasure-house of mighty kings,
Some one might show it at a joust of arms,
Saying, "King Arthur's sword, Excalibur,
Wrought by the lonely maiden of the Lake.
Nine years she wrought it, sitting in the deeps
Upon the hidden bases of the hills."
So might some old man speak in the aftertime
To all the people, winning reverence.
But now much honour and much fame were lost.'
   So spake he, clouded with his own conceit,
And hid Excalibur the second time,
And so strode back slow to the wounded King.
   Then spoke King Arthur, breathing heavily:
'What is it thou hast seen? or what hast heard?'
   And answer made the bold Sir Bedivere:
'I heard the water lapping on the crag,
And the long ripple washing in the reeds.'
   To whom replied King Arthur, much in wrath:
'Ah, miserable and unkind, untrue,
Unknightly, traitor-hearted! Woe is me!
Authority forgets a dying king,
Laid widow'd of the power in his eye
That bow'd the will. I see thee what thou art,
For thou, the latest-left of all my knights,
In whom should meet the offices of all,
Thou wouldst betray me for the precious hilt;
Either from lust of gold, or like a girl
Valuing the giddy pleasure of the eyes.
Yet, for a man may fail in duty twice,
And the third time may prosper, get thee hence:
But, if thou spare to fling Excalibur,
I will arise and slay thee with my hands.'
   Then quickly rose Sir Bedivere, and ran,
And, leaping down the ridges lightly, plunged
Among the bulrush-beds, and clutch'd the sword,
And strongly wheel'd and threw it. The great brand
Made lightnings in the splendour of the moon,
And flashing round and round, and whirl'd in an arch,

Shot like a streamer of the northern morn,
Seen where the moving isles of winter shock
By night, with noises of the northern sea.
So flash'd and fell the brand Excalibur:
But ere he dipt the surface, rose an arm
Clothed in white samite, mystic, wonderful,
And caught him by the hilt, and brandish'd him
Three times, and drew him under in the mere.
And lightly went the other to the King.
Then spoke King Arthur, drawing thicker breath:
'Now see I by thine eyes that this is done.
Speak out: what is it thou hast heard, or seen?'
    And answer made the bold Sir Bedivere:
'Sir King, I closed mine eyelids, lest the gems
Should blind my purpose, for I never saw,
Nor shall see, here or elsewhere, till I die,
Not tho' I live three lives of mortal men,
So great a miracle as yonder hilt.
Then with both hands I flung him, wheeling him;
But when I look'd again, behold an arm,
Clothed in white samite, mystic, wonderful,
That caught him by the hilt, and brandish'd him
Three times, and drew him under in the mere.'
    And answer made King Arthur, breathing hard:
'My end draws nigh; 'tis time that I were gone.
Make broad thy shoulders to receive my weight,
And bear me to the margin; yet I fear
My wound hath taken cold, and I shall die.'
    So saying, from the pavement he half rose,
Slowly, with pain, reclining on his arm,
And looking wistfully with wide blue eyes
As in a picture. Him Sir Bedivere
Remorsefully regarded thro' his tears,
And would have spoken, but he found not words,
Then took with care, and kneeling on one knee
O'er both his shoulders drew the languid hands,
And rising bore him thro' the place of tombs.
    But as he walk'd, King Arthur panted hard,
Like one that feels a nightmare on his bed

When all the house is mute. So sigh'd the King,
Muttering and murmuring at his ear 'Quick, quick!
I fear it is too late, and I shall die.'
But the other swiftly strode from ridge to ridge,
Clothed with his breath, and looking as he walk'd,
Larger than human on the frozen hills.
He heard the deep behind him, and a cry
Before. His own thought drove him like a goad.
Dry clash'd his harness in the icy caves
And barren chasms, and all to left and right
The bare black cliff clang'd round him, as he based
His feet on juts of slippery crag that rang
Sharp-smitten with the dint of armed heels—
And on a sudden, lo! the level lake,
And the long glories of the winter moon.

Then saw they how there hove a dusky barge,
Dark as a funeral scarf from stem to stern,
Beneath them; and descending they were ware
That all the decks were dense with stately forms
Black-stoled, black-hooded, like a dream—by these
Three Queens with crowns of gold—and from them rose
A cry that shiver'd to the tingling stars,
And, as it were one voice, an agony
Of lamentation, like a wind, that shrills
All night in a waste land, where no one comes,
Or hath come, since the making of the world.

Then murmur'd Arthur, 'Place me in the barge',
And to the barge they came. There those three Queens
Put forth their hands, and took the King, and wept.
But she, that rose the tallest of them all
And fairest, laid his head upon her lap,
And loosed the shatter'd casque, and chafed his hands,
And call'd him by his name, complaining loud,
And dropping bitter tears against his brow
Striped with dark blood: for all his face was white
And colourless, and like the wither'd moon
Smote by the fresh beam of the springing east;
And all his greaves and cuisses dash'd with drops
Of onset; and the light and lustrous curls—

That made his forehead like a rising sun
High from the dais-throne—were parch'd with dust;
Or, clotted into points and hanging loose,
Mix'd with the knightly growth that fringed his lips.
So like a shatter'd column lay the King;
Not like that Arthur who, with lance in rest,
From spur to plume a star of tournament,
Shot thro' the lists at Camelot, and charged
Before the eyes of ladies and of kings.
   Then loudly cried the bold Sir Bedivere,
'Ah! my Lord Arthur, whither shall I go?
Where shall I hide my forehead and my eyes?
For now I see the true old times are dead,
When every morning brought a noble chance,
And every chance brought out a noble knight.
Such times have been not since the light that led
The holy Elders with the gift of myrrh.
But now the whole ROUND TABLE is dissolved
Which was an image of the mighty world;
And I, the last, go forth companionless,
And the days darken round me, and the years,
Among new men, strange faces, other minds.'
   And slowly answer'd Arthur from the barge:
'The old order changeth, yielding place to new,
And God fulfils himself in many ways,
Lest one good custom should corrupt the world.
Comfort thyself: what comfort is in me?
I have lived my life, and that which I have done
May He within himself make pure! but thou,
If thou shouldst never see my face again,
Pray for my soul. More things are wrought by prayer
Than this world dreams of. Whereof, let thy voice
Rise like a fountain for me night and day.
For what are men better than sheep or goats
That nourish a blind life within the brain,
If, knowing God, they lift not hands of prayer
Both for themselves and those who call them friend?
For so the whole round earth is every way
Bound by gold chains about the feet of God.

But now farewell. I am going a long way
With these thou seest—if indeed I go—
(For all my mind is clouded with a doubt)
To the island-valley of Avilion;
Where falls not hail, or rain, or any snow,
Nor ever wind blows loudly; but it lies
Deep-meadow'd, happy, fair with orchard-lawns
And bowery hollows crown'd with summer sea,
Where I will heal me of my grievous wound.'
  So said he, and the barge with oar and sail
Moved from the brink, like some full-breasted swan
That, fluting a wild carol ere her death,
Ruffles her pure cold plume, and takes the flood
With swarthy webs. Long stood Sir Bedivere
Revolving many memories, till the hull
Look'd one black dot against the verge of dawn,
And on the mere the wailing died away.

# IV

# THE POET'S TRANSLATION

# HOMER

## *Iliad* VIII, 542–61

### (*a*)

This speech all Trojans did applaud; who from their traces los'd
Their sweating horse, which sev'rally with headstalls they repos'd,
And fast'ned by their chariots; when others brought from town
Fat sheep and oxen, instantly, bread, wine, and hewéd down
Huge store of wood. The winds transferr'd into the friendly sky
Their supper's savour; to the which they sat delightfully,
And spent all night in open field; fires round about them shin'd.
As when about the silver moon, when air is free from wind,
And stars shine clear, to whose sweet beams, high prospects, and
    the brows
Of all steep hills and pinnacles, thrust up themselves for shows,
And ev'n the lowly valleys joy to glitter in their sight,
When the unmeasur'd firmament bursts to disclose her light,
And all the signs in heav'n are seen, that glad the shepherd's heart;
So many fires disclos'd their beams, made by the Trojan part,
Before the face of Ilion, and her bright turrets show'd.
A thousand courts of guard kept fires, and ev'ry guard allow'd
Fifty stout men, by whom their horse ate oats and hard white corn,
And all did wishfully expect the silver-thronéd morn.

GEORGE CHAPMAN, 1611

### (*b*)

The leader spoke. From all his host around
Shouts of applause along the shores resound.
Each from the yoke the smoking steeds untied,
And fix'd their headstalls to his chariot-side.
Fat sheep and oxen from the town are led,
With generous wine, and all-sustaining bread.
Full hecatombs lay burning on the shore;
The winds to heaven the curling vapours bore.
Ungrateful offering to th'immortal powers!

Whose wrath hung heavy o'er the Trojan towers;
Nor Priam nor his sons obtained their grace;
Proud Troy they hated, and her guilty race.
  The troops exulting sat in order round,
And beaming fires illumined all the ground.
As when the moon, refulgent lamp of night,
O'er heaven's clear azure spreads her sacred light,
When not a breath disturbs the deep serene,
And not a cloud o'ercasts the solemn scene;
Around her throne the vivid planets roll,
And stars unnumber'd gild the glowing pole,
O'er the dark trees a yellower verdure shed,
And tip with silver every mountain's head;
Then shine the vales, the rocks in prospect rise,
A flood of glory bursts from all the skies:
The conscious swains, rejoicing in the sight,
Eye the blue vault, and bless the useful light.
So many flames before proud Ilion blaze,
And lighten glimmering Xanthus with their rays:
The long reflections of the distant fires
Gleam on the walls, and tremble on the spires.
A thousand piles the dusky horrors gild,
And shoot a shady lustre o'er the field.
Full fifty guards each flaming pile attend,
Whose umber'd arms, by fits, thick flashes send.
Loud neigh the coursers o'er their heaps of corn,
And ardent warriors wait the rising morn.

ALEXANDER POPE, 1715

(c)

Thus Hector spoke; the Trojans shouted loud:
Then from the yoke the sweating steeds they loosed,
And tethered each beside their several cars:
Next from the city speedily they brought
Oxen and sheep; the luscious wine procured;
Brought bread from out their houses, and good store
Of fuel gathered; wafted from the plain,
The winds to Heaven the savoury odours bore.

Full of proud hopes, upon the pass of war,
All night they camped, and frequent blazed their fires.
As when in Heaven, around the glittering moon
The stars shine bright amid the breathless air;
And every crag and every jutting peak
Stands boldly forth, and every forest glade;
Even to the gates of Heaven is opened wide
The boundless sky; shines each particular star
Distinct; joy fills the gazing shepherd's heart.
So bright, so thickly scattered o'er the plain,
Before the walls of Troy, between the ships
And Xanthus' stream, the Trojan watchfires blazed.
A thousand fires burnt brightly; and round each
Sat fifty warriors in the ruddy glare;
Champing the provender before them laid,
Barley and rye, the tethered horses stood
Beside the cars, and waited for the morn.

LORD DERBY, 1864


(*d*)

So Hector spoke; the Trojans roared applause,
Then loosed their sweating horses from the yoke,
And each beside his chariot bound his own;
And oxen from the city, and goodly sheep
In haste they drove, and honey-hearted wine
And bread from out the houses brought, and heaped
Their firewood, and the winds from off the plain
Rolled the rich vapour far into the heaven.
And these all night upon the bridge of war
Sat glorying; many a fire before them blazed:
As when in heaven the stars about the moon
Look beautiful, when all the winds are laid,
And every height comes out, and jutting peak
And valley, and the immeasurable heavens
Break open to their highest, and all the stars
Shine, and the shepherd gladdens in his heart:
So many a fire between the ships and stream
Of Xanthus blazed before the towers of Troy,

A thousand on the plain; and close by each
Sat fifty in the blaze of burning fire;
And eating hoary grain and pulse the steeds,
Fixt by their cars, waited the golden dawn.

LORD TENNYSON, 1868

## HOMER

*Odyssey* XXIV, 1–14

### (*a*)

Cyllenian Hermes, with his golden rod,
The Wooers' souls, that yet retain'd abode
Amidst their bodies, call'd in dreadful rout
Forth to th' Infernals; who came murmuring out.
And as amidst the desolate retreat
Of some vast cavern, made the sacred seat
Of austere spirits, bats with breasts and wings
Clasp fast the walls, and each to other clings,
But, swept off from their coverts, up they rise
And fly with murmurs in amazeful guise
About the cavern; so these, grumbling, rose
And flock'd together. Down before them goes
None-hurting Mercury to Hell's broad ways,
And straight to those straits, where the ocean stays
His lofty current in calm deeps, they flew.
Then to the snowy rock they next withdrew,
And to the close of Phoebus' orient gates.
The nation then of dreams, and then the states
Of those souls' idols that the weary dead
Gave up in earth, which in a flow'ry mead
Had habitable situatión.

GEORGE CHAPMAN, 1615

### (*b*)

And now Cyllenian Hermes summon'd forth
The spirits of the suitors; waving wide
The golden wand of power to seal all eyes

In slumber, and to ope them wide again,
He drove them gibbering down into the shades.
As when the bats within some hallow'd cave
Flit squeaking all around, for if but one
Fall from the rock, the rest all follow him,
In such connexion mutual they adhere;
So, after bounteous Mercury, the ghosts
Troop'd downward gibbering all the dreary way.
The Ocean's flood and the Leucadian rock,
The Sun's gate also and the land of Dreams
They pass'd, whence next into the meads they came
Of Asphodel, by shadowy forms possess'd,
Simulars of the dead.

WILLIAM COWPER, 1791

(c)

But now the ghosts of the men who were of the wooers' band
Called forth Cyllenian Hermes; and he had his staff in hand,
Lovely and golden, wherewith he lulleth the eyes of men,
Whomsoever he willeth, while others from slumber he rouseth
    again.
Therewith he roused and drave them, who gibbering went along;
As when in the inmost ingle of a wondrous den the throng
Of night-bats gibbereth fluttering, when one falleth off aloof
From their chain, where clustered together they hang from the
    rocky roof,
So fared their flock a-twittering, and Hermes void of wrong
Adown the dusky highway led all the band along:
There by the streams of Ocean and the White Rock went their band,
By the gates of the Sun they wended and by the dream-folk's land,
Till in no long while they were gotten to the meads of asphodel,
Wherein the ghosts, the pictures of outworn men-folk, dwell.

WILLIAM MORRIS, 1887

(d)

Now Hermes of Cyllene called to the world beyond
The wraiths of the fallen Suitors—in hand he bore his wand,
Fair-wrought in gold, wherewith he charms the eyes of men
To sleep, and out of slumber awakens them again.

105

With it he roused the Suitors, and led them—shrieking shrill
They followed; as squeaking flutter the hosts of bats that fill
The nooks of some great grotto if one shall chance to fall
From the chain that clusters clinging to the cavern's rocky wall.
So, gibbering, on Hermes the Saviour in his flight
They followed, where he led them on the mouldering paths of night—
Past the great gateway of the Sun, past Ocean's streams,
Past the White Rock they hastened, and past the Land of Dreams,
Until at the last they came to the Meadow of Asphodel,
Where the phantoms of the weary, the souls of the perished dwell....

F. L. LUCAS, 1948

## HOMERIC HYMN

### *To the Earth*

#### (a)

Mother of all things, the well-founded Earth,
My Muse shall memorize; who all the birth
Gives food that all her upper regions breed,
All that in her divine diffusions feed
In under continents, all those that live
In all the seas, and all the air doth give
Wing'd expeditions, of thy bounties eat;
Fair children, and fair fruits, thy labour's sweat,
O great in reverence; and referr'd to thee,
For life and death is all the pedigree
Of mortal humans. Happy then is he
Whom the innate propensions of thy mind
Stand bent to honour. He shall all things find
In all abundance; all his pastures yield
Herds in all plenties; all his roofs are fill'd
With rich possessions; he, in all the sway
Of laws best order'd, cuts out his own way
In cities shining with delicious dames,
And takes his choice of all those striving flames;
High happiness and riches, like his train,
Follow his fortunes, with delights that reign

In all their princes; glory invests his sons;
His daughters, with their crown'd selections
Of all the city, frolic through the meads,
And every one her call'd-for dances treads
Along the soft-flow'r of the claver-grass.
All this, with all those, ever comes to pass,
That thy love blesses, Goddess full of grace,
And treasurous Angel t' all the human race.
    Hail, then, Great Mother of the Deified Kind,
Wife to the cope of stars! Sustain a mind
Propitious to me for my praise, and give
(Answering my mind) my vows fit means to live.

GEORGE CHAPMAN, 1616

(b)

O universal Mother, who dost keep
From everlasting thy foundations deep,
Eldest of things, Great Earth, I sing of thee!
All shapes that have their dwelling in the sea,
All things that fly, or on the ground divine
Live, move, and there are nourished—these are thine;
These from thy wealth thou dost sustain; from thee
Fair babes are born, and fruits on every tree
Hang ripe and large, revered Divinity!

    The life of mortal men beneath thy sway
Is held; thy power both gives and takes away!
Happy are they whom thy mild favours nourish;
All things unstinted round them grow and flourish.
For them endures the life-sustaining field
Its load of harvest, and their cattle yield
Large increase, and their house with wealth is filled.
Such honoured dwell in cities fair and free,
The homes of lovely women, prosperously;
Their sons exult in youth's new budding gladness,
And their fresh daughters free from care or sadness,
With bloom-inwoven dance and happy song,
On the soft flowers the meadow-grass among,
Leap round them sporting—such delights by thee
Are given, rich Power, revered Divinity.

Mother of gods, thou Wife of starry Heaven,
Farewell! be thou propitious, and be given
A happy life for this brief melody,
Nor thou nor other songs shall unremembered be

P. B. SHELLEY, 1818

## ANACREON

### Ode XXXIII

#### (a)

Downward was the wheeling Bear
Driven by the Waggoner:
Men by powerful sleep opprest,
Gave their busie troubles rest:
Love, in this still depth of night,
Lately at my house did light;
Where perceiving all fast lockt,
At the door he boldly knockt.
'Who's that,' said I, 'that does keep
Such a noise, and breaks my sleep?'
'Ope,' saith Love, 'for pity hear;
'Tis a childe, thou need'st not fear,
Wet and weary, from his way
Led by this dark night astray.'
With compassion this I heard;
Light I struck; the door unbarr'd:
Where a little Boy appears,
Who wings, bow, and quiver bears;
Near the fire I made him stand,
With my own I chaft his hand;
And with kindly busie care
Wrung the chill drops from his hair:
When well warm'd he was, and dry,
'Now,' saith he, ''tis time to try
If my bow no hurt did get,
For methinks the string is wet.'
With that, drawing it, a dart
He let fly that pierc'd my heart:

Leaping then, and laughing said,
'Come my friend, with me be glad;
For my Bow thou see'st is sound
Since thy heart hath got a wound.'

THOMAS STANLEY, 1651

(*b*)

'Twas noon of night, when round the pole
The sullen Bear is seen to roll;
And mortals, wearied with the day,
Are slumbering all their cares away:
An infant, at that dreary hour,
Came weeping to my silent bower,
And wak'd me with a piteous prayer,
To shield him from the midnight air.
'And who art thou,' I waking cry,
'That bid'st my blissful visions fly?'
'Ah, gentle sire!' the infant said,
'In pity take me to thy shed;
Nor fear deceit: a lonely child
I wander o'er the gloomy wild.
Chill drops the rain, and not a ray
Illumes the drear and misty way!'

I heard the baby's tale of woe;
I heard the bitter night-winds blow,
And sighing for his piteous fate,
I trimm'd my lamp and op'd the gate.
'Twas Love! the little wandering sprite,
His pinion sparkled through the night.
I knew him by his bow and dart;
I knew him by my fluttering heart.
Fondly I take him in, and raise
The dying embers' cheering blaze;
Press from his dank and clinging hair
The crystals of the freezing air,
And in my hand and bosom hold
His little fingers thrilling cold.

And now the embers' genial ray
Had warm'd his anxious fears away;

'I pray thee,' said the wanton child,
(My bosom trembled as he smil'd,)
'I pray thee let me try my bow,
For through the rain I've wander'd so,
That much I fear, the midnight shower
Has injured its elastic power.'
The fatal bow the urchin drew;
Swift from the string the arrow flew;
As swiftly flew as glancing flame,
And to my inmost spirit came!
'Fare thee well,' I heard him say,
As laughing wild he wing'd away;
'Fare thee well, for now I know
The rain has not relax'd my bow;
It still can send a thrilling dart,
As thou shalt own with all thy heart!'

THOMAS MOORE, 1800

# CATULLUS

## *Ode* XXXI

### (a)

Gem of all isthmuses and isles that lie,
Fresh or salt water's children, in clear lake
Or ampler ocean, with what joy do I
Approach thee, Sirmio.  Oh! Am I awake,
Or dream that once again my eye beholds
Thee, and has looked its last on Thynian wolds?
Sweetest of sweets to me that pastime seems,
When the mind drops her burden: when—the pain
Of travel past—our own cot we regain
And nestle on the pillow of our dreams!
'Tis this one thought that cheers us as we roam.
Hail, O fair Sirmio! Joy, thy lord is here!
Joy too, ye waters of the Garda Mere!
And ring out, all ye laughter-peals of home.

C. S. CALVERLEY, 1862

(b)

Sirmio, thou dearest dear of strands
That Neptune strokes in lake and sea,
With what high joy from stranger lands
Doth thy old friend set foot on thee!
Yea, barely seems it true to me
That no Bithynia holds me now,
But calmly and assuringly
Around me stretchest homely Thou.

Is there a scene more sweet than when
Our clinging cares are undercast,
And, worn by alien moils and men,
The long untrodden sill repassed,
We press the pined for couch at last,
And find a full repayment there?
Then hail, sweet Sirmio; thou that wast,
And art, mine own unrivalled Fair!

THOMAS HARDY, 1887

## VIRGIL

*Aeneid* VI, 269–294

(a)

Obscure they went through dreary shades, that led
Along the waste dominions of the dead.
Thus wander travellers in woods by night,
By the moon's doubtful and malignant light,
When Jove in dusky clouds involves the skies,
And the faint crescent shoots by fits before their eyes.
  Just in the gate, and in the jaws of hell,
Revengeful Cares and sullen Sorrows dwell;
And pale Diseases, and repining Age,
Want, Fear, and Famine's unresisted rage;
Here Toils, and Death, and Death's half-brother Sleep
(Forms terrible to view), their sentry keep;
With anxious Pleasures of a guilty mind;
Deep Frauds before, and open Force behind;

The Furies' iron beds; and Strife, that shakes
Her hissing tresses, and unfolds her snakes.
Full in the midst of this infernal road
An elm displays her dusky arms abroad:
The god of sleep there hides his heavy head,
And empty dreams on every leaf are spread.
Of various forms unnumbered spectres more,
Centaurs, and double shapes, besiege the door.
Before the passage, horrid Hydra stands,
And Briareus with all his hundred hands;
Gorgons, Geryon with his triple frame,
And vain Chimæra vomits empty flame.
The chief unsheathed his shining steel, prepared,
Though seized with sudden fear, to force the guard,
Offering his brandished weapon at their face,
Had not the Sibyl stopped his eager pace,
And told him what those empty phantoms were—
Forms without bodies, and impassive air.

JOHN DRYDEN, 1697

(b)

They went obscure in lowering lone night
Through lodges of King Dis, untenanted,—
Featureless lands. Thus goes a forest pathway
Beneath the curst light of the wav'ring moon,
When Jove has gloomed the sky, and pitchy dark
Uncoloured all the world. In Hell's first reach
Fronting the very vestibule of Orcus
Griefs and the Cares have set their couches down,—
The vengeful Cares. There pale Diseases dwell,
Sad Eld and Fear and loathsome Poverty
And Hunger, that bad counsellor,—dire shapes—
And Death and Toil, and Sleep brother of Death
And soul-corrupting joys. Opposed he viewed
War the great murderer, and those steel bowers
The Furies deck for bridal, and Discord
Daft, with blood-ribbons on her serpent hair.
But straight in front a huge black knotted elm
Stood branching: here, they say, the Vain Dreams roost:—

There's not a leaf without one stuck behind!
Next he saw twisted beasts of the old tales:
Centaurs were stabled at the gates: Scyllas
Spread their twin shapes, Briareus his hundred arms.
And Lerna's beast behold hissing out fear,
Chimæra too, who fights with fire, and Gorgons
And Harpies, and a shade with a triple form!
Such was the horror seized Aeneas then
He made to meet their onset with cold steel,
And had th' instructed Sybil not advised
That these were gossamer vitalities
Flitting in stuffless mockery of form,
He'd have leapt on and lashed the empty air.

JAMES ELROY FLECKER, 1910

(*c*)

They wer' amid the shadows by night in loneliness obscure
Walking forth i' the void and vasty dominion of Ades;
As by an uncertain moonray secretly illumin'd
One goeth in the forest, when heav'n is gloomily clouded,
And black night hath robb'd the colours and beauty from all things.

Here in Hell's very jaws, the threshold of darkening Orcus,
Have the avenging Cares laid their sleepless habitation
Wailing Grief, pallid Infections, and heart-stricken Old-age,
Dismal Fear, unholy Famine, with low-grovelling Want,
Forms of spectral horror, gaunt Toil and Death the devourer,
And death's drowsy brother, Torpor; with whom, an inane rout,
All the Pleasures of Sin; there also the Furies in ambusht
Chamber of iron, afore whose bars wild War bloodyhanded
Raged, and mad Discord high brandished her venomous locks.

Midway of all this tract, with secular arms an immense elm
Reareth a crowd of branches, aneath whose leafy protection
Vain dreams thickly nestle, clinging unto the foliage on high:
And many strange creatures of monstrous form and features
Stable about th' entrance, Centaur and Scylla's abortion,
And hundred-handed Briareus, and Lerna's wild beast
Roaring amain, and clothed in frightful flame the Chimæra,
Gorgons and Harpies, and Pluto's three-bodied ogre.

In terror Aeneas upheld his sword to defend him,
With ready naked point confronting their dreaded onset:
And had not the Sibyl warn'd how these lively spirits were
All incorporeal, flitting in thin maskery of form,
He had assail'd their host, and wounded vainly the void air.

ROBERT BRIDGES, 1916

(*d*)

Vague forms in lonely darkness, they were going
Through void and shadow, through the empty realm
Like people in a forest, when the moonlight
Shifts with a baleful glimmer, and shadow covers
The sky, and all the colours turn to blackness.
At the first threshold, on the jaws of Orcus,
Grief and avenging Cares have set their couches,
And pale Diseases dwell, and sad Old Age,
Fear, evil-counselling Hunger, wretched Need,
Forms terrible to see, and Death, and Toil,
And Death's own brother, Sleep, and evil Joys,
Fantasies of the mind, and deadly War,
The Furies' iron chambers, Discord, raving,
Her snaky hair entwined in bloody bands.
An elm-tree loomed there, shadowy and huge,
The aged boughs outspread, beneath whose leaves,
Men say, the false dreams cling, thousands and thousands.
And there are monsters in the dooryard, Centaurs,
Scyllas, of double shape, the beast of Lerna,
Hissing most horribly, Briareus,
The hundred-handed giant, a Chimæra
Whose armament is fire, Harpies, and Gorgons,
A triple-bodied giant. In sudden panic
Aeneas drew his sword, the edge held forward,
Ready to rush and flail, however blindly,
Save that his wise companion warned him, saying
They had no substance, they were only phantoms
Flitting about, illusions without body.

ROLFE HUMPHRIES, 1951

# VIRGIL

## *Georgics* I, 311–34

### (a)

Now sing we stormy stars, when autumn weighs
The year, and adds to nights, and shortens days,
And suns declining shine with feeble rays;
What cares must then attend the toiling swain;
Or when the lowering spring, with lavish rain,
Beats down the slender stem and bearded grain,
While yet the head is green, or lightly swelled
With milky moisture, overlooks the field.
E'en when the farmer, now secure of fear,
Sends in the swains to spoil the finished year,
E'en while the reaper fills his greedy hands,
And binds the golden sheaves in brittle bands,
Oft have I seen a sudden storm arise,
From all the warring winds that sweep the skies:
The heavy harvest from the root is torn,
And whirled aloft, the lighter stubble borne:
With such a force the flying rack is driven,
And such a winter wears the face of heaven:
And oft whole sheets descend of sluicy rain,
Sucked by the spongy clouds from off the main:
The lofty skies at once come pouring down,
The promised crop and golden labours drown.
The dikes are filled; and with a roaring sound,
The rising rivers float the nether ground;
And rocks the bellowing voice of boiling seas rebound.
The father of the gods his glory shrouds,
Involved in tempests, and a night of clouds;
And from the middle darkness flashing out,
By fits he deals his fiery bolts about.
Earth feels the motions of her angry god:
Her entrails tremble, and her mountains nod,
And flying beasts in forests seek abode:
Deep horror seizes every human breast;

115

Their pride is humbled and their fear confessed,
While he from high his rolling thunder throws,
And fires the mountains with repeated blows:
The rocks are from their old foundation rent;
The winds redouble, and the rains augment:
The waves on heaps are dashed against the shore;
And now the woods, and now the billows, roar.

JOHN DRYDEN, 1697

(b)

Am I to tell you next of the storms and stars of Autumn?
The things, when days draw in and summer's heat is abating,
That men must guard against? The dangers of showery spring,
When the prick-eared harvest already bristles along the plains
And when in the green blade the milky grain is swelling?
   Well, often I've seen a farmer lead into his golden fields
The reapers and begin to cut the frail-stalked barley,
And winds arise that moment, starting a free-for-all,
Tearing up by the roots whole swathes of heavy corn
And hurling them high in the air: with gusts black as a hurricane
The storm sent flimsy blades and stubble flying before it.
Often, too, huge columns of water come in the sky
And clouds charged off the deep amass for dirty weather
With rain-squalls black: then the whole sky gives way, falls,
Floods with terrific rain the fertile crops and the labours
Of oxen; filled are the ditches, dry rivers arise in spate
Roaring, the sea foams and seethes up the hissing fjords.
The Father, enthroned in midnight cloud, hurls from a flashing
Right hand his lightning: the whole
Earth trembles at the shock; the beasts are fled, and human
Hearts are felled in panic throughout the nations: on Athos,
Rhodope or the Ceraunian massif his bolt flares down:
The south wind doubles its force and thicker falls the rain:
Now wail the woods with that gale tremendous, now the shores wail.

C. DAY LEWIS, 1940

# HORACE

## *Odes* I, v

### (*a*)

What slender youth, bedewed with liquid odours,
Courts thee on roses in some pleasant cave,
    Pyrrha? For whom bind'st thou
      In wreaths thy golden hair,
Plain in thy neatness? Oh, how oft shall he
On faith and changed gods complain, and seas
    Rough with black winds and storms
      Unwonted shall admire!
Who now enjoys thee credulous, all gold;
Who always vacant, always amiable,
    Hopes thee, of flattering gales
      Unmindful. Hapless they
To whom thou untried seem'st fair! Me, in my vowed
Picture, the sacred wall declares t'have hung
    My dank and dropping weeds
      To the stern God of Sea.

JOHN MILTON, 1673

### (*b*)

What graceful boy, dripping with rich perfume
Wooes thee 'mong roses in some grotto's shade?
    Pyrrha! for whom
    Dost thou thy yellow tresses braid
    In simple neatness artlessly arrayed?
Alas, how oft shall he who credulous dreams
    That all is Truth that truthful seems,
Basks in thy sun, nor doubts that he alone
Shall ever call thy golden grace his own,
Heedless of treacherous gales, and love not tried,—
How oft bewail thy broken faith, and chide
The changeful Gods, and stare with wondering eye
On rough seas blackening 'neath a cloud-swept sky!
    Most miserable they

Whom, falsely fair, thou glitterest to betray!
I, too, have hung on Neptune's hallowed shrine
My picture vowed, and garments dark with brine
To that all-powerful God whom winds and waves obey.

STEPHEN DE VERE, 1885

(c)

Pyrrha, what graceful boy now to thy rosy
couch besprinkled with liquid odours
    down in thy cave art thou tying?
    For whom, sprucely but simply,

curls that gold head?...Ah, how many teardrops
for that too volatile heart of thine he'll be shedding
    and for the changed Fates!
    Unused, he will start back

to see the black winds rousing the sea's anger,
who now delights in thee as pure, kind, golden,
    hopes so to prove thee ever,
    of winds' misfaith unwitting!

But O what grief will blast him unawares!
Already my dank garments, with a votive
    tablet upon the temple wall,
    I've hung up to the ruler of the sea.

G. S. FRASER, 1954

HORACE

*Odes* I, ix

(a)

Behold yon mountain's hoary height,
    Made higher with new mounts of snow;
Again behold the winter's weight
    Oppress the labouring woods below:
And streams, with icy fetters bound,
Benumb'd and cramp'd to solid ground.

With well-heap'd logs dissolve the cold,
   And feed the genial hearth with fires;
Produce the wine, that makes us bold,
   And sprightly wit and love inspires:
For what hereafter shall betide,
God, if 'tis worth his care, provide.

Let him alone, with what he made,
   To toss and turn the world below;
At his command the storms invade;
   The winds by his commission blow;
Till with a nod he bids 'em cease,
And then the calm returns, and all is peace.

To-morrow and her works defy,
   Lay hold upon the present hour,
And snatch the pleasures passing by,
   To put them out of fortune's power:
Nor love, nor love's delights disdain;
Whate'er thou gett'st to-day is gain.

Secure those golden early joys,
   That youth unsour'd with sorrow bears,
Ere withering time the taste destroys,
   With sickness and unwieldy years.
For active sports, for pleasing rest,
This is the time to be possess'd;
The best is but in season best.

The appointed hour of promis'd bliss,
   The pleasing whisper in the dark,
The half unwilling willing kiss,
   The laugh that guides thee to the mark,
When the kind nymph would coyness feign,
And hides but to be found again;
These, these are joys, the gods for youth ordain.

JOHN DRYDEN, 1693

*(b)*

Seest thou yon mountain laden with deep snow,
The groves beneath their fleecy burthen bow,
The streams, congealed, forget to flow,
Come, thaw the cold, and lay a cheerful pile
    Of fuel on the hearth;
Broach the best cask, and make old winter smile
    With seasonable mirth.

This be our part—let Heaven dispose the rest;
    If Jove command, the winds shall sleep,
    That now wage war upon the foamy deep,
And gentle gales spring from the balmy west.

    E'en let us shift to-morrow as we may,
        When to-morrow's passed away,
        We at least shall have to say,
        We have lived another day;
Your auburn locks will soon be silvered o'er,
Old age is at our heels, and youth returns no more.

WILLIAM COWPER, 1757

*(c)*

How dazzling white with drifted snow
Soracte stands! The woods below
    Are bowed to breaking with their burden;
The frozen rivers have ceased to flow.

Come, friend, let's drive away the cold:
Pile the logs high as hearth will hold,
    And bring me forth a flask of Sabine,
The strong, the mellow, the four years old.

All else entrust to heaven's will,
Which bids the battling winds be still—
    And waves grow calm, and peace possesses
The ash and cypress upon the hill.

No matter what the morrow prove:
Count each day gain the Powers above
    May grant us. Take what boyhood offers,
The fun and dancing and making love.

Leave gloom for when your hair is grey;
Youth is the time for sport and play—
   Then off to keep your tryst at twilight
And softly prattle an hour away,

Or by a tell-tale laugh to trace
The saucy charmer's hiding-place,
   And snatch a pledge from wrist or finger,
Surrendered with but a feign'd ill grace.

H. RACKHAM, 1950

## HORACE

*Odes* IV, vii

### (*a*)

The snow, dissolv'd no more is seen,
The fields and woods, behold! are green;
The changing year renews the plain,
The rivers know their banks again;
The sprightly nymph and naked grace
The mazy dance together trace;
The changing year's successive plan
Proclaims mortality to man;
Rough winter's blasts to spring give way,
Spring yields to summer's sov'reign ray;
Then summer sinks in autumn's reign,
And winter chills the world again;
Her losses soon the moon supplies,
But wretched man when once he lies
Where Priam and his sons are laid,
Is nought but ashes and a shade.
Who knows if Jove, who counts our score,
Will toss us in a morning more?
What with your friend you nobly share,
At least you rescue from your heir.
Not you, Torquatus, boast of Rome,
When Minos once has fix'd your doom,
Or eloquence, or splendid birth,
Or virtue, shall restore to earth.

Hippolytus, unjustly slain,
Diana calls to life in vain;
Nor can the might of Theseus rend
The chains of Hell that hold his friend.

SAMUEL JOHNSON, 1784

(b)

The snows are fled away, leaves on the shaws
And grasses in the mead renew their birth,
The river to the river-bed withdraws,
And altered is the fashion of the earth.

The Nymphs and Graces three put off their fear
And unapparelled in the woodland play,
The swift hour and the brief prime of the year
Say to the soul, *Thou wast not born for aye.*

Thaw follows frost; hard on the heel of spring
Treads summer sure to die, for hard on hers
Comes autumn, with his apples scattering;
Then back to wintertide, when nothing stirs.

But oh, whate'er the sky-led seasons mar,
Moon upon moon rebuilds it with her beams:
Come *we* where Tullus and where Ancus are,
And good Aeneas, we are dust and dreams.

Torquatus, if the gods in heaven shall add
The morrow to the day, what tongue has told?
Feast then thy heart, for what thy heart has had
The fingers of no heir will ever hold.

When thou descendest once the shades among,
The stern assize and equal judgement o'er,
Not thy long lineage nor thy golden tongue,
No, nor thy righteousness, shall friend thee more.

Night holds Hippolytus the pure of stain,
Diana steads him nothing, he must stay;
And Theseus leaves Pirithöus in the chain
The love of comrades cannot take away.

A. E. HOUSMAN, 1926

(*c*)

The snows are gone, grass in the fields is growing
  And foliage on the bough:
Earth's seasons change: the shrinking streams are flowing
  Within their channels low.

Now Nymphs and Graces all unclad may boldly
  Dance in the warmth of spring:
Each year, each hour that hastens night says coldly
  'Life is a passing thing.'

Frost yields to Zephyrs, spring to summer's fever,
  And summer will be sped
When autumn pours her plenteous fruit, and ever
  Comes winter, dull and dead.

Yet with the moons the seasons swiftly waken:
  We, when we once have passed
The way that good and rich and great have taken,
  Are dust and shades at last.

Who knows if God above will add tomorrow
  To this completed day?
What you spend now to keep your soul from sorrow
  No heir can waste away.

When you are dead and Minos once has o'er you
  His grand pronouncement made,
Your eloquence, your birth will not restore you,
  Nor your devotion aid.

Hippolytus was chaste, yet Dian never
  Frees him from night again.
Nor from Pirithöus can Theseus sever
  The links of Lethe's chain.

JAMES MACLEAN TODD, 1955

# DANTE

*Paradiso*, Canto XXXIII, 97–145

(*a*)

With fixed heed, suspense and motionless,
Wondering I gazed; and admiration still
Was kindled as I gazed. It may not be,
That one, who looks upon that light, can turn
To other object, willingly, his view.
For all the good, that will may covet, there
Is summ'd; and all, elsewhere defective found,
Complete. My tongue shall utter now, no more
E'en what remembrance keeps, than could the babe's,
That yet is moisten'd at his mother's breast.
Not that the semblance of the living light
Was changed, (that ever as at first remain'd,)
But that my vision quickening, in that sole
Appearance, still new miracles descried,
And toil'd me with the change. In that abyss
Of radiance, clear and lofty, seem'd, methought,
Three orbs of triple hue, clipt in one bound:
And, from another, one reflected seem'd,
As rainbow is from rainbow: and the third
Seem'd fire, breathed equally from both. O speech!
How feeble and how faint art thou, to give
Conception birth. Yet this to what I saw
Is less than little. O eternal Light!
Sole in Thyself that dwell'st; and of Thyself
Sole understood, past, present, or to come;
Thou smiledst, on that circling, which in Thee
Seem'd as reflected splendour, while I mused;
For I therein, methought, in its own hue
Beheld our image painted: steadfastly
I therefore pored upon the view. As one,
Who versed in geometric lore, would fain
Measure the circle; and, though pondering long
And deeply, that beginning, which he needs,

Finds not: e'en such was I, intent to scan
The novel wonder, and trace out the form,
How to the circle fitted, and therein ·
How placed: but the flight was not for my wing;
Had not a flash darted athwart my mind,
And, in the spleen, unfolded what it sought.
   Here vigour fail'd the towering fantasy:
But yet the will roll'd onward, like a wheel
In even motion, by the Love impell'd,
That moves the sun in Heaven and all the stars.

H. F. CARY, 1812

(b)

My mind in this wise wholly in suspense,
   Steadfast, immovable, attentive gazed,
   And evermore with gazing grew enkindled.
In presence of that light one such becomes,
   That to withdraw therefrom for other prospect
   It is impossible he e'er consent;
Because the good, which object is of will,
   Is gathered all in this, and out of it
   That is defective which is perfect there.
Shorter henceforward will my language fall
   Of what I yet remember, than an infant's
   Who still his tongue doth moisten at the breast.
Not because more than one unmingled semblance
   Was in the living light on which I looked,
   For it is always what it was before;
But through the sight, that fortified itself
   In me by looking, one appearance only
   To me was ever changing as I changed.
Within the deep and luminous subsistence
   Of the High Light appeared to me three circles,
   Of threefold colour and of one dimension,
And by the second seemed the first reflected
   As Iris is by Iris, and the third
   Seemed fire that equally from both is breathed.
O how all speech is feeble and falls short

Of my conceit, and this to what I saw
Is such, 'tis not enough to call it little!
O Light Eterne, sole in thyself that dwellest,
  Sole knowest thyself, and, known unto thyself
  And knowing, lovest and smilest on thyself!
That circulation, which being thus conceived
  Appeared in thee as a reflected light,
  When somewhat contemplated by mine eyes,
Within itself, of its own very colour
  Seemed to me painted with our effigy,
  Wherefore my sight was all absorbed therein.
As the geometrician, who endeavours
  To square the circle and discovers not,
  By taking thought, the principle he wants,
Even such was I at that new apparition;
  I wished to see how the image to the circle
  Conformed itself, and how it there finds place;
But my own wings were not enough for this,
  Had it not been that then my mind there smote
  A flash of lightning, wherein came its wish.
Here vigour failed the lofty fantasy:
  But now was turning my desire and will,
  Even as a wheel that equally is moved,
The Love which moves the sun and the other stars.

H. W. LONGFELLOW, 1867

(c)

Thus did my mind in the suspense of thought
  Gaze fixedly, all immovable and intent,
  And ever fresh fire from its gazing caught.
Man at that light becometh so content
  That to choose other sight and this reject,
  It is impossible that he consent,
Because the good which is the will's object
  Dwells wholly in it, and that within its pale
  Is perfect, which, without, hath some defect.
Even for my remembrance now must fail
  My words, and less than could an infant's store
  Of speech, who at the pap yet sucks, avail;

126

Not that within the living light was more
  Than one sole aspect of divine essence,
  Being still for ever as it was before,
But the one semblance, seen with more intense
  A faculty, even as over me there stole
  Change, was itself transfigured to my sense.
Within the clear profound Light's aureole
  Three circles from its substance now appeared,
  Of three colours, and each an equal whole.
One its reflection on the next conferred
  As rainbow upon rainbow, and the two
  Breathed equally the fire that was the third.
To my conception O how frail and few
  My words! and that, to what I looked upon,
  Is such that 'little' is more than is its due.
O Light Eternal, who in thyself alone
  Dwell'st and thyself know'st, and self-understood,
  Self-understanding, smilest on thine own!
That circle which, as I conceived it, glowed
  Within thee like reflection of a flame,
  Being by mine eyes a little longer wooed,
Deep in itself, with colour still the same,
  Seemed with our human effigy to fill,
  Wherefore absorbed in it my sight became.
As the geometer who bends all his will
  To measure the circle, and howsoe'er he try
  Fails, for the principle escapes him still,
Such at this mystery new-disclosed was I,
  Fain to understand how the image doth alight
  Upon the circle, and with its form comply.
But these my wings were fledged not for that flight,
  Save that my mind a sudden glory assailed
  And its wish came revealed to it in that light.
To the high imagination force now failed;
  But like to a wheel whose circling nothing jars
  Already on my desire and will prevailed
The Love that moves the sun and the other stars.

LAURENCE BINYON, 1943

127

# CHAUCER

*The Nonne Preestes Tale,* 1–16

## (a)

There lived, as authors tell, in days of yore,
A widow, somewhat old, and very poor:
Deep in a dell her cottage lonely stood,
Well thatched, and under covert of a wood.
 This dowager, on whom my tale I found,
Since last she laid her husband in the ground,
A simple sober life in patience led,
And had but just enough to buy her bread;
But huswifing the little Heaven had lent,
She duly paid a groat for quarter-rent;
And pinched her belly, with her daughters two,
To bring the year about with much ado.
 The cattle in her homestead were three sows,
An ewe called Mally, and three brinded cows.
Her parlour window stuck with herbs around
Of savoury smell; and rushes strewed the ground.
A maple dresser in her hall she had,
On which full many a slender meal she made,
For no delicious morsel passed her throat;
According to her cloth she cut her coat.
No poignant sauce she knew, no costly treat,
Her hunger gave a relish to her meat.

JOHN DRYDEN, 1699

## (b)

Once, long ago, there dwelt a poor old widow
In a small cottage by a little meadow
Beside a grove and standing in a dale.
This widow-woman of whom I tell my tale
Since the sad day when last she was a wife
Had led a very patient, simple life.
Little she had in capital or rent,

But still by making do with what God sent
She kept herself and her two daughters going.
Three hefty sows—no more—were all her showing,
Three cows as well; there was a sheep called Molly.
  Sooty her hall, her kitchen melancholy,
And there she ate full many a slender meal;
There was no sauce piquante to spice her veal,
No dainty morsel ever passed her throat,
According to her cloth she cut her coat.

NEVILL COGHILL, 1951

# V

# POEMS FOR APPRECIATION

**(1)** *Compare the treatment of nature in the two following passages:*

(a)

To hear the lark begin his flight,
And, singing, startle the dull night,
From his watch-tower in the skies,
Till the dappled dawn doth rise;
Then to come, in spite of sorrow,
And at my window bid good-morrow,
Through the sweet-brier or the vine,
Or the twisted eglantine;
While the cock, with lively din,
Scatters the rear of darkness thin;
And to the stack, or the barn-door,
Stoutly struts his dames before:
Oft list'ning how the hounds and horn
Cheerly rouse the slumb'ring morn,
From the side of some hoar hill,
Through the high wood echoing shrill:
Sometimes walking, not unseen,
By hedgerow elms, on hillocks green,
Right against the eastern gate
Where the great Sun begins his state,
Robed in flames and amber light,
The clouds in thousand liveries dight;
While the ploughman, near at hand,
Whistles o'er the furrow'd land,
And the milkmaid singeth blithe,
And the mower whets his scythe,
And every shepherd tells his tale
Under the hawthorn in the dale.

(b)

I love at early morn, from new-mown swath,
    To see the startled frog his route pursue;
To mark while, leaping o'er the dripping path,
    His bright sides scatter dew,

133

The early lark that from its bustle flies
To hail his matin new;
And watch him to the skies:
To note on hedgerow baulks, in moisture sprent,
The jetty snail creep from the mossy thorn,
With earnest heed, and tremulous intent,
Frail brother of the morn,
That from the tiny bents and misted leaves
Withdraws his timid horn,
And fearful vision weaves:
Or swallow heed on smoke-tanned chimney top,
Wont to be first unsealing morning's eye,
Ere yet the bee hath gleaned one wayward drop
Of honey on his thigh;
To see him seek morn's airy couch to sing
Until the golden sky
Bepaint his russet wing:
And sawning boy by tanning corn espy,
With clapping noise to startle birds away,
And hear him bawl to every passer-by
To know the hour of day;
And see the uncradled breeze, refreshed and strong,
With waking blossoms play,
And breathe aeolian song.

(2) *Compare the following passages as examples of dramatic speech:*

(*a*)

Illustrious England, ancient seat of kings,
Whose chivalry hath royalized thy fame,
That sounding bravely through terrestrial vales
Proclaiming conquests, spoils and victories,
Rings glorious echoes through the farthest world;
What warlike nation, trained in feats of arms,
What barbarous people, stubborn or untamed,
What climate under the meridian signs,
Or frozen zone under his brumal plage,
Erst have not quaked and trembled at the name
Of Britain and her mighty conquerors?

Her neighbour-nations, as Scotland, Denmark, France,
Awed with their deeds and jealous of her arms,
Have begged defensive and offensive leagues.
Thus Europe, rich and mighty in her kings,
Hath feared brave England, dreadful in her kings
And now, to eternize Albion's champions,
Equivalent with Trojans' ancient fame,
Comes lovely Edward from Jerusalem,
Veering before the wind, ploughing the sea,
His stretchèd sails filled with the breath of men,
That through the world admire his manliness.

### (b)

This royal throne of kings, this scepter'd isle,
This earth of majesty, this seat of Mars,
This other Eden, demi-paradise,
This fortress built by Nature for herself
Against infection and the hand of war,
This happy breed of men, this little world,
This precious stone set in the silver sea,
Which serves it in the office of a wall,
Or as a moat defensive to a house,
Against the envy of less happier lands,
This blessed plot, this earth, this realm, this England,
This nurse, this teeming womb of royal kings,
Feared by their breed and famous by their birth,
Renownèd for their deeds as far from home—
For Christian service and true chivalry—
As is the sepulchre in stubborn Jewry
Of the world's ransom blessèd Mary's Son:
This land of such dear souls, this dear, dear land,
Dear for her reputation through the world,
Is now leased out—I die pronouncing it—
Like to a tenement, or pelting farm:
England, bound in with the triumphant sea,
Whose rocky shore beats back the envious siege,
Of watery Neptune, is now bound in with shame,
With inky blots, and rotten parchment bonds:

That England, that was wont to conquer others
Hath made a shameful conquest of itself.
Ah! would the scandal vanish with my life,
How happy then were my ensuing death.

(3) *If you were compiling an anthology of poetry would you include any
of these poems? Give reasons for your choice or rejection of each poem.*

(*a*)

What bird so sings, yet so does wail?
O 'tis the ravished nightingale.
'Jug, jug, jug, jug, tereu', she cries,
And still her woes at midnight rise.
Brave prick-song! who is't now we hear?
None but the lark so shrill and clear;
Now at heaven's gates she claps her wings,
The morn not waking till she sings.
Hark, hark, with what a pretty throat,
Poor robin redbreast tunes his note;
Hark how the jolly cuckoos sing,
Cuckoo to welcome in the spring!
Cuckoo to welcome in the spring!

(*b*)

When first we hear the shy-come nightingales,
They seem to mutter o'er their songs in fear,
And, climb we e'er so soft the spinney rails,
All stops as if no bird was anywhere.
The kindled bushes with the young leaves thin
Let curious eyes to search a long way in,
Until impatience cannot see or hear
The hidden music; gets but little way
Upon the path—when up the songs begin,
Full loud a moment and then low again.
But when a day or two confirms her stay
Boldly she sings and loud for half the day;
And soon the village brings the woodman's tale
Of having heard the new-come nightingale.

(c)

What voice of gladness, hark!
In heaven is ringing?
From the sad fields the lark
Is upward winging.

High through the mournful mist that blots our day
Their songs betray them soaring in the grey.
See them! Nay, they
In sunlight swim; above the furthest stain
Of cloud attain; their hearts in music rain
Upon the plain.

Sweet birds, far out of sight
Your songs of pleasure
Dome us with joy as bright
As heaven's best azure.

(d)

Robin on a leafless bough,
Lord in Heaven, how he sings!
Now cold Winter's cruel wind
Makes playmates of poor, dead things.

How he sings for joy this morn!
How his breast doth pant and glow!
Look you how he stands and sings,
Half-way up his legs in snow!

If these crumbs of bread were pearls,
And I had no bread at home,
He should have them for that song;
Pretty Robin Redbreast, Come.

(e)

O blithe New-comer! I have heard,
I hear thee and rejoice:
O Cuckoo! shall I call thee Bird,
Or but a wandering Voice?

While I am lying on the grass
    Thy twofold shout I hear;
From hill to hill it seems to pass,
    At once far off and near.

Though babbling only to the vale
    Of sunshine and of flowers,
Thou bringest unto me a tale
    Of visionary hours.

Thrice welcome, darling of the Spring!
    Even yet thou art to me
No bird, but an invisible thing,
    A voice, a mystery;

The same whom in my school-boy days
    I listen'd to; that Cry
Which made me look a thousand ways
    In bush, and tree, and sky,

To seek thee did I often rove
    Through woods and on the green;
And thou wert still a hope, a love;
    Still long'd for, never seen!

And I can listen to thee yet;
    Can lie upon the plain
And listen, till I do beget
    That golden time again.

O blessèd Bird! the earth we pace
    Again appears to be
An unsubstantial, faery place,
    That is fit home for Thee!

(4) *Here are two versions of the same poem. What reasons can you find
for the changes in the second poem?*

(a)

A hiding tuft, a greenbarked yewtree,
    Holds the roof,
Dearest spot! The oaktree guards me,
    Tempestproof.

Full of bounty, there's an apple
   Like an inn!
A fistful of a bush of hazel,
   Branching, green.

A peaceful troop, a country gathering
   Pays a call,
And the foxes come to join them,
   Best of all.

To what feasts the woods invite me
   All about!
Water pure and herbs and cresses,
   Salmon, trout.

All a man could ask of comfort
   Round me grows
Haws and yewberries and strawberries,
   Nuts and sloes.

And when summer spreads its mantle,
   There's a sight!
Marjoram and leeks and pignuts
   Green and bright.

Bees and beetles, nature's singers,
   Croon and strum,
Geese pass over, duck in autumn,
   Dark streams hum.

In the year's most brilliant weather
   Heifers low
Through green fields, not harsh nor laboured,
   Tranquil, slow.


*(b)*

A hiding tuft, a greenbarked yewtree,
   Spreads its roof,
An oak keeps this dear spot and me
   Tempestproof.

I can fetch an apple from a tree
    Like an inn
Or can fill my fists where hazels
    Block the scene.

Inquirers from a neighbouring country
    Pay a call,
And the foxes come to join them,
    Best of all.

To what a diet the woods invite me
    All about!
Water pure and herbs and cresses,
    Salmon and trout.

All a man could ask of comfort
    Round me grows
Hips and haws and strawberries,
    Nuts and sloes.

And when summer spreads its mantle,
    There's a sight!
Marjoram and leeks and pignuts
    Show green and bright.

Bees and beetles, natural singers,
    Croon and strum,
Geese pass over, duck in autumn,
    Dark streams hum.

In the year's most brilliant weather
    Heifers low
Through green fields, not driven and beaten,
    Tranquil, slow.

(5) *Compare the following passages, indicating differences of tone and manner:*
(a)

In the worst inn's worst room, with mat half-hung,
The floors of plaister, and the walls of dung,
On once a flock-bed, but repair'd with straw,
With tape-ty'd curtains, never meant to draw,

The George and Garter dangling from that bed
Where tawdry yellow strove with dirty red,
Great *Villiers* lies—alas! how chang'd from him,
That life of pleasure, and that soul of whim!...
No Wit to flatter left of all his store!
No Fool to laugh at, which he valu'd more.
There, Victor of his health, of fortune, friends,
And fame, this lord of useless thousands ends.

### (*b*)

Such is that room which one rude beam divides,
And naked rafters form the sloping sides;
Where the vile bands that bind the thatch are seen,
And lath and mud are all that lie between;
Save one dull pane, that, coarsely patch'd, gives way
To the rude tempest, yet excludes the day:
Here, on a matted flock, with dust o'erspread,
The drooping wretch reclines his languid head;
For him no hand the cordial cup applies,
Or wipes the tear that stagnates in his eyes;
No friends with soft discourse his pain beguile,
Or promise hope till sickness wears a smile.

(6) *Examine the use of metaphor and personification in these poems and
say whether the poet's meaning is helped or obscured.*

### (*a*)

Yes, thou art gone! and round me too the night
  In ever-nearing circle weaves her shade.
    I see her veil draw soft across the day,
  I feel her slowly chilling breath invade
      The cheek grown thin, the brown hair sprent with grey;
        I feel her finger light
Laid pausefully upon life's headlong train;
    The foot less prompt to meet the morning dew,
    The heart less bounding at emotion new,
And hope, once crush'd, less quick to spring again.

141

And long the way appears, which seem'd so short
   To the unpractis'd eye of sanguine youth;
     And high the mountain-tops, in cloudy air,
  The mountain-tops where is the throne of Truth,
     Tops in life's morning-sun so bright and bare!
        Unbreachable the fort
  Of the long-batter'd world uplifts its wall.
    And strange and vain the earthly turmoil grows,
    And near and real the charm of thy repose,
And night as welcome as a friend would fall.

### (b)

In vain to me the smiling mornings shine,
   And reddening Phoebus lifts his golden fire;
The birds in vain their amorous descant join,
   Or cheerful fields resume their green attire.
These ears, alas! for other notes repine,
   A different object do these eyes require:
My lonely anguish melts no heart but mine;
   And in my breast the imperfect joys expire.
Yet morning smiles the busy race to cheer,
   And new-born pleasures bring to happier men:
The fields to all their wonted tribute bear:
   To warm their little loves the birds complain.
I fruitless mourn to him that cannot hear,
   And weep the more, because I weep in vain.

(7) *Compare and contrast the following poems in point of style, feeling and intention:*

### (a)

I heard a thousand blended notes,
While in a grove I sate reclined,
In that sweet mood when pleasant thoughts
Bring sad thoughts to the mind.

To her fair works did Nature link
The human soul that through me ran;
And much it grieved my heart to think
What man has made of man.

Through primrose tufts, in that green bower,
The periwinkle trailed its wreaths;
And 'tis my faith that every flower
Enjoys the air it breathes.

The birds around me hopped and played,
Their thoughts I cannot measure:—
But the least motion which they made,
It seemed a thrill of pleasure.

The budding twigs spread out their fan,
To catch the breezy air;
And I must think, do all I can,
That there was pleasure there.

If this belief from heaven be sent,
If such be Nature's holy plan,
Have I not reason to lament
What man has made of man?

(*b*)

Heart-halt and spirit-lame,
        City-opprest,
Unto this wood I came
        As to a nest;
Dreaming that sylvan peace
Offered the harrowed ease—
Nature a soft release
        From men's unrest.

But, having entered in,
        Great growth and small
Show them to men akin—
        Combatants all!
Sycamore shoulders oak,
Bines the slim saplings yoke,
Ivy-spun halters choke
        Elms stout and tall.

Touches from ash, O wych,
        Sting you like scorn!

143

You, too, brave hollies, twitch
    Sidelong from thorn.
Even the rank poplars bear
Illy a rival's air,
Cankering in black despair
    If overborne.

Since, then, no grace I find
    Taught me of trees,
Turn I back to my kind,
    Worthy as these.
There at least smiles abound,
There discourse trills around
There, now and then, are found
    Life-loyalties.

(8) *Compare the following passages, and try to explain in what respects one is better than the other:*

(*a*)

Nor was his name unheard or unador'd
In ancient Greece, and in Ausonian land
Men call'd him Mulciber; and how he fell
From Heav'n they fabl'd, thrown by angry Jove
Sheer o'er the Chrystal Battlements; from Morn
To Noon he fell, from Noon to dewy Eve,
A Summer's day; and with the setting Sun
Dropt from the Zenith like a falling Star
On Lemnos th' Ægæan Ile: thus they relate,
Erring; for he with his rebellious rout
Fell long before.

(*b*)

Falling, falling! Los fell and fell,
Sunk precipitant, heavy, down, down,
Times on times, night on night, day on day;
Truth has bounds, Error none: falling, falling;
Years on years, and ages on ages
Still he fell thro' the void, still a void
Found for falling day and night without end;

For though day or night was not, their spaces
Were measur'd by his incessant whirls
In the horrid vacuity bottomless.

(9) *Appraise the following two poems:*

(*a*)

There was an Indian, who had known no change,
Who strayed content along a sunlit beach
Gathering shells. He heard a sudden strange
Commingled noise: looked up; and gasped for speech.
For in the bay, where nothing was before,
Moving on the sea, by magic, huge canoes,
With bellying cloths on poles, and not one oar,
And fluttering coloured signs and clambering crews.

And he, in fear, this naked man alone,
His fallen hands forgetting all their shells,
His lips gone pale, knelt low behind a stone,
And stared, and saw, and did not understand,
Columbus's doom-burdened caravels
Slant to the shore, and all their seamen land.

(*b*)

Much have I travelled in the realms of gold,
And many goodly states and kingdoms seen;
Round many western islands have I been
Which bards in fealty to Apollo hold.
Oft of one wide expanse had I been told,
That deep-browed Homer ruled as his demesne:
Yet did I never breathe its pure serene
Till I heard Chapman speak out loud and bold:
Then felt I like some watcher of the skies
When a new planet swims into his ken;
Or like stout Cortez, when with eagle eyes
He stared at the Pacific—and all his men
Looked at each other with a wild surmise—
Silent, upon a peak in Darien.

145

(10) *Compare and contrast the two following poems:*

(*a*)

Since there's no help, come let us kiss and part;
Nay, I have done, you get no more of me;
And I am glad, yea, glad with all my heart,
That thus so cleanly I myself can free;
Shake hands for ever, cancel all our vows,
And when we meet at any time again,
Be it not seen in either of our brows
That we one jot of former love retain.
Now at the last gasp of love's latest breath,
When his pulse failing, passion speechless lies,
When faith is kneeling by his bed of death,
And innocence is closing up his eyes,
Now if thou would'st, when all have given him over,
From death to life thou might'st him yet recover.

(*b*)

All's over, then; does truth sound bitter
　　As one at first believes?
Hark, 'tis the sparrows' good-night twitter
　　About your cottage eaves!

And the leaf-buds on the vine are woolly,
　　I noticed that, to-day;
One day more bursts them open fully
　　—You know the red turns grey.

To-morrow we meet the same then, dearest?
　　May I take your hand in mine?
Mere friends are we,—well, friends the merest
　　Keep much that I'll resign:

For each glance of that eye so bright and black,
　　Though I keep with heart's endeavour,—
Your voice, when you wish the snowdrops back,
　　Though it stay in my soul for ever!—

Yet I will but say what mere friends say,
 Or only a thought stronger;
I will hold your hand but as long as all may,
 Or so very little longer!

(11) *Which of these two poems do you prefer, and why?*

(a)

Behold her, single in the field,
Yon solitary Highland lass!
Reaping and singing by herself;
Stop here, or gently pass!
Alone she cuts and binds the grain,
And sings a melancholy strain;
Oh, listen! for the vale profound
Is overflowing with the sound.

No nightingale did ever chaunt
More welcome notes to weary bands
Of travellers in some shady haunt,
Among Arabian sands:
A voice so thrilling ne'er was heard
In spring-time from the cuckoo-bird,
Breaking the silence of the seas
Among the farthest Hebrides.

Will no one tell me what she sings?
Perhaps the plaintive numbers flow
For old, unhappy, far-off things,
And battles long ago:
Or is it some more humble lay,
Familiar matter of to-day?
Some natural sorrow, loss, or pain,
That has been, and may be again?

Whate'er the theme, the maiden sang
As if her song could have no ending;
I saw her singing at her work,
And o'er the sickle bending;
I listen'd, till I had my fill;

And, as I mounted up the hill,
The music in my heart I bore,
Long after it was heard no more.

(*b*)

There was never a sound beside the wood but one,
And that was my long scythe whispering to the ground.
What was it it whispered? I knew not well myself;
Perhaps it was something about the heat of the sun,
Something, perhaps, about the lack of sound—
And that was why it whispered and did not speak.
It was no dream of the gift of idle hours,
Or easy gold at the hand of fay or elf:
Anything more than the truth would have seemed too weak
To the earnest love that laid the swale in rows,
Not without feeble-pointed spikes of flowers
(Pale orchises), and scared a bright green snake.
The fact is the sweetest dream that labour knows.
My long scythe whispered and left the hay to make.

(12) *Compare these two poems:*

(*a*)

The warm sun is failing, the bleak wind is wailing,
The bare boughs are sighing, the pale flowers are dying;
And the Year
On the earth her death-bed, in a shroud of leaves dead,
Is lying.
Come, Months, come away,
From November to May,
In your saddest array;
Follow the bier
Of the dead cold Year,
And like dim shadows watch by her sepulchre.

The chill rain is falling, the nipped worm is crawling,
The rivers are swelling, the thunder is knelling
For the Year;
The blithe swallows are flown, and the lizards each gone
To his dwelling.

Come, Months, come away;
Put on white, black and grey;
Let your light sisters play—
Ye, follow the bier
Of the dead cold Year,
And make her grave green with tear on tear.

### (b)

I saw old Autumn in the misty morn
Stand shadowless like Silence, listening
To silence, for no lonely bird would sing
Into his hollow ear from woods forlorn,
Nor lowly hedge nor solitary thorn;
Shaking his languid locks all dewy bright
With tangled gossamer that fell by night,
    Pearling his coronet of golden corn.

Where are the songs of Summer? With the sun,
Oping the dusky eyelids of the south,
Till shade and silence waken up as one,
And Morning sings with a warm odorous mouth.
Where are the merry birds? Away, away,
On panting wings through the inclement skies,
    Lest owls should prey
    Undazzled at noonday,
And tear with horny beak their lustrous eyes.

Where are the blossoms of Summer? In the west,
Blushing their last to the last sunny hours
When the mild Eve by sudden Night is prest
Like a tearful Proserpine, snatched from her flowers
    To a most gloomy breast.
Where is the pride of Summer—the green prime—
The many, many leaves all twinkling? Three
    On the mossed elm; three on the naked lime
Trembling—and one upon the old oak tree.
Where is the Dryad's immortality?
Gone into mournful cypress and dark yew,
Or wearing the long gloomy Winter through
    In the smooth holly's green eternity.

149

(13) *Write a careful comparison of these two poems:*

(*a*)

Ethereal minstrel! pilgrim of the sky!
Dost thou despise the earth where cares abound?
Or, while the wings aspire, are heart and eye
Both with thy nest upon the dewy ground?
Thy nest which thou canst drop into at will,
Those quivering wings composed, that music still!

Leave to the nightingale her shady wood;
A privacy of glorious light is thine;
Whence thou dost pour upon the world a flood
Of harmony, with instinct more divine;
Type of the wise who soar, but never roam;
True to the kindred points of Heaven and Home!

To the last point of vision, and beyond,
Mount, daring warbler!—that love-prompted strain,
('Twixt thee and thine a never-failing bond).
Thrills not the less the bosom of the plain:
Yet might'st thou seem, proud privilege! to sing
All independent of the leafy spring.

(*b*)

Above the russet clods the corn is seen
Sprouting its spiry points of tender green,
Where squats the hare, to terrors wide awake,
Like some brown clod the harrows failed to break.
Opening their golden caskets to the sun,
The buttercups make schoolboys eager run,
To see who shall be first to pluck the prize—
Up from their hurry see the Skylark flies,
And o'er her half-formed nest, with happy wings,
Winnows the air till in the cloud she sings,
Then hangs a dust spot in the sunny skies,
And drops and drops till in her nest she lies,
Which they unheeded passed—not dreaming then
That birds, which flew so high, would drop again
To nest upon the ground, which anything
May come at to destroy.  Had they the wing

Like such a bird, themselves would be too proud
And build on nothing but a passing cloud!
As free from danger as the heavens are free
From pain and toil, there would they build and be,
And sail about the world to scenes unheard
Of and unseen,—O were they but a bird!
So think they while they listen to its song,
And smile and fancy and so pass along;
While its low nest, moist with the dews of morn,
Lies safely, with the leveret, in the corn.

(14) *Examine these two versions of the same poem, say which you consider the revised version, and give your reasons.*

(*a*)

Two pewits sport and cry
Under the after sunset sky,
Whiter than the moon on high
That rides the black surge in the sky,
Than the pool it is mirrored by,
The only light under the sky;
Blacker than the earth. Their cry
Makes the sole sound under the sky.
They alone move, low or high.
And merrily they cry,
To the mischievous dark sky,
Plunging earthward, tossing high
They care not for the sigh
Of the traveller wondering why
So merrily they cry and fly,
They choose not between earth and sky,
While the moon's quarter silently
Rides, and earth rests as silently.

(*b*)

Under the after-sunset sky
Two pewits sport and cry,
More white than is the moon on high
Riding the dark surge silently;

More black than earth. Their cry
Is the one sound under the sky,
They alone move, now low, now high,
And merrily they cry
To the mischievous Spring sky,
Plunging earthward, tossing high,
Over the ghost who wonders why
So merrily they cry and fly,
Nor choose 'twixt earth and sky,
While the moon's quarter silently
Rides, and earth rests as silently.

(15) *Compare the manner of expression of these two passages:*

(*a*)

The Cock is crowing,
The stream is flowing,
The small birds twitter,
The lake doth glitter,
The green field sleeps in the sun;
The oldest and youngest
Are at work with the strongest;
The cattle are grazing,
Their heads never raising;
There are forty feeding like one!

Like an army defeated
The snow hath retreated,
And now doth fare ill
On the top of the bare hill;
The Ploughboy is whooping—anon—anon:
There's joy in the mountains;
There's life in the fountains;
Small clouds are sailing,
Blue sky prevailing;
The rain is over and gone!

(*b*)

A touch, a kiss! the charm was snapt.
  There rose a noise of striking clocks,
And feet that ran, and doors that clapt,
  And barking dogs, and crowing cocks;
A fuller light illumined all,
  A breeze through all the garden swept,
A sudden hubbub shook the hall,
  And sixty feet the fountain leapt.

The hedge broke in, the banner blew,
  The butler drank, the steward scrawl'd,
The fire shot up, the martin flew,
  The parrot scream'd, the peacock squall'd,
The maid and page renew'd their strife,
  The palace bang'd and buzz'd and clackt,
And all the long-pent stream of life
  Dash'd downward in a cataract.

(16) *Analyse the different effects produced on you by each of the following poems:*

(*a*)

We are slumberous poppies,
  Lords of Lethe downs,
Some awake, and some asleep,
  Sleeping in our crowns.
What perchance our dreams may know,
Let our serious beauty show.

Central depth of purple,
  Leaves more bright than rose,
Who shall tell what brightest thought
  Out of darkest grows?
Who, through what funereal pain,
Souls to love and peace again?

Visions aye are on us,
  Unto eyes of power,

Pluto's always setting sun,
   And Proserpine's bower:
There, like bees, the pale souls come
For our drink with drowsy hum.

Taste, ye mortals, also;
   Milky-hearted, we;
Taste, but with a reverent care;
   Active-patient be.
Too much gladness brings to gloom
Those who on the gods presume.

### (b)

The sleep-flower sways in the wheat its head,
Heavy with dreams, as that with bread:
The goodly grain and the sun-flushed sleeper
The reaper reaps, and Time the reaper.

I hang mid men my needless head,
And my fruit is dreams, as theirs is bread:
The goodly men and the sun-hazed sleeper
Time shall reap, but after the reaper
The world shall glean of me, me the sleeper.

(17) *Compare the following passages as examples of dramatic speech:*

### (a)

O you hard hearts, you cruel men of Rome,
Knew you not Pompey? Many a time and oft
Have you climb'd up to walls and battlements,
To towers and windows, yea, to chimney-tops,
Your infants in your arms, and there have sat
The livelong day, with patient expectation,
To see great Pompey pass the streets of Rome:
And when you saw his chariot but appear,
Have you not made an universal shout,
That Tiber trembled underneath her banks,
To hear the replication of your sounds
Made in her concave shores?

And do you now put on your best attire?
And do you now cull out a holiday?
And do you now strew flowers in his way,
That comes in triumph over Pompey's blood?

### (b)

All tongues speak of him, and the bleared sights
Are spectacled to see him: your prattling nurse
Into a rapture lets her baby cry,
While she chats him; the kitchen malkin pins
Her richest lockram 'bout her reechy neck,
Clambering the walls to eye him: stalls, bulks, windows,
Are smother'd up, leads fill'd, and ridges hors'd
With variable complexions, all agreeing
In earnestness to see him: seld-shown flamens
Do press among the popular throngs, and puff
To win a vulgar station: our veil'd dames
Commit the war of white and damask, in
Their nicely-gawded cheeks, to the wanton spoil
Of Phoebus' burning kisses: such a pother
As if that whatsoever god who leads him
Were slily crept into his human powers,
And gave him graceful posture.

(18) *Examine the following poems, and say what you find of interest
in each:*

### (a)

Spring, the sweet Spring, is the year's pleasant king;
Then blooms each thing, then maids dance in a ring,
Cold doth not sting, the pretty birds do sing—
      Cuckoo, jug-jug, pu-we, to-witta-woo!

The palm and may make country houses gay,
Lambs frisk and play, the shepherds pipe all day,
And we hear aye birds tune this merry lay—
      Cuckoo, jug-jug, pu-we, to-witta-woo!

The fields breathe sweet, the daisies kiss our feet,
Young lovers meet, old wives a-sunning sit,

In every street these tunes our ears do greet—
   Cuckoo, jug-jug, pu-we, to-witta-woo!
    Spring the sweet Spring!


(*b*)

Now fades the last long streak of snow,
   Now burgeons every maze of quick
   About the flowering squares, and thick
By ashen roots the violets blow.

Now rings the woodland loud and long,
   The distance takes a lovelier hue,
   And drown'd in yonder living blue
The lark becomes a sightless song.

Now dance the lights on lawn and lea,
   The flocks are whiter down the vale,
   And milkier every milky sail
On winding stream or distant sea;

Where now the seamew pipes, or dives
   In yonder greening gleam, and fly
   The happy birds, that change their sky
To build and brood; that live their lives

From land to land; and in my breast
   Spring wakens too; and my regret
   Becomes an April violet,
And buds and blossoms like the rest.


(*c*)

O thou with dewy locks, who lookest down
Through the clear windows of the morning, turn
Thine angel eyes upon our western isle,
Which in full choir hails thy approach, O Spring!

The hills tell one another, and the listening
Valleys hear; all our longing eyes are turn'd
Up to thy bright pavilions: issue forth
And let thy holy feet visit our clime!

Come o'er the eastern hills, and let our winds
Kiss thy perfumèd garments; let us taste
Thy morn and evening breath; scatter thy pearls
Upon our lovesick land that mourns for thee.

O deck her forth with thy fair fingers; pour
Thy soft kisses on her bosom; and put
Thy golden crown upon her languish'd head,
Whose modest tresses were bound up for thee.

### (d)

Now the full-throated daffodils,
Our trumpeters in gold,
Call resurrection from the ground
And bid the year be told.

To-day the almond-tree turns pink,
The first flush of spring;
Winds loll and gossip through the town
Her secret whispering.

Now too the bird must try his voice
Upon the morning air;
Down drowsy avenues he cries
A novel great affair.

He tells of royalty to be;
How with her train of rose,
Summer to coronation comes
Through waving wild hedgerows.

To-day crowds quicken in a street,
The fish leaps in the flood:
Look there, gasometer rises,
And here boughs swell to bud.

For our love's luck, our stowaway,
Stretches in his cabin;
Our youngster joy, barely conceived
Shows up beneath the skin.

Our joy was but a gusty thing
Without sinew or wit,
An infant flyaway; but now
We make a man of it.

(19) *Compare the following poems, paying particular attention to diction and imagery:*

(*a*)

Flowers of the willow-herb are wool;
Flowers of the briar berries red;
Speeding their seed as the breeze may rule,
Flowers of the thistle loosen the thread.
Flowers of the clematis drip in beard,
Slack from the fir-tree youngly climbed;
Chaplets in air, flies foliage seared;
Heeled upon earth, lie clusters rimed.

Where were skies of the mantle stained
Orange and scarlet, a coat of frieze
Travels from North till day has waned,
Tattered, soaked in the ditch's dyes;
Tumbles the rook under gray or slate;
Else unfolds us, damps to the bone;
Narrows the world to my neighbour's gate;
Paints me Life as a wheezy crone.

Now seems none but the spider lord;
Star in circle his web waits prey,
Silvering bush-mounds, blue brushing sward;
Slow runs the hour, swift flits the ray.
Now to his thread-shroud is he nigh,
Nigh to the tangle where wings are sealed,
He who frolicked the jewelled fly;
All is adroop on the down and the weald.

(*b*)

This darksome burn, horseback brown,
His rollcock highroad roaring down,
In coop and in comb the fleece of his foam
Flutes, and low to the lake falls home.

A windpuff-bonnet of fawn-froth
Turns and twindles over the broth
Of a pool so pitchblack, fell-frowning,
It rounds and rounds Despair to drowning.

Degged with dew, dappled with dew
Are the groins of the braes that the brook treads through,
Wiry heathpacks, flitches of fern,
And the beadbonny ash that sits over the burn.

What would the world be, once bereft
Of wet and of wildness? Let them be left,
O let them be left, wildness and wet;
Long live the weeds and the wilderness yet.

(20) *Comment on the versification of the following passages:*

*(a)*

In parchments then, large as his fields, hee drawes
Assurances, bigge, as gloss'd civill lawes,
So huge, that men (in our times forwardnesse)
Are Fathers of the Church for writing lesse.
These hee writes not; nor for these written payes,
Therefore spares no length; as in those first dayes
When Luther was profest, He did desire
Short *Pater nosters*, saying as a Fryer
Each day his beads, but having left those lawes,
Addes to Christs prayer, the Power and glory clause.
But when he sells or changes land, he 'impaires
His writings, and (unwatch'd) leaves out, *ses heires*,
As slily as any Commenter goes by
Hard words, or sense; or in Divinity
As controverters, in vouch'd Texts, leave out
Shrewd words, which might against them cleare the doubt.

*(b)*

Then strongly fencing ill-got wealth by law,
Indentures, Cov'nants, Articles they draw,
Large as the fields themselves, and larger far
Than Civil Codes, with all their Glosses are;

So vast, our new Divines, we must confess,
Are Fathers of the Church for writing less.
But let them write for you, each rogue impairs
The deeds, and dext'rously omits, *ses heires*:
No Commentator can more slily pass
O'er a learn'd, unintelligible place;
Or, in quotation, shrewd Divines leave out
Those words, that would against them clear the doubt.
So Luther thought the Pater-noster long,
When doom'd to say his beads and Even-song;
But having cast his cowl, and left those laws,
Adds to Christ's pray'r, the *Pow'r and Glory* clause.

(21) *Compare the following, stating the attitude of each poet to his subject; say which poem you prefer and give your reasons.*

(*a*)

When maidens such as Hester die,
Their place ye may not well supply,
Though ye among a thousand try,
    With vain endeavour.

A month or more hath she been dead,
Yet cannot I by force be led
To think upon the wormy bed,
    And her together.

A springy motion in her gait,
A rising step, did indicate
Of pride and joy no common rate,
    That flush'd her spirit.

I know not by what name beside
I shall it call:—if 'twas not pride,
It was a joy to that allied,
    She did inherit.

Her parents held the Quaker rule,
Which doth the human feeling cool,
But she was train'd in Nature's school,
    Nature had blest her.

A waking eye, a prying mind,
A heart that stirs, is hard to bind,
A hawk's keen sight ye cannot blind,
    Ye could not Hester.

My sprightly neighbour, gone before
To that unknown and silent shore,
Shall we not meet, as heretofore,
    Some summer morning,

When from thy cheerful eyes a ray
Hath struck a bliss upon the day,
A bliss that would not go away,
    A sweet fore-warning?


### (b)

Enough: and leave the rest to Fame.
'Tis to commend her but to name.
Courtship, which living she declin'd,
When dead to offer were unkind.
Where never any could speak ill,
Who would officious praises spill?
Nor can the truest wit or friend,
Without detracting, her commend.
To say she liv'd a virgin chaste,
In this age loose and all unlac't;
Nor was, when vice is so allow'd,
Of virtue or asham'd, or proud;
That her soul was on Heaven so bent
No minute but it came and went;
That ready her last debt to pay
She summ'd her life up ev'ry day;
Modest as morn; as mid-day bright;
Gentle as ev'ning; cool as night;
'Tis true: but all so weakly said;
'Twere more significant, *She's Dead*.

(22) *Examine these three successive drafts of Milton's 'Lycidas' and try to account for the changes.*

(*a*)

Bring the rathe primrose that unwedded dies
colouring the pale cheek of unenjoyed love
and the sad flower that strove
to write his own woes in the vermeil grain
next add Narcissus that still weeps in vain
the woodbine and the pansy freaked with jet
the glowing violet
the cowslip wan that hangs his pensive head
and every bud that sorrow's livery wears
let Daffadillies fill their cups with tears
bid Amaranthus all his beauty shed.

(*b*)

Bring the rathe primrose that forsaken dies
the tufted crow-toe and pale Gessamin
the white pink and the pansy freaked with jet
the glowing violet
the musk rose and the garish columbine
with cowslips wan that hang the pensive head
and every flower that sad escutcheon bears
let Daffadillies fill their cups with tears
bid Amaranthus all his beauties shed.

(*c*)

Bring the rathe primrose that forsaken dies,
The tufted crow-toe, and pale jessamine,
The white pink and the pansy freaked with jet,
The glowing violet,
The musk-rose, and the well-attired woodbine,
With cowslips wan that hang the pensive head,
And every flower that sad embroidery wears:
Bid amaranthus all his beauty shed,
And daffadillies fill their cups with tears.

**(23)** *Which of these do you consider the more important poem?*

(*a*)

Ah, Sun-flower! weary of time,
Who countest the steps of the sun;
Seeking after that sweet golden clime,
Where the traveller's journey is done;

Where the Youth pined away with desire,
And the pale Virgin shrouded in snow,
Arise from their graves, and aspire
Where my Sun-Flower wishes to go.

(*b*)

In that world we weary to attain,
   Love's furled banner floats at large unfurled;
There is no more doubt and no more pain
   In that world.

   There are gems and gold and inlets pearled;
There the verdure fadeth not again;
   There no clinging tendrils droop uncurled.

Here incessant tides stir up the main,
   Stormy miry depths aloft are hurled:
There is no more sea, or storm, or stain,
   In that world.

**(24)** *Compare the following poems, pointing out in what respects one is better than the other:*

(*a*)

I arise from dreams of thee
In the first sweet sleep of night,
When the winds are breathing low,
And the stars are shining bright:
I arise from dreams of thee,
And a spirit in my feet
Hath led me—who knows how?
To thy chamber window, Sweet!

The wandering airs they faint
On the dark, the silent stream—
The Champak odours fail
Like sweet thoughts in a dream;
The nightingale's complaint,
It dies upon her heart;—
As I must on thine,
Oh! beloved as thou art!

Oh lift me from the grass!
I die! I faint! I fail!
Let thy love in kisses rain
On my lips and eyelids pale.
My cheek is cold and white, alas!
My heart beats loud and fast;—
Oh! press it to thine own again,
Where it will break at last.

(*b*)

Blame not my cheeks, though pale with love they be;
The kindly heat unto my heart is flown,
To cherish it that is dismayed by thee,
Who art so cruel and unsteadfast grown:
For nature, called for by distressed hearts,
Neglects and quite forsakes the outward parts.

But they whose cheeks with careless blood are stained,
Nurse not one spark of love within their hearts,
And, when they woo, they speak with passion feigned,
For their fat love lies in their outward parts:
But in their breasts, where love his court should hold,
Poor Cupid sits and blows his nails for cold.

(25) *Make a critical examination of the style of the following poems:*

(*a*)

It will not shine again,
Its sad course is done;
I have seen the last ray wane
Of the cold, bright sun.

None but me beheld him dying,
Parting with the parting day;
Wind of evening, sadly sighing,
Bore his soul from earth away.

Coldly, bleakly, dreamily
Evening died on Elbe's shore;
Winds were in the cloudy sky,
Sighing, mourning ever more.

### (b)

The Day's grown old, the fainting Sun
Has but a little way to run,
And yet his Steeds, with all his skill,
Scarce lug the Chariot down the Hill.

With Labour spent, and Thirst opprest,
Whilst they strain hard to gain the West,
From Fetlocks hot drops melted light,
Which turns to Meteors in the Night.

The Shadows now so long do grow,
That Brambles like tall Cedars show,
Mole-hills seem Mountains, and the Ant
Appears a monstrous Elephant.

A very little little Flock
Shades thrice the ground that it would stock;
Whilst the small Stripling following them,
Appears a mighty *Polypheme*.

(26) *Compare and contrast the attitude shown to the subject in these two poems:*

### (a)

Remember me when I am gone away,
Gone far away into the silent land;
When you can no more hold me by the hand,
Nor I half turn to go yet turning stay.
Remember me when no more day by day
You tell me of our future that you plann'd:

Only remember me; you understand
It will be late to counsel then or pray.
Yet if you should forget me for a while
    And afterwards remember, do not grieve:
    For if the darkness and corruption leave
A vestige of the thoughts that once I had,
Better by far you should forget and smile
    Than that you should remember and be sad.

(b)

I tell you, hopeless grief is passionless;
    That only men incredulous of despair,
    Half-taught in anguish, through the midnight air
Beat upward to God's throne in loud access
Of shrieking and reproach. Full desertness
    In souls, as countries, lieth silent-bare
    Under the blanching, vertical eye-glare
Of the absolute Heavens. Deep-hearted man, express
Grief for the Dead in silence like to death:—
    Most like a monumental statue set
In everlasting watch and moveless woe
Till itself crumble to the dust beneath.
    Touch it: the marble eyelids are not wet:
If it could weep, it could arise and go.

(27) *Point out the special qualities in thought and manner of the following poems. Which do you prefer?*

(a)

My tongue-tied Muse in manners holds her still,
While comments of your praise, richly compiled,
Reserve their character with golden quill,
And precious phrase by all the Muses filed.
I think good thoughts, whilst other write good words,
And, like unletter'd clerk, still cry 'Amen'
To every hymn that able spirit affords,
In polish'd form of well-refined pen.

Hearing you praised, I say ''Tis so, 'tis true',
And to the most of praise add something more;
But that is in my thought, whose love to you,
Though words come hindmost, holds his rank before.
   Then others for the breath of words respect,
   Me for my dumb thoughts, speaking in effect.

## (b)

She is foremost of those that I would hear praised.
I have gone about the house, gone up and down
As a man does who has published a new book
Or a young girl dressed out in her new gown,
And though I have turned the talk by hook or crook
Until her praise should be the uppermost theme,
A woman spoke of some new tale she had read,
A man confusedly in a half dream
As though some other name ran in his head.
She is foremost of those that I would hear praised.
I will talk no more of books or the long war
But walk by the dry thorn until I have found
Some beggar sheltering from the wind, and there
Manage the talk until her name come round.
If there be rags enough he will know her name
And be well pleased remembering it, for in the old days,
Though she had young men's praise and old men's blame,
Among the poor both old and young gave her praise.

(28) *Discuss the differences between these three versions of the same
passage by Keats, and try to say in what order they were written.*

## (a)

   As when, upon a tranced summer-night,
   Those green-rob'd senators of mighty woods,
   Tall oaks, branch-charmed by the earnest stars,
   Dream, and so dream all night without a stir,
   Save from one gradual solitary gust
   Which comes upon the silence, and dies off,
   As if the ebbing air had but one wave;
   So came these words and went....

### (*b*)

As when, upon a tranced summer-night,
Those green-rob'd senators of mighty woods,
The Oaks stand charmed by the earnest Stars:
And thus all night without a stir they rest
Save from one sudden momentary gust
Which comes upon the silence and dies off
As if the Sea of Air had but one wave:
So came these words and went....

### (*c*)

As when upon a tranced summer-night
Forests, branch-charmed by the earnest stars,
Dream, and so dream all night without a noise,
Save from one gradual solitary gust,
Swelling upon the silence; dying off;
As if the ebbing air had but one wave;
So came these words and went....

(29) *Examine the following passages and say in what sense, and to
what extent, the style of each is dramatic.*

### (*a*)

Had it pleas'd heaven
To try me with affliction; had they rain'd
All kinds of sores and shames on my bare head,
Steep'd me in poverty to the very lips,
Given to captivity me and my utmost hopes,
I should have found in some place of my soul
A drop of patience: but, alas, to make me
The fixed figure for the time of scorn
To point his slow and moving finger at!
Yet could I bear that too; well, very well:
But there, where I have garner'd up my heart,
Where either I must live or bear no life,
The fountain from the which my current runs

Or else dries up; to be discarded thence!
Or keep it as a cistern for foul toads
To knot and gender in!

### (b)

Oh, you gods,
Give me a worthy patience! Have I stood
Naked, alone, the shock of many fortunes?
Have I seen mischiefs numberless and mighty
Grow like a sea upon me? Have I taken
Danger as stern as death into my bosom,
And laugh'd upon it, made it but a mirth,
And flung it by? Do I live now like him,
Under this tyrant King, that languishing
Hears his sad bell and sees his mourners? Do I
Bear all this bravely, and must sink at length
Under a woman's falsehood?

(30) *Comment on the diction, imagery, feeling of the following poems, making any comparisons or contrasts which seem to you relevant:*

### (a)

The world is too much with us; late and soon,
Getting and spending, we lay waste our powers:
Little we see in Nature that is ours;
We have given our hearts away, a sordid boon!
This Sea that bares her bosom to the moon;
The winds that will be howling at all hours,
And are up-gathered now like sleeping flowers;
For this, for everything, we are out of tune;
It moves us not.—Great God! I'd rather be
A Pagan suckled in a creed outworn;
So might I, standing on this pleasant lea,
Have glimpses that would make me less forlorn;
Have sight of Proteus rising from the sea;
Or hear old Triton blow his wreathèd horn.

(b)

The world is charged with the grandeur of God.
  It will flame out, like shining from shook foil;
  It gathers to a greatness, like the ooze of oil
Crushed. Why do men then now not reck his rod?
Generations have trod, have trod, have trod;
  And all is seared with trade; bleared, smeared with toil;
  And wears man's smudge and shares man's smell: the soil
Is bare now, nor can foot feel, being shod.

And for all this, nature is never spent;
  There lives the dearest freshness deep down things;
And though the last lights off the black West went,
  Oh, morning, at the brown brink eastward, springs—
Because the Holy Ghost over the bent
  World broods with warm breast and with ah! bright wings.

(31) *Discuss the effect of the imagery in the following:*

(a)

How sweet the moonlight sleeps upon this bank!
Here will we sit, and let the sounds of music
Creep in our ears: soft stillness and the night
Become the touches of sweet harmony.
Sit, Jessica. Look how the floor of heaven
Is thick inlaid with patines of bright gold:
There's not the smallest orb which thou behold'st
But in his motion like an angel sings,
Still quiring to the young-eyed cherubins;
Such harmony is in immortal souls;
But whilst this muddy vesture of decay
Doth grossly close it in, we cannot hear it.

(b)

With how sad steps, O Moon, thou climb'st the skies!
How silently, and with how wan a face!
What, may it be that even in heav'nly place
That busy archer his sharp arrows tries!

Sure, if that long-with-love-acquainted eyes
Can judge of love, thou feel'st a lover's case,
I read it in thy looks; thy languisht grace,
To me, that feel the like, thy state descries.
Then, ev'n of fellowship, O moon, tell me,
Is constant love deem'd there but want of wit?
Are beauties there as proud as here they be?
Do they above love to be lov'd, and yet
Those lovers scorn whom that love doth possess?
Do they call virtue there ungratefulness?

(32) *Write a detailed critical comparison of these two poems, stating
which you prefer and why.*

(*a*)

Nothing is so beautiful as spring—
When weeds, in wheels, shoot long and lovely and lush;
Thrush's eggs look little low heavens, and thrush
Through the echoing timber does so rinse and wring
The ear, it strikes like lightnings to hear him sing;
The glassy peartree leaves and blooms, they brush
The descending blue; that blue is all in a rush
With richness; the racing lambs too have fair their fling.

What is all this juice and all this joy?
A strain of the earth's sweet being in the beginning
In Eden garden.—Have, get, before it cloy,
Before it cloud, Christ, lord, and sour with sinning,
Innocent mind and Mayday in girl and boy,
Most, O maid's child, thy choice and worthy the winning.

(*b*)

When Spring comes back to England
    And crowns her brows with May,
Round the merry moonlit world
    She goes the greenwood way:
She throws a rose to Italy,
    A fleur-de-lys to France;
But round her regal morris-ring
    The seas of England dance

171

When Spring comes back to England
   And dons her robe of green,
There's many a nation garlanded,
   But England is the Queen;
She's Queen, She's Queen of all the world
   Beneath the laughing sky,
For the nations go a-Maying
   When they hear the New Year cry—

'Come over the water to England,
   My old love, my new love,
Come over the water to England
   In showers of flowery rain;
Come over the water to England,
   April, my true love,
And tell the heart of England
   The Spring is here again!'

(33) *Comment on the style, imagery and dramatic significance of the following passages, making any comparisons which you consider relevant:*

(*a*)

To be, or not to be: that is the question:
Whether 'tis nobler in the mind to suffer
The slings and arrows of outrageous fortune,
Or to take arms against a sea of troubles,
And by opposing end them. To die: to sleep:
No more; and by a sleep to say we end
The heart-ache, and the thousand natural shocks
That flesh is heir to, 'tis a consummation
Devoutly to be wish'd. To die, to sleep;
To sleep: perchance to dream: ay, there's the rub;
For in that sleep of death what dreams may come,
When we have shuffled off this mortal coil,
Must give us pause: there's the respect
That makes calamity of so long life;
For who would bear the whips and scorns of time,
The oppressor's wrong, the proud man's contumely,
The pangs of despised love, the law's delay,

The insolence of office, and the spurns
That patient merit of the unworthy takes,
When he himself might his quietus make
With a bare bodkin? who would fardels bear,
To grunt and sweat under a weary life,
But that the dread of something after death,
The undiscover'd country from whose bourn
No traveller returns, puzzles the will,
And makes us rather bear those ills we have
Than fly to others that we know not of?

### (*b*)

Be it so, for I submit; his doom is fair,
That dust I am, and shall to dust return.
O welcome hour, whenever! Why delays
His hand to execute what his decree
Fixed on this day? Why do I overlive?
Why am I mocked with death, and lengthened out
To deathless pain? How gladly would I meet
Mortality, my sentence, and be earth
Insensible! How glad would lay me down
As in my mother's lap! There should I rest,
And sleep secure; his dreadful voice no more
Would thunder in my ears; no fear of worse
To me and my offspring would torment me
With cruel expectation. Yet one doubt
Pursues me still—lest all I cannot die,
Lest that pure breath of life, the Spirit of Man
Which God inspired, cannot together perish
With this corporeal clod. Then, in the grave,
Or in some other dismal place, who knows
But I shall die a living death? O thought
Horrid, if true! Yet why? It was but breath
Of life that sinned: what dies but what had life
And sin? The body properly hath neither.

(34) *Establish a preference for one over the other of the following poems:*

(*a*)

On Wenlock Edge the wood's in trouble;
His forest fleece the Wrekin heaves;
The gale, it plies the saplings double,
And thick on Severn snow the leaves.

'Twould blow like this through holt and hanger
When Uricon the city stood:
'Tis the old wind in the old anger,
But then it threshed another wood.

Then, 'twas before my time, the Roman
At yonder heaving hill would stare:
The blood that warms an English yeoman,
The thoughts that hurt him, they were there.

There, like the wind through woods in riot,
Through him the gale of life blew high;
The tree of man was never quiet:
Then 'twas the Roman, now 'tis I.

The gale, it plies the saplings double,
It blows so hard, 'twill soon be gone:
Today the Roman and his trouble
Are ashes under Uricon.

(*b*)

A wind is brushing down the clover,
It sweeps the tossing branches bare,
Blowing the poising kestrel over
The crumbling ramparts of the Caer.

It whirls the scattered leaves before us
Along the dusty road to home,
Once it awakened into chorus
The heart-strings in the ranks of Rome.

There by the gusty coppice border
The shrilling trumpets broke the halt,
The Roman line, the Roman order,
Swayed forwards to the blind assault.

Spearman and charioteer and bowman
Charged and were scattered into spray,
Savage and taciturn the Roman
Hewed upwards in the Roman way.

There—in the twilight—where the cattle
Are lowing home across the fields,
The beaten warriors left the battle
Dead on the clansmen's wicker shields

The leaves whirl in the wind's riot
Beneath the Beacon's jutting spur,
Quiet are clan and chief, and quiet
Centurion and signifer.

(35) *Compare the following passages which are from early and late versions of Tennyson's 'Œnone':*

(*a*)

There is a dale in Ida, lovelier
Than any in old Ionia, beautiful
With emerald slopes of sunny sward, that lean
Above the loud glenriver, which hath worn
A path thro' steepdown granite walls below
Mantled with flowering tendriltwine. In front
The cedarshadowy valleys open wide.
Far-seen, high over all the God-built wall
And many a snowycolumned range divine,
Mounted with awful sculptures,—men and Gods,
The work of Gods—bright on the dark-blue sky
The windy citadel of Ilion
Shone, like the crown of Troas. Hither came
Mournful Œnone wandering forlorn
Of Paris, once her playmate. Round her neck,
Her neck all marblewhite and marblecold,
Floated her hair or seemed to float in rest.
She, leaning on a vine-entwined stone,
Sang to the stillness, till the mountain-shadow
Sloped downward to her seat from the upper cliff.

(*b*)

There lies a vale in Ida, lovelier
Than all the valleys of Ionian hills.
The swimming vapour slopes across the glen,
Puts forth an arm, and creeps from pine to pine,
And loiters, slowly drawn.  On either hand
The lawns and meadow-ledges midway down
Hang rich in flowers, and far below them roars
The long brook falling through the clov'n ravine
In cataract after cataract to the sea.
Behind the valley topmost Gargarus
Stands up and takes the morning: but in front
The gorges, opening wide apart, reveal
Troas and Ilion's column'd citadel,
The crown of Troas.
                    Hither came at noon
Mournful Œnone, wandering forlorn
Of Paris, once her playmate on the hills.
Her cheek had lost the rose, and round her neck
Floated her hair or seemed to float in rest.
She, leaning on a fragment twined with vine,
Sang to the stillness, till the mountain-shade
Sloped downward to her seat from the upper cliff.

(36) *Write a careful appreciation of these two poems:*

(*a*)

The sigh that heaves the grasses
    Whence thou wilt never rise
Is of the air that passes
    And knows not if it sighs.

The diamond tears adorning
    Thy low mound on the lea,
Those are the tears of morning
    That weeps, but not for thee.

*(b)*

A slumber did my spirit seal;
    I had no human fears:
She seemed a thing that could not feel
    The touch of earthly years.

No motion has she now, no force;
    She neither hears nor sees;
Rolled round in earth's diurnal course,
    With rocks, and stones, and trees.

(37) *Here are two versions of the same incident; state what is gained by the use of prose and verse respectively.*

*(a)*

So thus as they rode in the wood, there came a man flying all that ever he might. Wither wilt thou? said Beaumains. O lord, he said, help me, for here by in a slade are six thieves that have taken my lord, and bound him, so I am afeard lest they will slay him. Bring me hither, said Beaumains. And so they rode together until they came thereas was the knight bounden; and then he rode unto them, and struck one unto the death, and then another, and at the third stroke he slew the third thief, and then the other three fled. And he rode after them, and he overtook them; and then those three thieves turned again and assailed Beaumains hard, but at the last he slew them, and returned and unbound the knight.

slade: *valley.*

*(b)*

So till the dusk that follow'd evensong
Rode on the two, reviler and reviled;
Then after one long slope was mounted, saw
Bowl-shaped, thro' tops of many thousand pines
A gloomy-gladed hollow slowly sink
To westward—in the deeps whereof a mere,
Round as the red eye of an Eagle-owl,
Under the half-dead sunset glared; and shouts
Ascended, and there brake a servingman

Flying from out of the black wood, and crying,
'They have bound my lord to cast him in the mere.'
Then Gareth, 'Bound am I to right the wrong'd,
But straitlier bound am I to bide with thee.'
And when the damsel spake contemptuously,
'Lead, and I follow', Gareth cried again,
'Follow, I lead!' so down among the pines
He plunged; and there, blackshadow'd nigh the mere,
And mid-thigh-deep in bulrushes and reed,
Saw six tall men haling a seventh along,
A stone about his neck to drown him in it.
Three with good blows he quieted, but three
Fled thro' the pines; and Gareth loosed the stone
From off his neck, then in the mere beside
Tumbled it; oilily bubbled up the mere.
Last, Gareth loosed his bonds and on free feet
Set him, a stalwart Baron, Arthur's friend.

(38) *Establish a preference for one of these poems:*

(*a*)

'Twas at the season when the Earth upsprings
From slumber; as a spherèd angel's child,
Shadowing its eyes with green and golden wings,
    Stands up before its mother bright and mild,
Of whose soft voice the air expectant seems—
So stood before the sun, which shone and smiled
    To see it ride thus joyous from its dreams,
The fresh and radiant Earth. The hoary grove
Waxed green, and flowers burst forth like starry beams;
    The grass in the warm sun did start and move,
And sea-buds burst under the waves serene:—
How many a one, though none be near to love,
    Loves then the shade of his own soul, half seen
In any mirror—or the spring's young minions,
The wingèd leaves amid the copses green:
    How many a spirit then puts on the pinions
Of fancy, and outstrips the lagging blast,
And his own steps, and over wide dominions

Sweeps in his dream-drawn chariot, far and fast,
More fleet than storms. The wide world shrinks below,
When winter and despondency are past.

(*b*)

The glory of the beauty of the morning,—
The cuckoo crying over the untouched dew;
The blackbird that has found it, and the dove
That tempts me on to something sweeter than love;
White clouds ranged even and fair as new-mown hay;
The heat, the stir, the sublime vacancy
Of sky and meadow and forest and my own heart:—
The glory invites me, yet it leaves me scorning
All I can ever do, all I can be,
Beside the lovely of motion, shape, and hue,
The happiness I fancy fit to dwell
In beauty's presence. Shall I now this day
Begin to seek as far as heaven, as hell,
Wisdom or strength to match this beauty, start
And tread the pale dust pitted with small dark drops,
In hope to find whatever it is I seek,
Hearkening to short-lived happy-seeming things
That we know naught of, in the hazel copse?
Or must I be content with discontent
As larks and swallows are perhaps with wings?
And shall I ask at the day's end once more
What beauty is, and what I can have meant
By happiness? And shall I let all go,
Glad, weary, or both? Or shall I perhaps know
That I was happy oft and oft before,
Awhile forgetting how I am fast pent,
How dreary-swift, with naught to travel to,
Is Time? I cannot bite the day to the core.

(39) *Comment on the rhythm and structure of these sonnets. Show in what ways each poem is effective.*

### (a)

Avenge, O Lord! Thy slaughter'd saints, whose bones
Lie scatter'd on the Alpine mountains cold;
Even them who kept Thy truth so pure of old
When all our fathers worshipt stocks and stones
Forget not: In Thy book record their groans
Who were thy sheep, and in their ancient fold
Slain by the bloody Piemontese, that roll'd
Mother with infant down the rocks. Their moans
The vales redoubled to the hills, and they
To Heaven. Their martyr'd blood and ashes sow
O'er all the Italian fields, where still doth sway
The triple Tyrant, that from these may grow
A hundred-fold, who, having learnt Thy way,
Early may fly the Babylonian woe.

### (b)

This is my play's last scene; here heavens appoint
My pilgrimage's last mile; and my race
Idly, yet quickly run, hath this last pace;
My span's last inch, my minute's latest point;
And gluttonous Death will instantly unjoint
My body and soul, and I shall sleep a space;
But my ever-waking part shall see that face,
Whose fear already shakes my every joint.
Then, as my soul to heaven, her first seat, takes flight,
And earth-borne body in the earth shall dwell,
So fall my sins, that all may have their right,
To where they're bred and would press me to hell.
Impute me righteous, thus purged of evil,
For thus I leave the world, the flesh, the devil.

### (c)

But be contented: when that fell arrest
Without all bail shall carry me away,
My life hath in this line some interest,

Which for memorial still with thee shall stay.
When thou reviewest this, thou dost review
The very part was consecrate to thee:
The earth can have but earth, which is his due;
My spirit is thine, the better part of me:
So then thou hast but lost the dregs of life,
The prey of worms, my body being dead;
The coward conquest of a wretch's knife,
Too base of thee to be remembered.
The worth of that is that which it contains,
And that is this, and this with thee remains.

(40) *Compare and contrast the two following poems paying particular attention to their versification, diction, imagery and feeling:*

(*a*)

I caught this morning morning's minion, king-
     dom of daylight's dauphin, dapple-dawn-drawn Falcon, in his
          riding
Of the rolling level underneath him steady air, and striding
High there, how he rung upon the rein of a wimpling wing
In his ecstasy! then off, off forth on swing,
     As a skate's heel sweeps smooth on a bow-bend: the hurl and
          gliding
Rebuffed the big wind. My heart in hiding
Stirred for a bird,—the achieve of, the mastery of the thing!

Brute beauty and valour and act, oh, air, pride, plume, here
     Buckle! AND the fire that breaks from thee then, a billion
Times told lovelier, more dangerous, O my chevalier!
     No wonder of it: shéer plód makes plough down sillion
Shine, and blue-bleak embers, ah my dear,
     Fall, gall themselves, and gash gold-vermilion.

(*b*)

The hawk slipt out of the pine, and rose in the sunlit air:
Steady and still he poised; his shadow slept on the grass:
And the bird's song sickened and sank: she cowered with furtive
     stare,

Dumb, till the quivering dimness should flicker and shift and pass.
Suddenly down he dropped: she heard the hiss of his wing,
Fled with a scream of terror: oh, would she had dared to rest!
For the hawk at eve was full, and there was no bird to sing,
And over the heather drifted the down from a bleeding breast.

(41) *Compare these two lyrical poems, and say which you find the more satisfying:*

(*a*)

If I could shut the gate against my thoughts
    And keep out sorrow from this room within,
Or memory could cancel all the notes
    Of my misdeeds, and I unthink my sin;
How free, how clear, how clean my soul should lie,
Discharged of such a loathsome company!

Or were there other rooms without my heart
    That did not to my conscience join so near,
Where I might lodge the thoughts of sin apart
    That I might not their clam'rous crying hear;
What peace, what joy, what ease should I possess,
Freed from their horrors that my soul oppress!

But, O my Saviour, who my refuge art,
    Let thy dear mercies stand 'twixt them and me,
And be the wall to separate my heart
    So that I may at length repose me free;
That peace, and joy, and rest may be within,
And I remain divided from my sin.

(*b*)

When I sit reading all alone that secret book
Wherein I sigh to look,
How many spots there be
I wish I could not see,
Or from myself might flee!

Mine eyes for refuge then with zeal befix the skies,
My tears do cloud those eyes,
My sighs do blow them dry;
And yet I live to die
Myself I cannot fly.

Heaven, I implore, that knows my fault, what shall I do?
To Hell I dare not go;
The world first made me rue,
My self my griefs renew:
To whom then shall I sue?

Alas, my soul doth faint to draw this doubtful breath:
Is there no hope in death?
O yes, death ends my woes,
Death me from me will loose;
My self am all my foes.

(42) *How do the following poems differ in their treatment of the
subject? Which poem do you prefer?*

(*a*)

Fair pledges of a fruitful tree,
    Why do ye fall so fast?
    Your date is not so past;
But you may stay yet here a while,
    To blush and gently smile;
        And go at last.

What, were ye born to be
    An hour or half's delight;
    And so to bid goodnight?
'Twas pity Nature brought ye forth
    Merely to show your worth,
        And lose you quite.

But you are lovely leaves, where we
    May read how soon things have
    Their end, though ne'er so brave:
And after they have shown their pride,
    Like you a while: they glide
        Into the grave.

183

(*b*)

Little think'st thou, poor flower,
Whom I have watched six or seven days,
And seen thy birth, and seen what every hour
Gave to thy growth, thee to this height to raise,
And now dost laugh and triumph on this bough,
　　Little think'st thou
That it will freeze anon, and that I shall
Tomorrow find thee fallen, or not at all.

Little think'st thou poor heart
That labour'st yet to nestle thee,
And think'st by hovering here to get a part
In a forbidden or forbidding tree,
And hop'st her stiffness by long siege to bow:
　　Little think'st thou,
That thou tomorrow, ere that sun doth wake,
Must with this sun, and me a journey take.

(43) *Here are two drafts of the same poem. Compare them in some detail, and say which you consider the later version.*

(*a*)

Old Yew, which graspest at the stones
　　That name the under-lying dead,
　　Thy fibres net the dreamless head,
Thy roots are wrapt about the bones.

The seasons bring the flower again,
　　And bring the firstling to the flock;
　　And in the dusk of thee, the clock
Beats out the little lives of men.

O not for thee the glow, the bloom,
　　Who changest not in any gale,
　　Nor branding summer suns avail
To touch thy thousand years of gloom:

And gazing on thee, sullen tree,
   Sick for thy sullen hardihood,
   I seem to fail from out my blood
And grow incorporate into thee.

### (b)

Old warder of these buried bones,
   And answering now my random stroke
   With fruitful cloud and living smoke,
Dark yew, that graspest at the stones

And dippest towards the dreamless head,
   To thee too comes the golden hour
   When flower is feeling after flower;
But sorrow—fixt upon the dead,

And darkening the dark graves of men,—
   What whisper'd from her lying lips?
   Thy gloom is kindled at the tips,
And passes into gloom again.

(44) *Which of the two following invocations of disorder do you consider to be the more effective?*

### (a)

Now bind my brows with iron; and approach
The ragged'st hour that time and spite dare bring
To frown upon the enraged Northumberland!
Let heaven kiss earth! now let not Nature's hand
Keep the wild flood confined! let order die!
And let this world no longer be a stage
To feed contention in a lingering act;
But let one spirit of the first-born Cain
Reign in all bosoms, that, each heart being set
On bloody courses, the rude scene may end,
And darkness be the burier of the dead!

### (b)

I conjure you, by that which you profess,
Howe'er you come to know it, answer me:
Though you untie the winds, and let them fight

Against the churches; though the yesty-waves
Confound and swallow navigation up;
Though bladed corn be lodg'd, and trees blown down;
Though castles topple on their warders' heads;
Though palaces, and pyramids, do slope
Their heads to their foundations; though the treasure
Of nature's germens tumble all together,
Even till destruction sicken, answer me
To what I ask you.

(45) *Comment on the style, imagery, and dramatic significance of the following passages:*

(*a*)

Time hath, my lord, a wallet at his back
Wherein he puts alms for oblivion,
A great-sized monster of ingratitudes:
Those scraps are good deeds past, which are devour'd
As fast as they are made, forgot as soon
As done: perseverance, dear my lord,
Keeps honour bright: to have done, is to hang
Quite out of fashion, like a rusty mail
In monumental mockery. Take the instant way;
For honour travels in a strait so narrow,
Where one but goes abreast: keep then the path;
For emulation hath a thousand sons,
That one by one pursue: if you give way,
Or hedge aside from the direct forthright,
Like to an enter'd tide they all rush by
And leave you hindmost:
Or, like a gallant horse fall'n in first rank,
Lie there for pavement to the abject rear,
O'er-run and trampled on: then what they do in present,
Though less than yours in past, must o'ertop yours;
For time is like a fashionable host
That slightly shakes his parting guest by the hand,
And with his arms outstretch'd, as he would fly,
Grasps in the comer: welcome ever smiles,
And farewell goes out sighing.

(*b*)

These God-like Vertues wherefore dost thou hide?
Affecting private life, or more obscure
In savage Wilderness, wherefore deprive
All Earth her wonder at thy acts, thy self
The fame and glory, glory the reward
That sole excites to high attempts the flame
Of most erected Spirits, most temper'd pure
Ætherial, who all pleasures else despise,
All treasures and all gain esteem as dross,
And dignities and powers all but the highest?
Thy years are ripe, and over-ripe, the Son
Of Macedonian Philip had e're these
Won Asia and the Throne of Cyrus held
At his dispose, young Scipio had brought down
The Carthaginian pride, young Pompey quell'd
The Pontic King and in triumph had rode.
Yet years, and to ripe years judgment mature,
Quench not the thirst of glory, but augment.
Great Julius, whom now all the world admires,
The more he grew in years, the more inflam'd
With glory, wept that he had liv'd so long
Inglorious: but thou yet art not too late.

(46) *Point out the special qualities in thought and manner of these two
poems:*

(*a*)

Come not, when I am dead,
  To drop thy foolish tears upon my grave,
To trample round my fallen head,
  And vex the unhappy dust thou wouldst not save.
There let the wind sweep and the plover cry;
  But thou, go by.

Child if it were thine error or thy crime
  I care no longer, being all unblest:

Wed whom thou wilt, but I am sick of Time,
   And I desire to rest.
Pass on, weak heart, and leave me where I lie:
   Go by, go by.

(b)

No longer mourn for me when I am dead
Than you shall hear the surly sullen bell
Give warning to the world that I am fled
From this vile world, with vilest worms to dwell;
Nay, if you read this line, remember not
The hand that writ it; for I love you so,
That I in your sweet thoughts would be forgot,
If thinking on me then should make you woe.
O, if, I say, you look upon this verse
When I perhaps compounded am with clay,
Do not so much as my poor name rehearse,
But let your love even with my life decay;
   Lest the wise world should look into your moan,
   And mock you with me after I am gone.

(47) *Which of these is the more effective poem?*

(a)

The sun that in Breadalbane's lake doth fall
Was melting to the sea down golden Tay,
When a cry came along the peopled way,
'Sebastopol is ours!' From that wild call
I turned, and leaning on a time-worn wall
Quaint with the touch of many an ancient day,
The mappèd mould and mildewed marquetry
Knew with my focused soul; which bent down all
Its sense, power, passion, to the sole regard
Of each green minim, as it were but born
To that one use. I strode home stern and hard;
In my hot hands I laid my throbbing head,
And all the living world and all the dead
Began a march which did not end at morn.

188

(*b*)

The wind flapped loose, the wind was still,
Shaken out dead from tree and hill:
I had walked on at the wind's will,—
I sat now for the wind was still.

Between my knees my forehead was,—
My lips, drawn in, said not Alas!
My hair was over in the grass,
My naked ears heard the day pass.

My eyes, wide open, had the run
Of some ten weeds to fix upon;
Among those few out of the sun:
The woodspurge flowered, three cups in one.

From perfect grief there need not be
Wisdom or even memory:
One thing then learnt remains to me,—
The woodspurge has a cup of three.

(48) *Either compare the following poems, or write a detailed criticism
of one of them:*

(*a*)

Long expected one-and-twenty,
  Ling'ring year, at length is flown;
Pride and pleasure, pomp and plenty,
  Great Sir John, are now your own.

Loosen'd from the minor's tether,
  Free to mortgage or to sell;
Wild as wind, and light as feather,
  Bid the sons of thrift farewell.

Call the Betsies, Kates, and Jennies,
  All the names that banish care;
Lavish of your grandsire's guineas,
  Show the spirit of an heir.

All that prey on vice or folly
  Joy to see their quarry fly:
There the gamester, light and jolly,
  There the lender, grave and sly.

Wealth, my lad, was made to wander,
  Let it wander as it will;
Call the jockey, call the pander,
  Bid them come and take their fill.

When the bonny blade carouses,
  Pockets full, and spirits high—
What are acres? what are houses?
  Only dirt or wet or dry.

Should the guardian friend, or mother
  Tell the woes of wilful waste;
Scorn their counsel, scorn their pother,
  You can hang or drown at last.


### (b)

Shot? so quick, so clean an ending?
  Oh that was right, lad, that was brave:
Yours was not an ill for mending,
  'Twas best to take it to the grave.

Oh you had forethought, you could reason,
  And saw your road and where it led,
And early wise and brave in season
  Put the pistol to your head.

Oh soon, and better so than later
  After long disgrace and scorn,
You shot dead the household traitor,
  The soul that should not have been born.

Right you guessed the rising morrow
  And scorned to tread the mire you must:
Dust's your wages, son of sorrow,
  But men may come to worse than dust.

Souls undone, undoing others,—
  Long time since the tale began.
You would not live to wrong your brothers:
  Oh lad, you died as fits a man.

Now to your grave shall friend and stranger
  With ruth and some with envy come:
Undishonoured, clear of danger,
  Clean of guilt, pass hence and home.

Turn safe to rest, no dreams, no waking;
  And here, man, here's the wreath I've made:
'Tis not a gift that's worth the taking,
  But wear it and it will not fade.

(49) *Contrast the personalities shown in these two poems:*

### (a)

When I consider how my light is spent,
  Ere half my days in this dark world and wide,
  And that one Talent which is death to hide
Lodged with me useless, though my Soul more bent
To serve therewith my Maker and present
  My true account lest he returning chide,—
  Doth God exact day-labour, light denied?
I fondly ask; But Patience, to prevent
That murmur, soon replies: God doth not need
  Either man's work or his own gifts; who best
    Bear his mild yoke, they serve him best; his State
Is kingly. Thousands at his bidding speed
  And post o'er Land and Ocean without rest.
    They also serve who only stand and wait.

### (b)

When I have fears that I may cease to be
  Before my pen has gleaned my teeming brain,
Before high-piled books, in charact'ry,
  Hold like rich garners the full-ripened grain;
When I behold, upon the night's starred face,
  Huge cloudy symbols of a high romance,

191

And think that I may never live to trace
Their shadows with the magic hand of chance;
And when I feel, frail creature of an hour,
That I shall never look upon thee more,
Never have relish in the faery power
Of unreflecting love!—then on the shore
Of the wide world I stand alone, and think
Till Love and Fame to nothingness do sink.

(50) *Compare the following two poems as to subject matter and treatment:*

(*a*)

Proud Maisie is in the wood,
　　Walking so early;
Sweet Robin sits on the bush,
　　Singing so rarely.

'Tell me, thou bonny bird,
　　When shall I marry me?'
'When six braw gentlemen
　　Kirkward shall carry ye.'

'Who makes the bridal bed,
　　Birdie, say truly?'
'The grey-headed sexton
　　That delves the grave duly.

'The glow-worm o'er grave and stone
　　Shall light thee steady.
The owl from the steeple sing,
　　"Welcome, proud lady."'

(*b*)

Who said, 'Peacock Pie'?
　　The old King to the sparrow:
Who said, 'Crops are ripe'?
　　Rust to the harrow:
Who said, 'Where sleeps she now?
　　Where rests she now her head,
Bathed in eve's loveliness'?
　　That's what I said.

Who said, 'Ay, mum's the word'?
   Sexton to willow:
Who said, 'Green dusk for dreams,
   Moss for a pillow'?
Who said, 'All Time's delight
   Hath she for narrow bed;
Life's troubled bubble broken'?—
   That's what I said.

(51) *Compare these versions of a traditional ballad, and say which one you prefer:*

(*a*)

There were three rauens sat on a tree,
They were as black as they might be.

The one of them said to his mate,
'Where shall we our breakfast take?'

'Down in yonder greene field,
There lies a knight slain vnder his shield.

'His hounds they lie downe at his feete,
So well they can their master keepe.

'His haukes they flie so eagerly,
There's no fowle dare him come nie.'

Downe there comes a fallow doe,
As great with young as she might goe.

She lift vp his bloudy hed,
And kist the wounds that were so red.

She got him vp vpon her backe,
And carried him to earthen lake.

She buried him before the prime,
She was dead herselfe ere euen-song time.

God send euery gentleman,
Such haukes, such hounds, and such a leman.

(*b*)

As I was walking all alane,
I heard twa corbies making a mane;
The tane unto the t'other did say,
'Where sall we gang to dine to-day?'

'In behint yon auld fail dyke,
I wot there lies a new-slain knight;
And naebody kens that he lies there,
But his hawk, his hound, and his lady fair.

'His hound is to the hunting gane,
His hawk to fetch the wild-fowl hame,
His lady's ta'en another mate,
So we may make our dinner sweet.

'Ye'll sit on his white hause-bane,
And I'll pike out his bonny blue een;
Wi' ae lock o' his gowden hair
We'll theek our nest when it grows bare.

'Mony a one for him makes mane,
But nane sall ken whare he is gane;
Oer his white banes, when they are bare
The wind sall blaw for evermair.'

(52) *Which of these two is the better poem?*

(*a*)

Love bade me welcome; yet my soul drew back,
    Guilty of dust and sin.
But quick-eyed Love, observing me grow slack
    From my first entrance in,
Drew nearer to me, sweetly questioning
    If I lack'd anything.

'A guest', I answer'd, 'worthy to be here':
    Love said, 'You shall be he.'

'I, the unkind, ungrateful? Ah, my dear,
  I cannot look on Thee.'
Love took my hand and smiling did reply,
  'Who made the eyes but I?'

'Truth, Lord; but I have marr'd them: let my shame
  Go where it doth deserve.'
'And you know not', says Love, 'Who bore the blame?'
  'My dear, then will I serve.'
 You must sit down', says Love, 'and taste my meat.'
  So I did sit and eat.


### (b)

'Lord, in Thy Courts
    Are seats so green bestow'd,
  As there resorts
    Along the dusty road
A cavalcade,—King, Bishop, Knight, and Judge:
And though I toil behind and meanly trudge,
Let me, too, lie upon that pleasant sward,
    For I am weary, Lord.

'Christ, at thy board
    Are wines and dishes drest
  That do afford
    Contentment to the best.
And though with poverty my bed hath been
These many years and my refreshment lean,
With plenty now at last my soul acquaint,
    Dear Master, for I faint!'

But through the grille,
    'Where is thy Robe?' said He,
  'Wouldst eat thy fill,
    Yet shirk civility?'
'My Robe, alas! There was a little child
That shivered by the road'—Swiftly God smiled;
'I was that Child,' said He, and raised the pin;
    'Dear friend, enter thou in!'

(53) *How do the following passages differ in their treatment of the subject?*

(*a*)

Enquirer, cease, petitions yet remain,
Which heav'n may hear, nor deem religion vain.
Still raise for good the supplicating voice,
But leave to heav'n the measure and the choice.
Safe in his pow'r, whose eyes discern afar
The secret ambush of a specious prayer.
Implore his aid, in his decisions rest,
Secure whate'er he gives, he gives the best.

(*b*)

Therefore to whom turn I but to Thee, the ineffable Name?
  Builder and maker, Thou, of houses not made with hands!
What, have fear of change from Thee who art ever the same?
  Doubt that Thy power can fill the heart that Thy power expands?
There shall never be one lost good! What was, shall live as before;
  The evil is null, is nought, is silence implying sound;
What was good, shall be good, with, for evil, so much good more;
  On the earth the broken arcs; in the heaven, a perfect round.

(54) *Compare the following poems. What attitude to their subject do the writers show? Which poem do you prefer?*

(*a*)

Because I could not stop for Death,
He kindly stopped for me;
The carriage held but just ourselves
And Immortality.

We slowly drove, he knew no haste,
And I had put away
My labour and my leisure too,
For his civility.

We passed the school where children played,
Their lessons scarcely done;
We passed the fields of gazing grain,
We passed the setting sun.

We paused before a house that seemed
A swelling on the ground;
The roof was scarcely visible,
The cornice but a mound.

Since then 'tis centuries; but each
Feels shorter than the day
I first surmised the horses' heads
Were toward eternity.

(*b*)

Good-bye, Winter
The days are getting longer,
The tea-leaf in the teacup
Is herald of a stranger.

Will he bring me business
Or will he bring me gladness
Or will he come for cure
Of his own sickness?

With a pedlar's burden
Walking up the garden
Will he come to beg
Or will he come to bargain?

Will he come to pester,
To cringe or to bluster,
A promise in his palm
Or a gun in his holster?

Will his name be John
Or will his name be Jonah,
Crying to repent
On the island of Iona?

Will his name be Jason
Looking for a seaman
Or a mad crusader
Without rhyme or reason?

What will be his message—
War or work or marriage?
News as new as dawn
Or an old adage?

Will he give a champion
Answer to my question
Or will his words be dark
And his ways evasion?

Will his name be love
And all his talk be crazy
Or will his name be Death
And his message easy?

(55) *Compare the following, and say which you consider to be the more important poem:*

(*a*)

The rose was sick and smiling died;
And, being to be sanctified,
About the bed there sighing stood
The sweet and flowery sisterhood:
Some hung the head, while some did bring,
To wash her, water from the spring;
Some laid her forth, while others wept,
But all a solemn fast there kept:
The holy sisters, some among,
The sacred dirge and trental sung.
But ah! what sweets smelt everywhere,
As Heaven had spent all perfumes there.
At last, when prayers for the dead
And rites were all accomplished,
They, weeping, spread a lawny loom,
And closed her up as in a tomb.

(*b*)

O Rose, thou art sick!
The invisible worm
That flies in the night,
In the howling storm,

Has found out thy bed
Of crimson joy,
And his dark secret love
Does thy life destroy.

(56) *Discuss the meaning, and give your critical opinion of the quality of these two poems:*

*(a)*

Batter my heart, three-person'd God; for, you
As yet but knock, breathe, shine, and seek to mend;
That I may rise, and stand, o'erthrow me, and bend
Your force, to break, blow, burn and make me new.
I, like an usurped town, to another due,
Labour to admit you, but O, to no end.
Reason, your viceroy in me, me should defend,
But is captiv'd, and proves weak or untrue.
Yet dearly I love you, and would be loved fain,
But am betroth'd unto your enemy:
Divorce me, untie, or break that knot again,
Take me to you, imprison me, for I
Except you enthrall me, never shall be free,
Nor ever chaste, except you ravish me.

*(b)*

The Lord will happiness divine
 On contrite hearts bestow:
Then tell me, gracious God, is mine
 A contrite heart, or no?

I hear, but seem to hear in vain,
 Insensible as steel;
If ought is felt, 'tis only pain,
 To feel I cannot feel.

I sometimes think myself inclin'd
 To love thee, if I could;
But often feel another mind,
 Averse to all that's good.

199

My best desires are faint and few,
   I fain would strive for more;
But when I cry, 'My strength renew',
   Seem weaker than before.

Thy saints are comforted I know,
   And love thy house of pray'r;
I therefore go where others go,
   But find no comfort there.

Oh make this heart rejoice, or ache;
   Decide this doubt for me;
And if it be not broken, break,
   And heal it, if it be.

(57) *Discuss the characteristics and peculiarities of the following two poems:*

(a)

You should be done with blossoming by now.
Yet here are leaves closer than any bough
That welcomes ivy. True, you were a tree
And stood with others in a marching line,
Less regular than this, of spruce and pine,
And boasted branches rather than a trunk.
This is your final winter, all arms shrunk
To one cross-bar bearing haphazardly
Four rusty strands. You cannot hope to feel
The electric sap run through those veins of steel.
The birds know this; the birds have hoodwinked you,
Crowding about you as they used to do.
The rainy robins huddled on your wire
And those black birds with shoulders dipped in fire
Have made you dream these vines; these tendrils are
A last despair in green, familiar
To derelicts of earth as well as sea.
Do not believe them, there is mockery
In their cool little jets of song. They know
What everyone but you learned long ago:
The stream of stories humming through your head
Is not your own. You dream. But you are dead.

(*b*)

Here come the line-gang pioneering by.
They throw a forest down less cut than broken.
They plant dead trees for living, and the dead
They string together with a living thread.
They string an instrument against the sky
Wherein words, whether beaten out or spoken,
Will run as hushed as when they were a thought.
But in no hush they string it: they go past
With shouts afar to pull the cable taut,
To hold it hard until they make it fast,
To ease away—they have it. With a laugh
And oaths of towns that set the wild at naught,
They bring the telephone and the telegraph.

(58) *Comment on the following passages, and say which of the two is the more convincing:*

(*a*)

...Most souls, 'tis true, but peep out once an age,
Dull, sullen prisoners in the body's cage;
Dim lights of life, that burn a length of years,
Useless, unseen, as lamps in sepulchres;
Like eastern kings, a lazy state they keep,
And close confined to their own palace, sleep....
Yet shall thy grave with rising flowers be dressed,
And the green turf lie lightly on thy breast:
There shall the morn her earliest tears bestow,
There the first roses of the year shall blow;
While angels with their silver wings o'ershade
The ground, now sacred by thy relics made.
So peaceful rests, without a stone, a name,
What once had beauty, titles, wealth and fame.
How loved, how honoured once, avails thee not
To whom related, or by whom begot;
A heap of dust alone remains of thee:
'Tis all thou art, and all the proud shall be!
Poets themselves must fall, like those they sung,
Deaf the praised ear and mute the tuneful tongue.

Ev'n he whose soul now melts in mournful lays
Shall shortly want the generous tear he pays;
Then from his closing eyes thy form shall part,
And the last pang shall tear thee from his heart:
Life's idle business at one gasp be o'er,
The Muse forgot, and thou beloved no more!

## (b)

Sleep on, my Love, in thy cold bed,
Never to be disquieted!
My last good night! Thou wilt not wake
Till I thy fate shall overtake:
Till age or grief or sickness must
Marry my body to that dust
It so much loves; and fill the room
My heart keeps empty in thy tomb.
Stay for me there; I will not fail
To meet thee in that hollow vale;
And think not much of my delay;
I am already on the way,
And follow thee with all the speed
Desire can make or sorrows breed.
Each minute is a short degree,
And ev'ry hour a step towards thee.
At night, when I betake to rest,
Next morn I rise nearer my West
Of Life, almost by eight hours' sail
Than when sleep breathed his drowsy gale....
The thought of this bids me go on,
And wait my dissolution
With hope and comfort. Dear (forgive
The crime) I am content to live
Divided, with but half a heart,
Till we shall meet and never part.

(59) *Point out the special qualities in thought and manner of the following passages:*

(a)

Happy those early days, when I
Shined in my Angel-infancy!
Before I understood this place
Appointed for my second race,
Or taught my soul to fancy aught
But a white celestial thought;
When yet I had not walked above
A mile or two from my first Love,
And looking back—at that short space—
Could see a glimpse of His bright face:
When on some gilded cloud, or flower,
My gazing soul would dwell an hour,
And in those weaker glories spy
Some shadows of eternity;
Before I taught my tongue to wound
My Conscience with a sinful sound,
Or had the black art to dispense
A several sin to every sense,
But felt through all this fleshly dress
Bright shoots of everlastingness.

O how I long to travel back,
And tread again that ancient track!
That I might once more reach that plain,
Where first I left my glorious train;
From whence th' enlightened spirit sees
That shady City of Palm trees.
But ah! my soul with too much stay
Is drunk, and staggers in the way!
Some men a forward motion love,
But I by backward steps would move;
And when this dust falls to the urn,
In that state I came, return.

*(b)*

The thought of our past years in me doth breed
Perpetual benediction: not indeed
For that which is most worthy to be blest,
Delight and liberty, the simple creed
Of childhood, whether busy or at rest,
With new-fledged hope still fluttering in his breast:
    Not for these I raise
    The song of thanks and praise;
But for those obstinate questionings
Of sense and outward things,
Fallings from us, vanishings,
Blank misgivings of a creature
Moving about in worlds not realised,
High instincts, before which our mortal nature
Did tremble like a guilty thing surprised:
    But for those first affections,
    Those shadowy recollections,
      Which, be they what they may,
Are yet the fountain-light of all our day,
Are yet a master-light of all our seeing;
    Uphold us, cherish, and have power to make
Our noisy years seem moments in the being
    Of the eternal silence: truths that wake,
      To perish never;
Which neither listlessness, nor mad endeavour,
    Nor man nor boy
Nor all that is at enmity with joy,
Can utterly abolish or destroy!
    Hence in a season of calm weather
      Though inland far we be,
      Our souls have sight of that immortal sea
    Which brought us hither;
    Can in a moment travel thither,
And see the children sport upon the shore,
And hear the mighty waters rolling evermore.

(60) *Explain clearly the similarities and differences you find in the thought in these poems, and comment on their poetic merits:*

(*a*)

Brave flowers, that I could gallant it like you
    And be as little vaine!
You come abroad, and make a harmlesse shew,
    And to your bedds of Earth againe;
You are not proud, you know your birth
For your Embroiderd garments are from Earth.

You doe obey your moneths, and times, but I
    Would have it ever Springe,
My fate would know noe Winter, never dye,
    Nor thinke of such a thing;
Oh that I could my bed of Earth but view
And Smile, and looke as chearefully as you:

Oh teach me to see Death, and not to feare,
    But rather to take truce;
How often have I seene you at a Beere,
    And there looke fresh and spruce;
You fragrant flowers then teach me that my breath
Like yours may sweeten, and perfume my death.

(*b*)

I made a posie, while the day ran by;
Here will I smell my remnant out, and tie
    My life within this band.
But time did beckon to the flowers, and they
By noon most cunningly did steal away
    And wither'd in my hand.

My hand was next to them, and then my heart:
I took, without more thinking, in good part
    Time's gentle admonition:
Who did so sweetly death's sad taste convey,
Making my minde to smell my fatall day,
    Yet sug'ring the suspicion.

Farewell, deare flowers, sweetly your time ye spent,
Fit, while ye liv'd, for smell or ornament,
    And after death for cures.
I follow straight without complaints or grief,
Since, if my scent be good, I care not if
    It be as short as yours.

# APPENDIX

# TEXTS OF THE POEMS OF
# SECTION IV

## HOMER, *Iliad* VIII, 542–61

ὣς Ἕκτωρ ἀγόρευ᾽, ἐπὶ δὲ Τρῶες κελάδησαν.
οἱ δ᾽ ἵππους μὲν λῦσαν ὑπὸ ζυγοῦ ἱδρώοντας,
δῆσαν δ᾽ ἱμάντεσσι παρ᾽ ἅρμασιν οἷσιν ἕκαστος·
ἐκ πόλιος δ᾽ ἄξοντο βόας καὶ ἴφια μῆλα
καρπαλίμως, οἶνον δὲ μελίφρονα οἰνίζοντο,
σῖτόν τ᾽ ἐκ μεγάρων, ἐπὶ δὲ ξύλα πολλὰ λέγοντο.
κνίσην δ᾽ ἐκ πεδίου ἄνεμοι φέρον οὐρανὸν εἴσω.
Οἱ δὲ μέγα φρονέοντες ἐπὶ πτολέμοιο γεφύρας
ἥατο παννύχιοι, πυρὰ δέ σφισι καίετο πολλά.
ὡς δ᾽ ὅτ᾽ ἐν οὐρανῷ ἄστρα φαεινὴν ἀμφὶ σελήνην
φαίνετ᾽ ἀριπρεπέα, ὅτε τ᾽ ἔπλετο νήνεμος αἰθήρ·
ἔκ τ᾽ ἔφανεν πᾶσαι σκοπιαὶ καὶ πρώονες ἄκροι
καὶ νάπαι· οὐρανόθεν δ᾽ ἄρ᾽ ὑπερράγη ἄσπετος αἰθήρ,
πάντα δὲ εἴδεται ἄστρα, γέγηθε δέ τε φρένα ποιμήν·
τόσσα μεσηγὺ νεῶν ἠδὲ Ξάνθοιο ῥοάων
Τρώων καιόντων πυρὰ φαίνετο Ἰλιόθι πρό.
χίλι᾽ ἄρ᾽ ἐν πεδίῳ πυρὰ καίετο, πὰρ δε ἑκάστῳ
ἥατο πεντήκοντα σέλαι πυρὸς αἰθομένοιο.
ἵπποι δὲ κρῖ λευκὸν ἐρεπτόμενοι καὶ ὀλύρας
ἑσταότες παρ᾽ ὄχεσφιν ἐΰθρονον Ἠῶ μίμνον.

## HOMER, *Odyssey* XXIV, 1–14

Ἑρμῆς δὲ ψυχὰς Κυλλήνιος ἐξεκαλεῖτο
ἀνδρῶν μνηστήρων· ἔχε δὲ ῥάβδον μετὰ χερσὶ
καλὴν χρυσείην, τῇ τ᾽ ἀνδρῶν ὄμματα θέλγει
ὧν ἐθέλει, τοὺς δ᾽ αὖτε καὶ ὑπνώοντας ἐγείρει·
τῇ ῥ᾽ ἄγε κινήσας, ταὶ δὲ τρίζουσαι ἕποντο.
ὡς δ᾽ ὅτε νυκτερίδες μυχῷ ἄντρου θεσπεσίοιο

APPENDIX

τρίζουσαι ποτέονται, ἐπεί κέ τις ἀποπέσῃσιν
ὁρμαθοῦ ἐκ πέτρης, ἀνά τ' ἀλλήλῃσιν ἔχονται,
ὣς αἱ τετριγυῖαι ἅμ' ἤϊσαν· ἄρχε δ' ἄρα σφιν
Ἑρμείας ἀκάκητα κατ' εὐρώεντα κέλευθα.
πὰρ δ' ἴσαν Ὠκεανοῦ τε ῥοὰς καὶ Λευκάδα πέτρην,
ἠδὲ παρ' Ἠελίοιο πύλας καὶ δῆμον ὀνείρων
ἤϊσαν· αἶψα δ' ἵκοντο κατ' ἀσφοδελὸν λειμῶνα,
ἔνθα τε ναίουσι ψυχαί, εἴδωλα καμόντων.

HOMERIC HYMN, *To the Earth*

Γαῖαν παμμήτειραν ἀείσομαι ἠϋθέμεθλον
πρεσβίστην, ἣ φέρβει ἐπὶ χθονὶ πάνθ' ὁπόσ' ἐστίν·
ἠμὲν ὅσα χθόνα δῖαν ἐπέρχεται ἠδ' ὅσα πόντον,
ἠδ' ὅσα πωτῶνται, τάδε φέρβεται ἐκ σέθεν ὄλβου.
ἐκ σέο δ' εὔπαιδές τε καὶ εὔκαρποι τελέθουσι
πότνια, σεῦ δ' ἔχεται δοῦναι βίον ἠδ' ἀφελέσθαι
θνητοῖς ἀνθρώποισιν· ὁ δ' ὄλβιος ὅν κε σὺ θυμῷ
πρόφρων τιμήσῃς· τῷ τ' ἄφθονα πάντα πάρεστι.
βρίθει μέν σφιν ἄρουρα φερέσβιος, ἠδὲ κατ' ἀγροὺς
κτήνεσιν εὐθηνεῖ, οἶκος δ' ἐμπίπλαται ἐσθλῶν·
αὐτοὶ δ' εὐνομίῃσι πόλιν κάτα καλλιγύναικα
κοιρανέουσ', ὄλβος δὲ πολὺς καὶ πλοῦτος ὀπηδεῖ·
παῖδες δ' εὐφροσύνῃ νεοθηλέϊ κυδιόωσι,
παρθενικαί τε χοροῖς φερεσανθέσιν εὔφρονι θυμῷ
παίζουσαι σκαίρουσι κατ' ἄνθεα μαλθακὰ ποίης,
οὕς κε σὺ τιμήσῃς σεμνὴ θεὰ ἄφθονε δαῖμον.
Χαῖρε θεῶν μήτηρ, ἄλοχ' Οὐρανοῦ ἀστερόεντος,
πρόφρων δ' ἀντ' ᾠδῆς βίοτον θυμήρε' ὄπαζε·
αὐτὰρ ἐγὼ καὶ σεῖο καὶ ἄλλης μνήσομ' ἀοιδῆς.

ANACREON, *Ode* XXXIII

Μεσονυκτίοις ποθ' ὥραις,
στρέφεται ὅτ' Ἄρκτος ἤδη
κατὰ χεῖρα τὴν Βοώτου,
μερόπων δὲ φῦλα πάντα
κέαται κόπῳ δαμέντα,

τότ᾽ Ἔρως ἐπισταθείς μευ
θυρέων ἔκοπτ᾽ ὀχῆας.
τίς, ἔφην, θύρας ἀράσσει;
κατά μευ σχίζεις ὀνείρους.
ὁ δ᾽ Ἔρως, ἄνοιγε, φησίν·
βρέφος εἰμί, μὴ φόβησαι·
βρέχομαι δὲ κἀσέληνον
κατὰ νύκτα πεπλάνημαι.
ἐλέησα ταῦτ᾽ ἀκούσας,
ἀνὰ δ᾽ εὐθὺ λύχνον ἅψας
ἀνέῳξα, καὶ βρέφος μέν
ἐσορῶ φέροντα τόξον
πτέρυγάς τε καὶ φαρέτρην.
παρὰ δ᾽ ἱστίην καθῖσα,
παλάμαις τε χεῖρας αὐτοῦ
ἀνέθαλπον, ἐκ δὲ χαίτης
ἀπέθλιβον ὑγρὸν ὕδωρ.
ὁ δ᾽, ἐπεὶ κρύος μεθῆκεν,
φέρε, φησί, πειράσωμεν
τόδε τόξον, εἴ τι μοι νῦν
βλάβεται βραχεῖσα νευρή.
τανύει δὲ καί με τύπτει
μέσον ἧπαρ, ὥσπερ οἶστρος·
ἀνὰ δ᾽ ἅλλεται καχάζων,
ξένε δ᾽, εἶπε, συγχάρηθι·
κέρας ἀβλαβὲς μέν ἐστιν,
σὺ δὲ καρδίην πονήσεις.


CATULLUS, *Ode* XXXI

Paene insularum, Sirmio, insularumque
ocelle, quascumque in liquentibus stagnis
marique vasto fert uterque Neptunus;
quam te libenter quamque laetus inviso,
vix mi ipse credens Thuniam atque Bithunos
liquisse campos et videre te in tuto.
o quid solutis est beatius curis?
cum mens onus reponit, ac peregrino

labore fessi venimus larem ad nostrum,
desideratoque acquiescimus lecto.
hoc est quod unum est pro laboribus tantis.
salve o venusta Sirmio atque hero gaude;
gaudete vosque o Lydiae lacus undae;
ridete quidquid est domi cachinnorum.

VIRGIL, *Aeneid* VI, 269–294

perque domos Ditis vacuas et inania regna:
quale per incertam lunam sub luce maligna
est iter in silvis, ubi caelum condidit umbra
Iuppiter, et rebus nox abstulit atra colorem.
vestibulum ante ipsum primis in faucibus Orci
Luctus et ultrices posuere cubilia Curae;
pallentesque habitant Morbi tristisque Senectus,
et Metus et malesuada Fames ac turpis Egestas,
terribiles visu formae, Letumque Labosque;
tum consanguineus Leti Sopor et mala mentis
Gaudia, mortiferumque adverso in limine Bellum,
ferreique Eumenidum thalami et Discordia demens
vipereum crinem vittis innexa cruentis.
  In medio ramos annosaque bracchia pandit
ulmus opaca, ingens, quam sedem Somnia vulgo
vana tenere ferunt, foliisque sub omnibus haerent.
multaque praeterea variarum monstra ferarum,
Centauri in foribus stabulant Scyllaeque biformes
et centumgeminus Briareus ac belua Lernae
horrendum stridens, flammisque armata Chimaera,
Gorgones Harpyiaeque et forma tricorporis umbrae.
corripit hic subita trepidus formidine ferrum
Aeneas strictamque aciem venientibus offert,
et ni docta comes tenuis sine corpore vitas
admoneat volitare cava sub imagine formae,
inruat et frustra ferro diverberet umbras.

## VIRGIL, *Georgics* I, 311–34

Quid tempestates autumni et sidera dicam,
atque, ubi iam breviorque dies et mollior aestas,
quae vigilanda viris? vel cum ruit imbriferum ver,
spicea iam campis cum messis inhorruit et cum
frumenta in viridi stipula lactentia turgent?
saepe ego, cum flavis messorem induceret arvis
agricola et fragili iam stringeret hordea culmo,
omnia ventorum concurrere proelia vidi,
quae gravidam late segetem ab radicibus imis
sublimem expulsam eruerent; ita turbine nigro
ferret hiems culmumque levem stipulasque volantis.
saepe etiam immensum caelo venit agmen aquarum
et foedam glomerant tempestatem imbribus atris
collectae ex alto nubes; ruit arduus aether,
et pluvia ingenti sata laeta boumque labores
diluit; implentur fossae et cava flumina crescunt
cum sonitu fervetque fretis spirantibus aequor.
ipse pater media nimborum in nocte corusca
fulmina molitur dextra: quo maxima motu
terra tremit; fugere ferae et mortalia corda
per gentis humilis stravit pavor: ille flagranti
aut Athon aut Rhodopen aut alta Ceraunia telo
deicit; ingeminant Austri et densissimus imber:
nunc nemora ingenti vento, nunc litora plangunt.

## HORACE, *Odes* I, V

Quis multa gracilis te puer in rosa
perfusus liquidis urget odoribus
    grato, Pyrrha, sub antro?
        cui flavam religas comam

simplex munditiis? heu quotiens fidem
mutatosque deos flebit et aspera
    nigris aequora ventis
        emirabitur insolens,

qui nunc te fruitur credulus aurea,
qui semper vacuam, semper amabilem
   sperat, nescius aurae
     fallacis. miseri, quibus

intemptata nites. me tabula sacer
votiva paries indicat uvida
   suspendisse potenti
     vestimenta maris deo.


HORACE, *Odes* I, ix

Vides ut alta stet nive candidum
Soracte, nec iam sustineant onus
   silvae laborantes, geluque
     flumina constiterint acuto.

dissolve frigus ligna super foco
large reponens atque benignius
   deprome quadrimum Sabina,
     o Thaliarche, merum diota:

permitte divis cetera, qui simul
stravere ventos aequore fervido
   deproeliantis, nec cupressi
     nec veteres agitantur orni.

quid sit futurum cras fuge quaerere et
quem Fors dierum cumque dabit lucro
   appone, nec dulcis amores
     sperne puer neque tu choreas,

donec virenti canities abest
morosa. nunc et campus et areae
   lenesque sub noctem susurri
     composita repetantur hora,

nunc et latentis proditor intimo
gratus puellae risus ab angulo
   pignusque dereptum lacertis
     aut digito male pertinaci.

## HORACE, *Odes* IV, vii

Diffugere nives, redeunt iam gramina campis
    arboribusque comae;
mutat terra vices, et decrescentia ripas
    flumina praetereunt;
Gratia cum Nymphis geminisque sororibus audet
    ducere nuda choros.
immortalia ne speres, monet annus et almum
    quae rapit hora diem:
frigora mitescunt Zephyris, ver proterit aestas
    interitura simul
pomifer Autumnus fruges effuderit, et mox
    bruma recurrit iners.
damna tamen celeres reparant caelestia lunae:
    nos ubi decidimus
quo pater Aeneas, quo Tullus dives et Ancus,
    pulvis et umbra sumus.
quis scit an adiciant hodiernae crastina summae
    tempora di superi?
cuncta manus avidas fugient heredis, amico
    quae dederis animo.
cum semel occideris et de te splendida Minos
    fecerit arbitria,
non, Torquate, genus, non te facundia, non te
    restituet pietas;
infernis neque enim tenebris Diana pudicum
    liberat Hippolytum,
nec Lethaea valet Theseus abrumpere caro
    vincula Perithoo.

## DANTE, *Paradiso*, Canto XXXIII, 97–145

Così la mente mia, tutta sospesa,
    mirava fissa, immobile e attenta,
    e sempre di mirar faciesi accesa.
A quella luce cotal si diventa,
    che volgersi da lei per altro aspetto
    è impossibil che mai si consenta;

però che il ben, ch' è del volere obietto,
  tutto s' accoglie in lei; e fuor di quella
  è defettivo ciò ch' è lì perfetto.
Omai sarà più corta mia favella,
  pur a quel ch' io ricordo, che d' un fante
  che bagni ancor la lingua a la mammella.
Non perchè più ch' un semplice sembiante
  fosse nel vivo lume ch' io mirava,
  che tal è sempre qual s' era davante;
ma per la vista che s' avvalorava
  in me guardando, una sola parvenza,
  mutandom' io, a me si travagliava.
Ne la profonda e chiara sussistenza
  de l' alto lume parvermi tre giri
  di tre colori e d' una contenenza;
e l' un da l' altro come iri da iri
  parea reflesso, e 'l terzo parea foco
  che quinci e quindi igualmente si spiri.
Oh quanto è corto il dire e come fioco
  al mio concetto! e questo, a quel ch' i' vidi,
  è tanto, che non basta a dicer 'poco'.
O luce etterna che sola in te sidi,
  sola t' intendi, e da te intelletta
  e intendente te ami e arridi!
Quella circulazion che sì concetta
  pareva in te come lume reflesso,
  da li occhi miei alquanto circunspetta,
dentro da sè, del suo colore stesso,
  mi parve pinta de la nostra effige;
  per che 'l mio viso in lei tutto era messo.
Qual è 'l geometra che tutto s' affige
  per misurar lo cerchio, e non ritrova,
  pensando, quel principio ond' elli indige,
tal era io a quella vista nova:
  veder volea come si convenne
  l' imago al cerchio e come vi s' indova;
ma non eran da ciò le proprie penne:
  se non che la mia mente fu percossa
  da un fulgore in che sua voglia venne.

A l' alta fantasia qui mancò possa;
  ma già volgeva il mio disio e il velle,
  sì come rota ch' igualmente è mossa,
l' amor che move il sole e l' altre stelle.

CHAUCER, *The Nonne Preestes Tale*, 1–16

A povre widwe, somdel stape in age,
Was whylom dwelling in a narwe cotage,
Bisyde a grove, stonding in a dale.
This widwe, of which I telle yow my tale,
Sin thilke day that she was last a wyf,
In pacience hadde a ful simple lyf,
For litel was hir catel and hir rente;
By housbondrye, of such as God hir sente,
She fond hir-self, and eek hir doghtren two.
Three large sowes hadde she, and namo,
Three kine, and eek a sheep that highte Malle,
Ful sooty was hir bour, and eek hir halle,
In which she ate ful many a sclendre meel.
Of poynant sauce hir needed never a deel.
No deyntee morsel passed thurgh hir throte;
Hir dyete was accordant to hir cote.

# NOTES ON THE MANUSCRIPT
# POEMS OF SECTION I

[In preparing these notes I am greatly indebted to *English Poetical Autographs*, by Desmond Flower and A. N. L. Munby. A.F.S.]

WILLIAM SHAKESPEARE. The play, *Sir Thomas More*, written, presumably, by Anthony Munday, has some passages which such eminent Shakespearean scholars as J. Dover Wilson, A. W. Pollard, W. W. Greg, and R. W. Chapman maintain to be not only by Shakespeare but in his autograph. One of these passages is reproduced here. (See *Shakespeare's Hand in the Play of Sir Thomas More*, Cambridge, 1923.)

GEORGE HERBERT. *Perfection*, composed by Herbert, was written down by another hand and corrected by the poet. The last verse, replacing the one deleted, is entirely in Herbert's autograph. This well-known poem was first published in *The Temple*, 1633.

JOHN MILTON. The poet writes of *Lycidas*, 'In this Monody the Author bewails a learned Friend, unfortunately drown'd in his passage from Chester on the Irish Seas, 1637.' This reproduction is of part of an early draft of the poem, written at Horton in November 1637, and published in the following year.

THOMAS GRAY. *The Elegy* was begun in 1742, soon after the death of Gray's friend, Richard West, and the poet continued to work upon the poem 'at irregular intervals during the next eight years'. The poem was first published in 1751 by Robert Dodsley, advised by Horace Walpole. This draft is in the Memorial Buildings at Eton College.

WILLIAM COWPER. Cowper wrote *The Halibut* in a letter dated 25 April 1784 to his friend Mary Unwin. It was not published till 1824, when Cowper's letters were first edited.

GEORGE CRABBE. *Jane Adair*, reproduced from one of Crabbe's autograph notebooks, is part of a longer poem entitled *Tracy*. Composed early in 1813, it was not published till 1907.

WILLIAM BLAKE. These first versions of *The Tyger* are written on two facing pages of the most famous of Blake's notebooks, known as the

Rossetti MS. The poem appeared in *Songs of Experience*, which Blake engraved and published himself in 1794.

WILLIAM WORDSWORTH. The basis of the manuscript of *The Waggoner* is a careful transcript made by Sara Hutchinson in 1806 from the rough drafts of the poems. Upon this transcript Wordsworth laboured during a period of thirteen years, as he himself records. The passage reproduced here has been worked over, cancelled and revised in Wordsworth's hand.

S. T. COLERIDGE. *Lewti* was first published in the *Morning Post*, 13 April 1798. Though intended for inclusion in the *Lyrical Ballads*, it was withdrawn at the last moment. It was included in the *Annual Anthology*, 1800, and *Sibylline Leaves* in 1817.

LORD BYRON. *Oh! Snatch'd away in Beauty's Bloom* was written at the request of Byron's friend the Hon. Douglas Kinnaird for a *Selection of Hebrew Melodies*, and was published, with the music by the composer Isaac Nathan, in April 1815.

P. B. SHELLEY. Among Shelley's manuscript fragments occur two undated translations; one, of a part of Bion's *Lament for Adonis*, is reproduced here; the other is a part of Moschus' *Elegy on the Death of Bion*. These were first published by H. Buxton Forman in 1876.

JOHN KEATS. This is a reproduction of the first draft of the *Ode to a Nightingale* made by the poet on 30 April 1819. His friend Charles Brown said that Keats wrote it under the plum-tree in the garden at Wentworth Place, Hampstead. The poem was published in the July number of *Annals of the Fine Arts* for 1819, and reprinted in *Lamia and other Poems*, 1820.

T. L. BEDDOES. The poet sent a copy of *Dream Pedlary* to his friend Kelsall in a letter dated 19 July 1830. The poem is reproduced here from the MS. of an early version in the British Museum.

LORD TENNYSON. *Milton: Alcaics*, an experiment in quantity, was first printed in *The Cornhill Magazine*, December 1863. It was reprinted in *Idylls of the Hearth*, 1864, subsequently known as *Enoch Arden and other Poems*.

ROBERT BROWNING. This passage from *The Ring and the Book* is reproduced from the MS. copy of the poem in the British Museum on which Browning worked 'four full years unintermittingly' from 1864. The poem was published in four volumes in the winter of 1868–69.

E. B. BROWNING. *The Runaway Slave at Pilgrim's Point* was written at Pisa in the autumn of 1847, and sent to America. It was published in Boston, in *The Liberty Bell*, in 1848, and separately in England in 1849.

D. G. ROSSETTI. This is a reproduction of the first draft of *Love's Compass* published in *Poems*, 1870. It was one of the group of sonnets which later formed part of *The House of Life*.

CHRISTINA ROSSETTI. *Sleeping at Last* was written about 1893. It was published in 1896 in a posthumous volume entitled *New Poems* edited by the poet's brother W. M. Rossetti.

A. C. SWINBURNE. This is a reproduction of part of the first draft of *Rococo* in the large collection of Swinburne's MS. poems in the British Museum. The poem was first published in *Poems and Ballads*, 1866.

G. M. HOPKINS. *Starlight Night* was written on 24 February 1877. Robert Bridges kept a MS. book in which he pasted Hopkins' poems, in the author's handwriting, as he received them. This is a reproduction of the draft in the MS. book now in the Bodleian Library. The poem was first published in Miles' *Poets and Poetry of the Century*, 1897.

EDWARD THOMAS. This first draft of *Adlestrop*, in the thin exercise book in the British Museum containing many of Thomas's manuscript poems, was written in 1916 and published in the following year.

RUPERT BROOKE. This is a reproduction of the first of several drafts of *The Soldier*. This sonnet first appeared in *New Numbers*, 1914. It was reprinted in *1914 and Other Poems* in the year 1915. The MSS. are in the Library of King's College, Cambridge.

WILFRED OWEN. The amendments to *Anthem for Dead Youth* were made in pencil by Siegfried Sassoon when, at Craiglockhart, near Edinburgh, in September 1917, Wilfred Owen showed him the first draft of the sonnet which is reproduced here. The title was changed later to *Anthem for Doomed Youth*.

ISAAC ROSENBERG. The first draft of *Moses*, part of which is reproduced here, was written in 1916 on rough scraps of paper. Rosenberg's only publications during his life were three pamphlets: *Night and Day*, *Youth*, and *Moses, A Play*, all published at his own expense.

# IDENTIFICATION OF THE POEMS
## OF SECTION V

1. (a) JOHN MILTON, from *L'Allegro*, ll. 41–68
   (b) JOHN CLARE, *Summer Images*
2. (a) GEORGE PEELE, from *Edward I*, ll. 11–32
   (b) WILLIAM SHAKESPEARE, from *Richard II*, II. i. 39–68
3. (a) THOMAS NASHE, *Spring's Welcome*
   (b) JOHN CLARE, *Early Nightingale*
   (c) ROBERT BRIDGES, *Larks*
   (d) W. H. DAVIES, *Robin Redbreast*
   (e) WILLIAM WORDSWORTH, *To the Cuckoo*
4. (a) FRANK O'CONNOR, from the Irish
   (b) Revised version by W. B. YEATS
5. (a) ALEXANDER POPE, from *Moral Essays*, ll. 299–314
   (b) GEORGE CRABBE, from *The Village*, Book I, ll. 252–263
6. (a) MATTHEW ARNOLD, from *Thyrsis*, ll. 131–150
   (b) THOMAS GRAY, *Sonnet: On the Death of Richard West*
7. (a) WILLIAM WORDSWORTH, *Lines Written in Early Spring*
   (b) THOMAS HARDY, *In a Wood*
8. (a) JOHN MILTON, from *Paradise Lost*, Book I, ll. 738–748
   (b) WILLIAM BLAKE, from *The Book of Los*, ch. II, ll. 76–85
9. (a) SIR JOHN SQUIRE, *There was an Indian*
   (b) JOHN KEATS, *On First Looking into Chapman's Homer*
10. (a) MICHAEL DRAYTON, *Love's Farewell*
    (b) ROBERT BROWNING, *The Lost Mistress*
11. (a) WILLIAM WORDSWORTH, *The Solitary Reaper*
    (b) ROBERT FROST, *Mowing*
12. (a) P. B. SHELLEY, *Autumn: A Dirge*
    (b) THOMAS HOOD, *Ode: Autumn*
13. (a) WILLIAM WORDSWORTH, *To a Skylark*
    (b) JOHN CLARE, *The Skylark*
14. EDWARD THOMAS, *Two Pewits*; (b) is the revised version
15. (a) WILLIAM WORDSWORTH, *Written in March*
    (b) LORD TENNYSON, from *The Day-Dream: The Revival*, ll. 1–16

16. (a) LEIGH HUNT, *Poppies*
    (b) FRANCIS THOMPSON, from *The Poppy*, ll. 64–72
17. (a) WILLIAM SHAKESPEARE, from *Julius Caesar*, I. i. 39–54
    (b) WILLIAM SHAKESPEARE, from *Coriolanus*, II. i. 201–218
18. (a) THOMAS NASHE, from *Summer's Last Will and Testament: Song*
    (b) LORD TENNYSON, from *In Memoriam*, CXV
    (c) WILLIAM BLAKE, *To Spring*
    (d) C. DAY LEWIS, *Now the Full-throated Daffodils*
19. (a) GEORGE MEREDITH, *Seed-Time*
    (b) G. M. HOPKINS, *Inversnaid*
20. (a) JOHN DONNE, from *Satyre II*, ll. 87–102
    (b) ALEXANDER POPE, from *The Satires of Dr Donne Versified. Satire II*, ll. 93–108
21. (a) CHARLES LAMB, *To Hester*
    (b) ANDREW MARVELL, *An Epitaph*
22. JOHN MILTON, from *Lycidas*, ll. 142–150
23. (a) WILLIAM BLAKE, *Ah! Sun-flower*
    (b) CHRISTINA ROSSETTI, from *Divers Worlds. Time and Eternity. His Banner over me was Love*
24. (a) P. B. SHELLEY, *The Indian Serenade*
    (b) THOMAS CAMPION, from *A Book of Airs*, No. 14
25. (a) EMILY BRONTË, *Sunset (Fragment)*
    (b) CHARLES COTTON, from *Evening Quatrains*, ll. 1–16
26. (a) CHRISTINA ROSSETTI, *Remember*
    (b) E. B. BROWNING, *Grief*
27. (a) WILLIAM SHAKESPEARE, *Sonnet 85*
    (b) W. B. YEATS, *Her Praise*
28. JOHN KEATS, from *Hyperion*, Book I, ll. 72–79. The order of the three versions is (b), (a), (c).
29. (a) WILLIAM SHAKESPEARE, from *Othello*, IV. ii. 47–62
    (b) BEAUMONT AND FLETCHER, from *Philaster*, III. ii. 107–120
30. (a) WILLIAM WORDSWORTH, *The World is too much with us*
    (b) G. M. HOPKINS, *God's Grandeur*
31. (a) WILLIAM SHAKESPEARE, from *The Merchant of Venice*, V. i. 54–65
    (b) SIR PHILIP SIDNEY, *Sonnet*

32. (*a*) G. M. HOPKINS, *Spring*
    (*b*) ANON.
33. (*a*) WILLIAM SHAKESPEARE, from *Hamlet*, III. i. 56–82
    (*b*) JOHN MILTON, from *Paradise Lost*, Book X, ll. 769–791
34. (*a*) A. E. HOUSMAN, from *A Shropshire Lad*, XXXI
    (*b*) JOHN MASEFIELD, *On Malvern Hill*
35. LORD TENNYSON, from *Oenone*, ll. 1–22
36. (*a*) A. E. HOUSMAN, from *Last Poems*, XXVII
    (*b*) WILLIAM WORDSWORTH, *A Slumber did my spirit seal*
37. (*a*) SIR THOMAS MALORY, from *Le Morte d'Arthur*, Book VII, chap. V
    (*b*) LORD TENNYSON, from *Idylls of the King, Gareth and Lynette*, ll. 773–799
38. (*a*) P. B. SHELLEY, from *Prince Athanase*, Part II, Fragment iv, ll. 240–260
    (*b*) EDWARD THOMAS, *The Glory*
39. (*a*) JOHN MILTON, *On the late Massacre in Piedmont*
    (*b*) JOHN DONNE, *Holy Sonnets* VI
    (*c*) WILLIAM SHAKESPEARE, *Sonnet* 74
40. (*a*) G. M. HOPKINS, *The Windhover: To Christ our Lord*
    (*b*) A. C. BENSON, *The Hawk*
41. (*a*) JOHN DANYEL, from *Songs*
    (*b*) ROBERT JONES, from *The Musical Dream*
42. (*a*) ROBERT HERRICK, *To Blossoms*
    (*b*) JOHN DONNE, *The Blossom*
43. LORD TENNYSON, from *In Memoriam*; (*b*) is the later version
44. (*a*) WILLIAM SHAKESPEARE, from *Henry IV, Pt II*, I. i. 150–157
    (*b*) WILLIAM SHAKESPEARE, from *Macbeth*, IV. i. 47–58
45. (*a*) WILLIAM SHAKESPEARE, from *Troilus and Cressida*, III. iii. 144–169
    (*b*) JOHN MILTON, from *Paradise Regained*, Book III, ll. 21–42
46. (*a*) LORD TENNYSON, from *English Idylls and other Poems*
    (*b*) WILLIAM SHAKESPEARE, *Sonnet* 71
47. (*a*) SYDNEY DOBELL, *The Botanist's Vision*
    (*b*) D. G. ROSSETTI, *The Woodspurge*
48. (*a*) DR JOHNSON, *Improviso, on a young heir's coming of age*
    (*b*) A. E. HOUSMAN, from *A Shropshire Lad*, XLIV

49. (*a*) JOHN MILTON, *On his Blindness*
    (*b*) JOHN KEATS, *Sonnet: When I have fears*
50. (*a*) SIR WALTER SCOTT, *Proud Maisie*
    (*b*) WALTER DE LA MARE, *The Song of the Mad Prince*
51. ANON.
52. (*a*) GEORGE HERBERT, *Love*
    (*b*) SIR ARTHUR QUILLER-COUCH, *Lord, in Thy Courts*
53. (*a*) DR JOHNSON, from *The Vanity of Human Wishes*, ll. 339–346
    (*b*) ROBERT BROWNING, from *Abt Vogler*, Stanza IX, ll. 65–72
54. (*a*) EMILY DICKINSON, *The Chariot*
    (*b*) LOUIS MACNEICE, *Prognosis*
55. (*a*) ROBERT HERRICK, *The Funeral Rites of the Rose*
    (*b*) WILLIAM BLAKE, *The Sick Rose*
56. (*a*) JOHN DONNE, *Holy Sonnets* XIV
    (*b*) WILLIAM COWPER, *The Contrite Heart*
57. (*a*) LOUIS UNTERMEYER, *To a Telegraph Pole*
    (*b*) ROBERT FROST, *The Line-Gang*
58. (*a*) ALEXANDER POPE, from *Elegy to the Memory of an Unfortunate Lady*, ll. 17–22 and ll. 63–82
    (*b*) HENRY KING, from *The Exequy*, ll. 81–100 and ll. 114–119
59. (*a*) HENRY VAUGHAN, *The Retreat*
    (*b*) WILLIAM WORDSWORTH, from *Intimations of Immortality from Recollections of Early Childhood*, ll. 137–171
60. (*a*) HENRY KING, *A Contemplation upon Flowers*
    (*b*) GEORGE HERBERT, *Life*

# BOOK LIST

The following books are suggested for further study:

F. W. BATESON, *English Poetry: A Critical Introduction* (Longmans).

C. M. BOWRA, *The Heritage of Symbolism* (Macmillan/St. Martin's).

——, *The Creative Experiment* (Macmillan).

NORMAN CALLAN, *Poetry in Practice* (Lindsay Drummond).

T. S. ELIOT, *Selected Essays* (Faber/Harcourt).

——, *The Use of Poetry and the Use of Criticism* (Faber/Barnes and Noble).

——, *The Music of Poetry* (Glasgow University Publications).

W. EMPSON, *Seven Types of Ambiguity* (Chatto and Windus/New Directions).

A. H. GARDINER, *The Theory of Speech and Language* (Oxford University Press).

ROBERT GRAVES, *On English Poetry* (Heinemann).

A. E. HOUSMAN, *The Name and Nature of Poetry* (Cambridge University Press).

W. P. KER, *Collected Essays* (Macmillan).

——, *Epic and Romance* (Macmillan/Dover Publications).

——, *Form and Style in Poetry* (Macmillan).

F. R. LEAVIS, *New Bearings in English Poetry* (Chatto and Windus/ University of Michigan).

——, *Revaluation* (Chatto and Windus/W. W. Norton).

F. R. LEAVIS (ed.), *Determinations* (Chatto and Windus).

C. DAY LEWIS, *A Hope for Poetry* (Blackwell).

——, *The Poetic Image* (Cape/Oxford University Press).

C. S. LEWIS, *Rehabilitations* (Oxford University Press).

F. L. LUCAS, *The Decline and Fall of the Romantic Ideal* (Cambridge University Press).

P. H. B. LYON, *The Discovery of Poetry* (Arnold).

LOUIS MACNEICE, *Modern Poetry* (Oxford University Press).

JOHN PRESS, *The Fire and the Fountain* (Oxford University Press).

HERBERT READ, *Form in Modern Poetry* (Sheed and Ward).

——, *Phases of English Poetry* (Hogarth Press).

I. A. RICHARDS, *Principles of Literary Criticism* (Kegan Paul/ Harcourt).

——, *Practical Criticism* (Kegan Paul).

——, *Science and Poetry* (Kegan Paul).

M. R. RIDLEY, *Poetry and the Ordinary Reader* (Bell).

STEPHEN SPENDER, *The Destructive Element* (Cape/Saifer).

——, *World within World* (Hamish Hamilton).

——, *The Making of a Poem* (Hamish Hamilton/W. W. Norton).

MARTIN TURNELL, *Poetry and Crisis* (Sands).

EDMUND WILSON, *Axel's Castle* (Scribner's).

——, *The Wound and the Bow* (W. H. Allen/Oxford University Press).

CATALOGUE OF DOVER BOOKS

# Literature, History of Literature

**ARISTOTLE'S THEORY OF POETRY AND THE FINE ARTS, edited by S. H. Butcher.** The celebrated Butcher translation of this great classic faced, page by page, with the complete Greek text. A 300 page introduction discussing Aristotle's ideas and their influence in the history of thought and literature, and covering art and nature, imitation as an aesthetic form, poetic truth, art and morality, tragedy, comedy, and similar topics. Modern Aristotelian criticism discussed by John Gassner. lxxvi + 421pp. 5⅜ x 8. T42 Paperbound $2.00

**INTRODUCTIONS TO ENGLISH LITERATURE, edited by B. Dobrée.** Goes far beyond ordinary histories, ranging from the 7th century up to 1914 (to the 1940's in some cases.) The first half of each volume is a specific detailed study of historical and economic background of the period and a general survey of poetry and prose, including trends of thought, influences, etc. The second and larger half is devoted to a detailed study of more than 5000 poets, novelists, dramatists; also economists, historians, biographers, religious writers, philosophers, travellers, and scientists of literary stature, with dates, lists of major works and their dates, keypoint critical bibliography, and evaluating comments. The most compendious bibliographic and literary aid within its price range.

**Vol. I. THE BEGINNINGS OF ENGLISH LITERATURE TO SKELTON, (1509), W. L. Renwick, H. Orton.** 450pp. 5⅛ x 7⅞. T75 Clothbound $4.50

**Vol. II. THE ENGLISH RENAISSANCE, 1510-1688, V. de Sola Pinto.** 381pp. 5⅛ x 7⅞. T76 Clothbound $4.50

**Vol. III. AUGUSTANS AND ROMANTICS, 1689-1830, H. Dyson, J. Butt.** 320pp. 5⅛ x 7⅞. T77 Clothbound $4.50

**Vol. IV. THE VICTORIANS AND AFTER, 1830-1940's, E. Batho, B. Dobrée.** 360pp. 5⅛ x 7⅞. T78 Clothbound $4.50

**EPIC AND ROMANCE, W. P. Ker.** Written by one of the foremost authorities on medieval literature, this is the standard survey of medieval epic and romance. It covers Teutonic epics, Icelandic sagas, Beowulf, French chansons de geste, the Roman de Troie, and many other important works of literature. It is an excellent account for a body of literature whose beauty and value has only recently come to be recognized. Index. xxiv + 398pp. 5⅜ x 8. T355 Paperbound $2.00

**THE POPULAR BALLAD, F. B. Gummere.** Most useful factual introduction; fund of descriptive material; quotes, cites over 260 ballads. Examines, from folkloristic view, structure; choral, ritual elements; meter, diction, fusion; effects of tradition, editors; almost every other aspect of border, riddle, kinship, sea, ribald, supernatural, etc., ballads. Bibliography. 2 indexes. 374pp. 5⅜ x 8. T548 Paperbound $1.85

**MASTERS OF THE DRAMA, John Gassner.** The most comprehensive history of the drama in print, covering drama in every important tradition from the Greeks to the Near East, China, Japan, Medieval Europe, England, Russia, Italy, Spain, Germany, and dozens of other drama producing nations. This unsurpassed reading and reference work encompasses more than 800 dramatists and over 2000 plays, with biographical material, plot summaries, theatre history, etc. "Has no competitors in its field," THEATRE ARTS. "Best of its kind in English," NEW REPUBLIC. Exhaustive 35 page bibliography. 77 photographs and drawings. Deluxe edition with reinforced cloth binding, headbands, stained top. xxii + 890pp. 5⅜ x 8. T100 Clothbound $6.95

**THE DEVELOPMENT OF DRAMATIC ART, D. C. Stuart.** The basic work on the growth of Western drama from primitive beginnings to Eugene O'Neill, covering over 2500 years. Not a mere listing or survey, but a thorough analysis of changes, origins of style, and influences in each period; dramatic conventions, social pressures, choice of material, plot devices, stock situations, etc.; secular and religious works of all nations and epochs. "Generous and thoroughly documented researches," Outlook. "Solid studies of influences and playwrights and periods," London Times. Index. Bibliography. xi + 679pp. 5⅜ x 8. T693 Paperbound $2.75

**A SOURCE BOOK IN THEATRICAL HISTORY (SOURCES OF THEATRICAL HISTORY), A. M. Nagler.** Over 2000 years of actors, directors, designers, critics, and spectators speak for themselves in this potpourri of writings selected from the great and formative periods of western drama. On-the-spot descriptions of masks, costumes, makeup, rehearsals, special effects, acting methods, backstage squabbles, theatres, etc. Contemporary glimpses of Molière rehearsing his company, an exhortation to a Roman audience to buy refreshments and keep quiet, Goethe's rules for actors, Belasco telling of $6500 he spent building a river, Restoration actors being told to avoid "lewd, obscene, or indecent postures," and much more. Each selection has an introduction by Prof. Nagler. This extraordinary, lively collection is ideal as a source of otherwise difficult to obtain material, as well as a fine book for browsing. Over 80 illustrations. 10 diagrams. xxiii + 611pp. 5⅜ x 8. T515 Paperbound $3.00

**WORLD DRAMA, B. H. Clark.** The dramatic creativity of a score of ages and eras — all in two handy compact volumes. Over ⅓ of this material is unavailable in any other current edition! 46 plays from Ancient Greece, Rome, Medieval Europe, France, Germany, Italy, England, Russia, Scandinavia; India, China, Japan, etc. — including classic authors like Aeschylus, Sophocles, Euripides, Aristophanes, Plautus, Marlowe, Jonson, Farquhar, Goldsmith, Cervantes, Molière, Dumas, Goethe, Schiller, Ibsen, and many others. This creative collection avoids hackneyed material and includes only completely first-rate works which are relatively little known or difficult to obtain. "The most comprehensive collection of important plays from all literature available in English," SAT. REV. OF LITERATURE. Introduction. Reading lists. 2 volumes. 1364pp. 5⅜ x 8. Vol. 1, T57 Paperbound **$2.50**
Vol. 2, T59 Paperbound **$2.50**

**MASTERPIECES OF THE RUSSIAN DRAMA, edited with introduction by G. R. Noyes.** This only comprehensive anthology of Russian drama ever published in English offers complete texts, in 1st-rate modern translations, of 12 plays covering 200 years. Vol. 1: "The Young Hopeful," Fonvisin; "Wit Works Woe," Griboyedov; "The Inspector General," Gogol; "A Month in the Country," Turgenev; "The Poor Bride," Ostrovsky; "A Bitter Fate," Pisemsky. Vol. 2: "The Death of Ivan the Terrible," Alexey Tolstoy "The Power of Darkness," Lev Tolstoy; "The Lower Depths," Gorky; "The Cherry Orchard," Chekhov; "Professor Storitsyn," Andreyev; "Mystery Bouffe," Mayakovsky. Bibliography. Total of 902pp. 5⅜ x 8.
Vol. 1 T647 Paperbound **$2.25**
Vol. 2 T648 Paperbound **$2.00**

**EUGENE O'NEILL: THE MAN AND HIS PLAYS, B. H. Clark.** Introduction to O'Neill's life and work. Clark analyzes each play from the early THE WEB to the recently produced MOON FOR THE MISBEGOTTEN and THE ICEMAN COMETH revealing the environmental and dramatic influences necessary for a complete understanding of these important works. Bibliography. Appendices. Index. ix + 182pp. 5⅜ x 8. T379 Paperbound **$1.35**

**THE HEART OF THOREAU'S JOURNALS, edited by O. Shepard.** The best general selection from Thoreau's voluminous (and rare) journals. This intimate record of thoughts and observations reveals the full Thoreau and his intellectual development more accurately than any of his published works: self-conflict between the scientific observer and the poet, reflections on transcendental philosophy, involvement in the tragedies of neighbors and national causes, etc. New preface, notes, introductions. xii + 228pp. 5⅜ x 8. T741 Paperbound **$1.50**

**H. D. THOREAU: A WRITER'S JOURNAL, edited by L. Stapleton.** A unique new selection from the Journals concentrating on Thoreau's growth as a conscious literary artist, the ideals and purposes of his art. Most of the material has never before appeared outside of the complete 14-volume edition. Contains vital insights on Thoreau's projected book on Concord, thoughts on the nature of men and government, indignation with slavery, sources of inspiration, goals in life. Index. xxxiii + 234pp. 5⅜ x 8. T678 Paperbound **$1.65**

**THE HEART OF EMERSON'S JOURNALS, edited by Bliss Perry.** Best of these revealing Journals, originally 10 volumes, presented in a one volume edition. Talks with Channing, Hawthorne, Thoreau, and Bronson Alcott; impressions of Webster, Everett, John Brown, and Lincoln; records of moments of sudden understanding, vision, and solitary ecstasy. "The essays do not reveal the power of Emerson's mind . . . as do these hasty and informal writings," N.Y. Times. Preface by Bliss Perry. Index. xiii + 357pp. 5⅜ x 8. T477 Paperbound **$1.85**

**FOUNDERS OF THE MIDDLE AGES, E. K. Rand.** This is the best non-technical discussion of the transformation of Latin pagan culture into medieval civilization. Covering such figures as Tertullian, Gregory, Jerome, Boethius, Augustine, the Neoplatonists, and many other literary men, educators, classicists, and humanists, this book is a storehouse of information presented clearly and simply for the intelligent non-specialist. "Thoughtful, beautifully written," AMERICAN HISTORICAL REVIEW. "Extraordinarily accurate," Richard McKeon, THE NATION. ix + 365pp. 5⅜ x 8. T369 Paperbound **$2.00**

**PLAY-MAKING: A MANUAL OF CRAFTSMANSHIP, William Archer.** With an extensive, new introduction by John Gassner, Yale Univ. The permanently essential requirements of solid play construction are set down in clear, practical language: theme, exposition, foreshadowing, tension, obligatory scene, peripety, dialogue, character, psychology, other topics. This book has been one of the most influential elements in the modern theatre, and almost everything said on the subject since is contained explicitly or implicitly within its covers. Bibliography. Index. xlii + 277pp. 5⅜ x 8. T651 Paperbound **$1.75**

**HAMBURG DRAMATURGY, G. E. Lessing.** One of the most brilliant of German playwrights of the eighteenth-century age of criticism analyzes the complex of theory and tradition that constitutes the world of theater. These 104 essays on aesthetic theory helped demolish the regime of French classicism, opening the door to psychological and social realism, romanticism. Subjects include the original functions of tragedy; drama as the rational world; the meaning of pity and fear, pity and fear as means for purgation and other Aristotelian concepts; genius and creative force; interdependence of poet's language and actor's interpretation; truth and authenticity; etc. A basic and enlightening study for anyone interested in aesthetics and ideas, from the philosopher to the theatergoer. Introduction by Prof. Victor Lange. xxii + 265pp. 4½ x 6⅜. T32 Paperbound **$1.45**

# Orientalia

**ORIENTAL RELIGIONS IN ROMAN PAGANISM, F. Cumont.** A study of the cultural meeting of east and west in the Early Roman Empire. It covers the most important eastern religions of the time from their first appearance in Rome, 204 B.C., when the Great Mother of the Gods was first brought over from Syria. The ecstatic cults of Syria and Phrygia — Cybele, Attis, Adonis, their orgies and mutilatory rites; the mysteries of Egypt — Serapis, Isis, Osiris, the dualism of Persia, the elevation of cosmic evil to equal stature with the deity, Mithra; worship of Hermes Trismegistus; Ishtar, Astarte; the magic of the ancient Near East, etc. Introduction. 55pp. of notes; extensive bibliography. Index. xxiv + 298pp. 5⅜ x 8.
**T321 Paperbound $2.00**

**THE MYSTERIES OF MITHRA, F. Cumont.** The definitive coverage of a great ideological struggle between the west and the orient in the first centuries of the Christian era. The origin of Mithraism, a Persian mystery religion, and its association with the Roman army is discussed in detail. Then utilizing fragmentary monuments and texts, in one of the greatest feats of scholarly detection, Dr. Cumont reconstructs the mystery teachings and secret doctrines, the hidden organization and cult of Mithra. Mithraic art is discussed, analyzed, and depicted in 70 illustrations. 239pp. 5⅜ x 8.
**T323 Paperbound $1.85**

**CHRISTIAN AND ORIENTAL PHILOSOPHY OF ART, A. K. Coomaraswamy.** A unique fusion of philosopher, orientalist, art historian, and linguist, the author discusses such matters as: the true function of aesthetics in art, the importance of symbolism, intellectual and philosophic backgrounds, the role of traditional culture in enriching art, common factors in all great art, the nature of medieval art, the nature of folklore, the beauty of mathematics, and similar topics. 2 illustrations. Bibliography. 148pp. 5⅜ x 8.
**T378 Paperbound $1.35**

**TRANSFORMATION OF NATURE IN ART, A. K. Coomaraswamy.** Unabridged reissue of a basic work upon Asiatic religious art and philosophy of religion. The theory of religious art in Asia and Medieval Europe (exemplified by Meister Eckhart) is analyzed and developed. Detailed consideration is given to Indian medieval aesthetic manuals, symbolic language in philosophy, the origin and use of images in India, and many other fascinating and little known topics. Glossaries of Sanskrit and Chinese terms. Bibliography. 41pp. of notes. 245pp. 5⅜ x 8.
**T368 Paperbound $1.75**

**BUDDHIST LOGIC, F.Th. Stcherbatsky.** A study of an important part of Buddhism usually ignored by other books on the subject: the Mahayana buddhistic logic of the school of Dignaga and his followers. First vol. devoted to history of Indian logic with Central Asian continuations, detailed exposition of Dignaga system, including theory of knowledge, the sensible world (causation, perception, ultimate reality) and mental world (judgment, inference, logical fallacies, the syllogism), reality of external world, and negation (law of contradiction, universals, dialectic). Vol. II contains translation of Dharmakirti's Nyayabindu with Dharmamottara's commentary. Appendices cover translations of Tibetan treatises on logic, Hindu attacks on Buddhist logic, etc. The basic work, one of the products of the great St. Petersburg school of Indian studies. Written clearly and with an awareness of Western philosophy and logic; meant for the Asian specialist and for the general reader with only a minimum of background. Vol. I, xii + 559pp. Vol. II, viii + 468pp. 5⅜ x 8½.
**T955 Vol. I Paperbound $2.50**
**T956 Vol. II Paperbound $2.50**
**The set $5.00**

**THE TEXTS OF TAOISM.** The first inexpensive edition of the complete James Legge translations of the Tao Te King and the writings of Chinese mystic Chuang Tse. Also contains several shorter treatises: the T'ai Shang Tractate of Actions and Their Retributions; the King Kang King, or Classic of Purity; the Yin Fu King, or Classic of the Harmony of the Seen and Unseen; the Yu Shu King, or Classic of the Pivot of Jade; and the Hsia Yung King, or Classic of the Directory for a Day. While there are other translations of the Tao Te King, this is the only translation of Chuang Tse and much of other material. Extensive introduction discusses differences between Taoism, Buddhism, Confucianism; authenticity and arrangement of Tao Te King and writings of Chuang Tse; the meaning of the Tao and basic tenets of Taoism; historical accounts of Lao-tse and followers; other pertinent matters. Clarifying notes incorporated into text. Originally published as Volumes 39, 40 of SACRED BOOKS OF THE EAST series, this has long been recognized as an indispensible collection. Sinologists, philosophers, historians of religion will of course be interested and anyone with an elementary course in Oriental religion or philosophy will understand and profit from these writings. Index. Appendix analyzing thought of Chuang Tse. Vol. I, xxiii + 396pp. Vol. II, viii + 340pp. 5⅜ x 8½.
**T990 Vol. I Paperbound $2.25**
**T991 Vol. II Paperbound $2.25**

# Philosophy, Religion

**GUIDE TO PHILOSOPHY, C. E. M. Joad.** A modern classic which examines many crucial problems which man has pondered through the ages: Does free will exist? Is there plan in the universe? How do we know and validate our knowledge? Such opposed solutions as subjective idealism and realism, chance and teleology, vitalism and logical positivism, are evaluated and the contributions of the great philosophers from the Greeks to moderns like Russell, Whitehead, and others, are considered in the context of each problem. "The finest introduction," BOSTON TRANSCRIPT. Index. Classified bibliography. 592pp. 5⅜ x 8.
T297 Paperbound **$2.00**

**HISTORY OF ANCIENT PHILOSOPHY, W. Windelband.** One of the clearest, most accurate comprehensive surveys of Greek and Roman philosophy. Discusses ancient philosophy in general, intellectual life in Greece in the 7th and 6th centuries B.C., Thales, Anaximander, Anaximenes, Heraclitus, the Eleatics, Empedocles, Anaxagoras, Leucippus, the Pythagoreans, the Sophists, Socrates, Democritus (20 pages), Plato (50 pages), Aristotle (70 pages), the Peripatetics, Stoics, Epicureans, Sceptics, Neo-platonists, Christian Apologists, etc. 2nd German edition translated by H. E. Cushman. xv + 393pp. 5⅜ x 8.
T357 Paperbound **$1.85**

**ILLUSTRATIONS OF THE HISTORY OF MEDIEVAL THOUGHT AND LEARNING, R. L. Poole.** Basic analysis of the thought and lives of the leading philosophers and ecclesiastics from the 8th to the 14th century—Abailard, Ockham, Wycliffe, Marsiglio of Padua, and many other great thinkers who carried the torch of Western culture and learning through the "Dark Ages": political, religious, and metaphysical views. Long a standard work for scholars and one of the best introductions to medieval thought for beginners. Index. 10 Appendices. xiii + 327pp. 5⅜ x 8.
T674 Paperbound **$2.00**

**PHILOSOPHY AND CIVILIZATION IN THE MIDDLE AGES, M. de Wulf.** This semi-popular survey covers aspects of medieval intellectual life such as religion, philosophy, science, the arts, etc. It also covers feudalism vs. Catholicism, rise of the universities, mendicant orders, monastic centers, and similar topics. Unabridged. Bibliography. Index. viii + 320pp. 5⅜ x 8.
T284 Paperbound **$1.85**

**AN INTRODUCTION TO SCHOLASTIC PHILOSOPHY, Prof. M. de Wulf.** Formerly entitled SCHOLASTICISM OLD AND NEW, this volume examines the central scholastic tradition from St. Anselm, Albertus Magnus, Thomas Aquinas, up to Suarez in the 17th century. The relation of scholasticism to ancient and medieval philosophy and science in general is clear and easily followed. The second part of the book considers the modern revival of scholasticism, the Louvain position, relations with Kantianism and Positivism. Unabridged. xvi + 271pp. 5⅜ x 8.
T296 Clothbound **$3.50**
T283 Paperbound **$1.75**

**A HISTORY OF MODERN PHILOSOPHY, H. Höffding.** An exceptionally clear and detailed coverage of western philosophy from the Renaissance to the end of the 19th century. Major and minor men such as Pomponazzi, Bodin, Boehme, Telesius, Bruno, Copernicus, da Vinci, Kepler, Galileo, Bacon, Descartes, Hobbes, Spinoza, Leibniz, Wolff, Locke, Newton, Berkeley, Hume, Erasmus, Montesquieu, Voltaire, Diderot, Rousseau, Lessing, Kant, Herder, Fichte, Schelling, Hegel, Schopenhauer, Comte, Mill, Darwin, Spencer, Hartmann, Lange, and many others, are discussed in terms of theory of knowledge, logic, cosmology, and psychology. Index. 2 volumes, total of 1159pp. 5⅜ x 8.
T117 Vol. 1, Paperbound **$2.25**
T118 Vol. 2, Paperbound **$2.25**

**ARISTOTLE, A. E. Taylor.** A brilliant, searching non-technical account of Aristotle and his thought written by a foremost Platonist. It covers the life and works of Aristotle; classification of the sciences; logic; first philosophy; matter and form; causes; motion and eternity; God; physics; metaphysics; and similar topics. Bibliography. New Index compiled for this edition. 128pp. 5⅜ x 8.
T280 Paperbound **$1.00**

**THE SYSTEM OF THOMAS AQUINAS, M. de Wulf.** Leading Neo-Thomist, one of founders of University of Louvain, gives concise exposition to central doctrines of Aquinas, as a means toward determining his value to modern philosophy, religion. Formerly "Medieval Philosophy Illustrated from the System of Thomas Aquinas." Trans. by E. Messenger. Introduction. 151pp. 5⅜ x 8.
T568 Paperbound **$1.25**

**LEIBNIZ, H. W. Carr.** Most stimulating middle-level coverage of basic philosophical thought of Leibniz. Easily understood discussion, analysis of major works: "Theodicy," "Principles of Nature and Grace," "Monadology"; Leibniz's influence; intellectual growth; correspondence; disputes with Bayle, Malebranche, Newton; importance of his thought today, with reinterpretation in modern terminology. "Power and mastery," London Times. Bibliography. Index. 226pp. 5⅜ x 8.
T624 Paperbound **$1.35**

**THE SENSE OF BEAUTY, G. Santayana.** A revelation of the beauty of language as well as an important philosophic treatise, this work studies the "why, when, and how beauty appears, what conditions an ·object must fulfill to be beautiful, what elements of our nature make us sensible of beauty, and what the relation is between the constitution of the object and the excitement of our susceptibility." "It is doubtful if a better treatment of the subject has since been published," PEABODY JOURNAL. Index. ix + 275pp. 5⅜ x 8.
T238 Paperbound **$1.00**

**PROBLEMS OF ETHICS, Moritz Schlick.** The renowned leader of the "Vienna Circle" applies the logical positivist approach to a wide variety of ethical problems: the source and means of attaining knowledge, the formal and material characteristics of the good, moral norms and principles, absolute vs. relative values, free will and responsibility, comparative importance of pleasure and suffering as ethical values, etc. Disarmingly simple and straightforward despite complexity of subject. First English translation, authorized by author before his death, of a thirty-year old classic. Translated and with an introduction by David Rynin. Index. Foreword by Prof. George P. Adams. xxi + 209pp. 5⅜ x 8.     T946 Paperbound **$1.60**

**AN INTRODUCTION TO EXISTENTIALISM, Robert G. Olson.** A new and indispensable guide to one of the major thought systems of our century, the movement that is central to the thinking of some of the most creative figures of the past hundred years. Stresses Heidegger and Sartre, with careful and objective examination of the existentialist position, values—freedom of choice, individual dignity, personal love, creative effort—and answers to the eternal questions of the human condition. Scholarly, unbiased, analytic, unlike most studies of this difficult subject, Prof. Olson's book is aimed at the student of philosophy as well as at the reader with no formal training who is looking for an absorbing, accessible, and thorough introduction to the basic texts. Index. xv + 221pp. 5⅜ x 8½.     T55 Paperbound **$1.65**

**SYMBOLIC LOGIC, C. I. Lewis and C. H. Langford.** Since first publication in 1932, this has been among most frequently cited works on symbolic logic. Still one of the best introductions both for beginners and for mathematicians, philosophers. First part covers basic topics which easily lend themselves to beginning study. Second part is rigorous, thorough development of logistic method, examination of some of most difficult and abstract aspects of symbolic logic, including modal logic, logical paradoxes, many-valued logic, with Prof. Lewis' own contributions. 2nd revised (corrected) edition. 3 appendixes, one new to this edition. 524pp. 5⅜ x 8.     S170 Paperbound **$2.00**

**WHITEHEAD'S PHILOSOPHY OF CIVILIZATION, A. H. Johnson.** A leading authority on Alfred North Whitehead synthesizes the great philosopher's thought on civilization, scattered throughout various writings, into unified whole. Analysis of Whitehead's general definition of civilization, his reflections on history and influences on its development, his religion, including his analysis of Christianity, concept of solitariness as first requirement of personal religion, and so on. Other chapters cover views on minority groups, society, civil liberties, education. Also critical comments on Whitehead's philosophy. Written with general reader in mind. A perceptive introduction to important area of the thought of a leading philosopher of our century. Revised index and bibliography. xii + 211pp. 5⅜ x 8½.
T996 Paperbound **$1.50**

**WHITEHEAD'S THEORY OF REALITY, A. H. Johnson.** Introductory outline of Whitehead's theory of actual entities, the heart of his philosophy of reality, followed by his views on nature of God, philosophy of mind, theory of value (truth, beauty, goodness and their opposites), analyses of other philosophers, attitude toward science. A perspicacious lucid introduction by author of dissertation on Whitehead, written under the subject's supervision at Harvard. Good basic view for beginning students of philosophy and for those who are simply interested in important contemporary ideas. Revised index and bibliography. xiii + 267pp. 5⅜ x 8½.
T989 Paperbound **$2.00**

**MIND AND THE WORLD-ORDER, C. I. Lewis.** Building upon the work of Peirce, James, and Dewey, Professor Lewis outlines a theory of knowledge in terms of "conceptual pragmatism." Dividing truth into abstract mathematical certainty and empirical truth, the author demonstrates that the traditional understanding of the a priori must be abandoned. Detailed analyses of philosophy, metaphysics, method, the "given" in experience, knowledge of objects, nature of the a priori, experience and order, and many others. Appendices. xiv + 446pp. 5⅜ x 8.     T359 Paperbound **$2.25**

**SCEPTICISM AND ANIMAL FAITH, G. Santayana.** To eliminate difficulties in the traditional theory of knowledge, Santayana distinguishes between the independent existence of objects and the essence our mind attributes to them. Scepticism is thereby established as a form of belief, and animal faith is shown to be a necessary condition of knowledge. Belief, classical idealism, intuition, memory, symbols, literary psychology, and much more, discussed with unusual clarity and depth. Index. xii + 314pp. 5⅜ x 8.     T235 Clothbound **$3.50**
T236 Paperbound **$1.75**

**LANGUAGE AND MYTH, E. Cassirer.** Analyzing the non-rational thought processes which go to make up culture, Cassirer demonstrates that beneath both language and myth there lies a dominant unconscious "grammar" of experience whose categories and canons are not those of logical thought. His analyses of seemingly diverse phenomena such as Indian metaphysics, the Melanesian "mana," the Naturphilosophie of Schelling, modern poetry, etc., are profound without being pedantic. Introduction and translation by Susanne Langer. Index. x + 103pp. 5⅜ x 8.     T51 Paperbound **$1.25**

# CATALOGUE OF DOVER BOOKS

**AN ESSAY CONCERNING HUMAN UNDERSTANDING, John Locke.** Edited by A. C. Fraser. Unabridged reprinting of definitive edition; only complete edition of "Essay" in print. Marginal analyses of almost every paragraph; hundreds of footnotes; authoritative 140-page biographical, critical, historical prolegomena. Indexes. 1170pp. 5⅜ x 8.
T530 Vol. 1 (Books 1, 2) Paperbound **$2.50**
T531 Vol. 2 (Books 3, 4) Paperbound **$2.50**
2 volume set **$5.00**

**THE PHILOSOPHY OF HISTORY, G. W. F. Hegel.** One of the great classics of western thought which reveals Hegel's basic principle: that history is not chance but a rational process, the realization of the Spirit of Freedom. Ranges from the oriental cultures of subjective thought to the classical subjective cultures, to the modern absolute synthesis where spiritual and secular may be reconciled. Translation and introduction by J. Sibree. Introduction by C. Hegel. Special introduction for this edition by Prof. Carl Friedrich. xxxix + 447pp. 5⅜ x 8.
T112 Paperbound **$2.25**

**THE PHILOSOPHY OF HEGEL, W. T. Stace.** The first detailed analysis of Hegel's thought in English, this is especially valuable since so many of Hegel's works are out of print. Dr. Stace examines Hegel's debt to Greek idealists and the 18th century and then proceeds to a careful description and analysis of Hegel's first principles, categories, reason, dialectic method, his logic, philosophy of nature and spirit, etc. Index. Special 14 x 20 chart of Hegelian system. x + 526pp. 5⅜ x 8.
T254 Paperbound **$2.45**

**THE WILL TO BELIEVE and HUMAN IMMORTALITY, W. James.** Two complete books bound as one. THE WILL TO BELIEVE discusses the interrelations of belief, will, and intellect in man; chance vs. determinism, free will vs. determinism, free will vs. fate, pluralism vs. monism; the philosophies of Hegel and Spencer, and more. HUMAN IMMORTALITY examines the question of survival after death and develops an unusual and powerful argument for immortality. Two prefaces. Index. Total of 429pp. 5⅜ x 8.
T291 Paperbound **$2.00**

**THE WORLD AND THE INDIVIDUAL, Josiah Royce.** Only major effort by an American philosopher to interpret nature of things in systematic, comprehensive manner. Royce's formulation of an absolute voluntarism remains one of the original and profound solutions to the problems involved. Part One, Four Historical Conceptions of Being, inquires into first principles, true meaning and place of individuality. Part Two, Nature, Man, and the Moral Order, is application of first principles to problems concerning religion, evil, moral order. Introduction by J. E. Smith, Yale Univ. Index. 1070pp. 5⅜ x 8.
T561 Vol. 1 Paperbound **$2.75**
T562 Vol. 2 Paperbound **$2.75**
Two volume set **$5.50**

**THE PHILOSOPHICAL WRITINGS OF PEIRCE, edited by J. Buchler.** This book (formerly THE PHILOSOPHY OF PEIRCE) is a carefully integrated exposition of Peirce's complete system composed of selections from his own work. Symbolic logic, scientific method, theory of signs, pragmatism, epistemology, chance, cosmology, ethics, and many other topics are treated by one of the greatest philosophers of modern times. This is the only inexpensive compilation of his key ideas. xvi + 386pp. 5⅜ x 8.
T217 Paperbound **$2.00**

**EXPERIENCE AND NATURE, John Dewey.** An enlarged, revised edition of the Paul Carus lectures which Dewey delivered in 1925. It covers Dewey's basic formulation of the problem of knowledge, with a full discussion of other systems, and a detailing of his own concepts of the relationship of external world, mind, and knowledge. Starts with a thorough examination of the philosophical method; examines the interrelationship of experience and nature; analyzes experience on basis of empirical naturalism, the formulation of law, role of language and social factors in knowledge; etc. Dewey's treatment of central problems in philosophy is profound but extremely easy to follow. ix + 448pp. 5⅜ x 8.
T471 Paperbound **$2.00**

**THE PHILOSOPHICAL WORKS OF DESCARTES.** The definitive English edition of all the major philosophical works and letters of René Descartes. All of his revolutionary insights, from his famous "Cogito ergo sum" to his detailed account of contemporary science and his astonishingly fruitful concept that all phenomena of the universe (except mind) could be reduced to clear laws by the use of mathematics. An excellent source for the thought of men like Hobbes, Arnauld, Gassendi, etc., who were Descarte's contemporaries. Translated by E. S. Haldane and G. Ross. Introductory notes. Index. Total of 842pp. 5⅜ x 8.
T71 Vol. 1, Paperbound **$2.00**
T72 Vol. 2, Paperbound **$2.00**

**THE CHIEF WORKS OF SPINOZA.** An unabridged reprint of the famous Bohn edition containing all of Spinoza's most important works: Vol. I: The Theologico-Political Treatise and the Political Treatise. Vol. II: On The Improvement Of Understanding, The Ethics, Selected Letters. Profound and enduring ideas on God, the universe, pantheism, society, religion, the state, democracy, the mind, emotions, freedom and the nature of man, which influenced Goethe, Hegel, Schelling, Coleridge, Whitehead, and many others. Introduction. 2 volumes. 826pp. 5⅜ x 8.
T249 Vol. I, Paperbound **$1.50**
T250 Vol. II, Paperbound **$1.50**

**THE ANALYSIS OF MATTER, Bertrand Russell.** A classic which has retained its importance in understanding the relation between modern physical theory and human perception. Logical analysis of physics, prerelativity physics, causality, scientific inference, Weyl's theory, tensors, invariants and physical interpretations, periodicity, and much more is treated with Russell's usual brilliance. "Masterly piece of clear thinking and clear writing," NATION AND ATHENAEUM. "Most thorough treatment of the subject," THE NATION. Introduction. Index. 8 figures. viii + 408pp. 5⅜ x 8.  S231 Paperbound **$1.95**

**CONCEPTUAL THINKING (A LOGICAL INQUIRY), S. Körner.** Discusses origin, use of general concepts on which language is based, and the light they shed on basic philosophical questions. Rigorously examines how different concepts are related; how they are linked to experience; problems in the field of contact between exact logical, mathematical, and scientific concepts, and the inexactness of everyday experience (studied at length). This work elaborates many new approaches to the traditional problems of philosophy—epistemology, value theories, metaphysics, aesthetics, morality. "Rare originality . . . brings a new rigour into philosophical argument," Philosophical Quarterly. New corrected second edition. Index. vii + 301pp. 5⅜ x 8  T516 Paperbound **$1.75**

**INTRODUCTION TO SYMBOLIC LOGIC, S. Langer.** No special knowledge of math required — probably the clearest book ever written on symbolic logic, suitable for the layman, general scientist, and philosopher. You start with simple symbols and advance to a knowledge of the Boole-Schroeder and Russell-Whitehead systems. Forms, logical structure, classes, the calculus of propositions, logic of the syllogism, etc., are all covered. "One of the clearest and simplest introductions," MATHEMATICS GAZETTE. Second enlarged, revised edition. 368pp. 5⅜ x 8.  S164 Paperbound **$1.85**

**LANGUAGE, TRUTH AND LOGIC, A. J. Ayer.** A clear, careful analysis of the basic ideas of Logical Positivism. Building on the work of Schlick, Russell, Carnap, and the Viennese School, Mr. Ayer develops a detailed exposition of the nature of philosophy, science, and metaphysics; the Self and the World; logic and common sense, and other philosophic concepts. An aid to clarity of thought as well as the first full-length development of Logical Positivism in English. Introduction by Bertrand Russell. Index. 160pp. 5⅜ x 8.  T10 Paperbound **$1.25**

**ESSAYS IN EXPERIMENTAL LOGIC, J. Dewey.** Based upon the theory that knowledge implies a judgment which in turn implies an inquiry, these papers consider the inquiry stage in terms of: the relationship of thought and subject matter, antecedents of thought, data and meanings. 3 papers examine Bertrand Russell's thought, while 2 others discuss pragmatism and a final essay presents a new theory of the logic of values. Index. viii + 444pp. 5⅜ x 8.  T73 Paperbound **$2.25**

**TRAGIC SENSE OF LIFE, M. de Unamuno.** The acknowledged masterpiece of one of Spain's most influential thinkers. Between the despair at the inevitable death of man and all his works and the desire for something better, Unamuno finds that "saving incertitude" that alone can console us. This dynamic appraisal of man's faith in God and in himself has been called "a masterpiece" by the ENCYCLOPAEDIA BRITANNICA. xxx + 332pp. 5⅜ x 8.  T257 Paperbound **$2.00**

**HISTORY OF DOGMA, A. Harnack.** Adolph Harnack, who died in 1930, was perhaps the greatest Church historian of all time. In this epoch-making history, which has never been surpassed in comprehensiveness and wealth of learning, he traces the development of the authoritative Christian doctrinal system from its first crystallization in the 4th century down through the Reformation, including also a brief survey of the later developments through the Infallibility decree of 1870. He reveals the enormous influence of Greek thought on the early Fathers, and discusses such topics as the Apologists, the great councils, Manichaeism, the historical position of Augustine, the medieval opposition to indulgences, the rise of Protestantism, the relations of Luther's doctrines with modern tendencies of thought, and much more. "Monumental work; still the most valuable history of dogma . . . luminous analysis of the problems . . . abounds in suggestion and stimulus and can be neglected by no one who desires to understand the history of thought in this most important field," Dutcher's Guide to Historical Literature. Translated by Neil Buchanan. Index. Unabridged reprint in 4 volumes. Vol I: Beginnings to the Gnostics and Marcion. Vol II & III: 2nd century to the 4th century Fathers. Vol IV & V: 4th century Councils to the Carlovingian Renaissance. Vol VI & VII: Period of Clugny (c. 1000) to the Reformation, and after. Total of cii + 2407pp. 5⅜ x 8.

**THE GUIDE FOR THE PERPLEXED, Maimonides.** One of the great philosophical works of all time and a necessity for everyone interested in the philosophy of the Middle Ages in the Jewish, Christian, and Moslem traditions. Maimonides develops a common meeting-point for the Old Testament and the Aristotelian thought which pervaded the medieval world. His ideas and methods predate such scholastics as Aquinas and Scotus and throw light on the entire problem of philosophy or science vs. religion. 2nd revised edition. Complete unabridged Friedländer translation. 55 page introduction to Maimonides's life, period, etc., with an important summary of the GUIDE. Index. lix + 414pp. 5⅜ x 8.  T351 Paperbound **$2.00**

# Social Sciences

**SOCIAL THOUGHT FROM LORE TO SCIENCE, H. E. Barnes and H. Becker.** An immense survey of sociological thought and ways of viewing, studying, planning, and reforming society from earliest times to the present. Includes thought on society of preliterate peoples, ancient non-Western cultures, and every great movement in Europe, America, and modern Japan. Analyzes hundreds of great thinkers: Plato, Augustine, Bodin, Vico, Montesquieu, Herder, Comte, Marx, etc. Weighs the contributions of utopians, sophists, fascists and communists; economists, jurists, philosophers, ecclesiastics, and every 19th and 20th century school of scientific sociology, anthropology, and social psychology throughout the world. Combines topical, chronological, and regional approaches, treating the evolution of social thought as a process rather than as a series of mere topics. "Impressive accuracy, competence, and discrimination . . . easily the best single survey," Nation. Thoroughly revised, with new material up to 1960. 2 indexes. Over 2200 bibliographical notes. Three volume set. Total of 1586pp. 5⅜ x 8.

T901 Vol I   Paperbound **$2.50**
T902 Vol II  Paperbound **$2.50**
T903 Vol III Paperbound **$2.50**
The set **$7.50**

**FOLKWAYS, William Graham Sumner.** A classic of sociology, a searching and thorough examination of patterns of behaviour from primitive, ancient Greek and Judaic, Medieval Christian, African, Oriental, Melanesian, Australian, Islamic, to modern Western societies. Thousands of illustrations of social, sexual, and religious customs, mores, laws, and institutions. Hundreds of categories: Labor, Wealth, Abortion, Primitive Justice, Life Policy, Slavery, Cannibalism, Uncleanness and the Evil Eye, etc. Will extend the horizon of every reader by showing the relativism of his own culture. Prefatory note by A. G. Keller. Introduction by William Lyon Phelps. Bibliography. Index. xiii + 692pp. 5⅜ x 8.                     T508 Paperbound **$2.49**

**PRIMITIVE RELIGION, P. Radin.** A thorough treatment by a noted anthropologist of the nature and origin of man's belief in the supernatural and the influences that have shaped religious expression in primitive societies. Ranging from the Arunta, Ashanti, Aztec, Bushman, Crow, Fijian, etc., of Africa, Australia, Pacific Islands, the Arctic, North and South America, Prof. Radin integrates modern psychology, comparative religion, and economic thought with first-hand accounts gathered by himself and other scholars of primitive initiations, training of the shaman, and other fascinating topics. "Excellent," NATURE (London). Unabridged reissue of 1st edition. New author's preface. Bibliographic notes. Index. x + 322pp. 5⅜ x 8.
T393 Paperbound **$2.00**

**PRIMITIVE MAN AS PHILOSOPHER, P. Radin.** A standard anthropological work covering primitive thought on such topics as the purpose of life, marital relations, freedom of thought, symbolism, death, resignation, the nature of reality, personality, gods, and many others. Drawn from factual material gathered from the Winnebago, Oglala Sioux, Maori, Baganda, Batak, Zuni, among others, it does not distort ideas by removing them from context but interprets strictly within the original framework. Extensive selections of original primitive documents. Bibliography. Index. xviii + 402pp. 5⅜ x 8.             T392 Paperbound **$2.25**

**A TREATISE ON SOCIOLOGY, THE MIND AND SOCIETY, Vilfredo Pareto.** This treatise on human society is one of the great classics of modern sociology. First published in 1916, its careful catalogue of the innumerable manifestations of non-logical human conduct (Book One); the theory of "residues," leading to the premise that sentiment not logic determines human behavior (Book Two), and of "derivations," beliefs derived from desires (Book Three); and the general description of society made up of non-elite and elite, consisting of "foxes" who live by cunning and "lions" who live by force, stirred great controversy. But Pareto's passion for isolation and classification of elements and factors, and his allegiance to scientific method as the key tool for scrutinizing the human situation made his a truly twentieth-century mind and his work a catalytic influence on certain later social commentators. These four volumes (bound as two) require no special training to be appreciated and any reader who wishes to gain a complete understanding of modern sociological theory, regardless of special field of interest, will find them a must. Reprint of revised (corrected) printing of original edition. Translated by Andrew Bongiorno and Arthur Livingston. Index. Bibliography. Appendix containing index-summary of theorems. 48 diagrams. Four volumes bound as two. Total of 2063pp. 5⅜ x 8½.           The set Clothbound **$15.00**

**THE POLISH PEASANT IN EUROPE AND AMERICA, William I. Thomas, Florian Znaniecki.** A seminal sociological study of peasant primary groups (family and community) and the disruptions produced by a new industrial system and immigration to America. The peasant's family, class system, religious and aesthetic attitudes, and economic life are minutely examined and analyzed in hundreds of pages of primary documentation, particularly letters between family members. The disorientation caused by new environments is scrutinized in detail (a 312-page autobiography of an immigrant is especially valuable and revealing) in an attempt to find common experiences and reactions. The famous "Methodological Note" sets forth the principles which guided the authors. When out of print this set has sold for as much as $50. 2nd revised edition. 2 vols. Vol. 1: xv + 1115pp. Vol. 2: 1135pp. Index. 6 x 9.
T478 Clothbound 2 vol. set **$12.50**

# Say It language phrase books

These handy phrase books (128 to 196 pages each) make grammatical drills unnecessary for an elementary knowledge of a spoken foreign language. Covering most matters of travel and everyday life each volume contains:

Over 1000 phrases and sentences in immediately useful forms — foreign language plus English.

Modern usage designed for Americans. Specific phrases like, "Give me small change," and "Please call a taxi."

Simplified phonetic transcription you will be able to read at sight.

The only completely indexed phrase books on the market.

Covers scores of important situations: — Greetings, restaurants, sightseeing, useful expressions, etc.

These books are prepared by native linguists who are professors at Columbia, N.Y.U., Fordham and other great universities. Use them independently or with any other book or record course. They provide a supplementary living element that most other courses lack. Individual volumes in:

| | | | |
|---|---|---|---|
| Russian 75¢ | Italian 75¢ | Spanish 75¢ | German 75¢ |
| Hebrew 75¢ | Danish 75¢ | Japanese 75¢ | Swedish 75¢ |
| Dutch 75¢ | Esperanto 75¢ | Modern Greek 75¢ | Portuguese 75¢ |
| Norwegian 75¢ | Polish 75¢ | French 75¢ | Yiddish 75¢ |
| Turkish 75¢ | | English for German-speaking people 75¢ | |
| English for Italian-speaking people 75¢ | | English for Spanish-speaking people 75¢ | |

Large clear type. 128-196 pages each. 3½ x 5¼. Sturdy paper binding.

# Listen and Learn language records

LISTEN & LEARN is the only language record course designed especially to meet your travel and everyday needs. It is available in separate sets for FRENCH, SPANISH, GERMAN, JAPANESE, RUSSIAN, MODERN GREEK, PORTUGUESE, ITALIAN and HEBREW, and each set contains three 33⅓ rpm long-playing records—1½ hours of recorded speech by eminent native speakers who are professors at Columbia, New York University, Queens College.

Check the following special features found only in LISTEN & LEARN:

- **Dual-language recording. 812 selected phrases and sentences,** over 3200 words, spoken first in English, then in their foreign language equivalents. A suitable pause follows each foreign phrase, allowing you time to repeat the expression. You learn by unconscious assimilation.

- **128 to 206-page manual** contains everything on the records, plus a simple phonetic pronunciation guide.

- **Indexed for convenience. The only set on the market** that is completely indexed. No more puzzling over where to find the phrase you need. Just look in the rear of the manual.

- **Practical.** No time wasted on material you can find in any grammar. LISTEN & LEARN covers central core material with phrase approach. Ideal for the person with limited learning time.

- **Living, modern expressions,** not found in other courses. Hygienic products, modern equipment, shopping—expressions used every day, like "nylon" and "air-conditioned."

- **Limited objective.** Everything you learn, no matter where you stop, is immediately useful. You have to finish other courses, wade through grammar and vocabulary drill, before they help you.

- **High-fidelity recording.** LISTEN & LEARN records equal in clarity and surface-silence any record on the market costing up to $6.

"Excellent . . . the spoken records . . . impress me as being among the very best on the market," **Prof. Mario Pei,** Dept. of Romance Languages, Columbia University. "Inexpensive and well-done . . . it would make an ideal present," CHICAGO SUNDAY TRIBUNE. "More genuinely helpful than anything of its kind which I have previously encountered," **Sidney Clark,** well-known author of "ALL THE BEST" travel books.

UNCONDITIONAL GUARANTEE. Try LISTEN & LEARN, then return it within 10 days for full refund if you are not satisfied.

Each set contains three twelve-inch 33⅓ records, manual, and album.

| | | | |
|---|---|---|---|
| SPANISH | the set $5.95 | GERMAN | the set $5.95 |
| FRENCH | the set $5.95 | ITALIAN | the set $5.95 |
| RUSSIAN | the set $5.95 | JAPANESE | the set $5.95 |
| PORTUGUESE | the set $5.95 | MODERN GREEK | the set $5.95 |
| MODERN HEBREW | the set $5.95 | | |

# Puzzles, Mathematical Recreations

**SYMBOLIC LOGIC and THE GAME OF LOGIC, Lewis Carroll.** "Symbolic Logic" is not concerned with modern symbolic logic, but is instead a collection of over 380 problems posed with charm and imagination, using the syllogism, and a fascinating diagrammatic method of drawing conclusions. In "The Game of Logic" Carroll's whimsical imagination devises a logical game played with 2 diagrams and counters (included) to manipulate hundreds of tricky syllogisms. The final section, "Hit or Miss" is a lagniappe of 101 additional puzzles in the delightful Carroll manner. Until this reprint edition, both of these books were rarities costing up to $15 each. Symbolic Logic: Index. xxxi + 199pp. The Game of Logic: 96pp. 2 vols. bound as one. 5⅜ x 8. T492 Paperbound **$1.50**

**PILLOW PROBLEMS and A TANGLED TALE, Lewis Carroll.** One of the rarest of all Carroll's works, "Pillow Problems" contains 72 original math puzzles, all typically ingenious. Particularly fascinating are Carroll's answers which remain exactly as he thought them out, reflecting his actual mental process. The problems in "A Tangled Tale" are in story form, originally appearing as a monthly magazine serial. Carroll not only gives the solutions, but uses answers sent in by readers to discuss wrong approaches and misleading paths, and grades them for insight. Both of these books were rarities until this edition, "Pillow Problems" costing up to $25, and "A Tangled Tale" $15. Pillow Problems: Preface and Introduction by Lewis Carroll. xx + 109pp. A Tangled Tale: 6 illustrations. 152pp. Two vols. bound as one. 5⅜ x 8. T493 Paperbound **$1.50**

**AMUSEMENTS IN MATHEMATICS, Henry Ernest Dudeney.** The foremost British originator of mathematical puzzles is always intriguing, witty, and paradoxical in this classic, one of the largest collections of mathematical amusements. More than 430 puzzles, problems, and paradoxes. Mazes and games, problems on number manipulation, unicursal and other route problems, puzzles on measuring, weighing, packing, age, kinship, chessboards, joiners', crossing river, plane figure dissection, and many others. Solutions. More than 450 illustrations. vii + 258pp. 5⅜ x 8. T473 Paperbound **$1.25**

**THE CANTERBURY PUZZLES, Henry Dudeney.** Chaucer's pilgrims set one another problems in story form. Also Adventures of the Puzzle Club, the Strange Escape of the King's Jester, the Monks of Riddlewell, the Squire's Christmas Puzzle Party, and others. All puzzles are original, based on dissecting plane figures, arithmetic, algebra, elementary calculus and other branches of mathematics, and purely logical ingenuity. "The limit of ingenuity and intricacy," The Observer. Over 110 puzzles. Full Solutions. 150 illustrations. vii + 225pp. 5⅜ x 8. T474 Paperbound **$1.25**

**MATHEMATICAL EXCURSIONS, H. A. Merrill.** Even if you hardly remember your high school math, you'll enjoy the 90 stimulating problems contained in this book and you will come to understand a great many mathematical principles with surprisingly little effort. Many useful shortcuts and diversions not generally known are included: division by inspection, Russian peasant multiplication, memory systems for pi, building odd and even magic squares, square roots by geometry, dyadic systems, and many more. Solutions to difficult problems. 50 illustrations. 145pp. 5⅜ x 8. T350 Paperbound **$1.00**

**MAGIC SQUARES AND CUBES, W. S. Andrews.** Only book-length treatment in English, a thorough non-technical description and analysis. Here are nasik, overlapping, pandiagonal, serrated squares; magic circles, cubes, spheres, rhombuses. Try your hand at 4-dimensional magical figures! Much unusual folklore and tradition included. High school algebra is sufficient. 754 diagrams and illustrations. viii + 419pp. 5⅜ x 8. T658 Paperbound **$1.85**

**CALIBAN'S PROBLEM BOOK: MATHEMATICAL, INFERENTIAL AND CRYPTOGRAPHIC PUZZLES, H. Phillips (Caliban), S. T. Shovelton, G. S. Marshall.** 105 ingenious problems by the greatest living creator of puzzles based on logic and inference. Rigorous, modern, piquant; reflecting their author's unusual personality, these intermediate and advanced puzzles all involve the ability to reason clearly through complex situations; some call for mathematical knowledge, ranging from algebra to number theory. Solutions. xi + 180pp. 5⅜ x 8. T736 Paperbound **$1.25**

**MATHEMATICAL PUZZLES FOR BEGINNERS AND ENTHUSIASTS, G. Mott-Smith.** 188 mathematical puzzles based on algebra, dissection of plane figures, permutations, and probability, that will test and improve your powers of inference and interpretation. The Odic Force, The Spider's Cousin, Ellipse Drawing, theory and strategy of card and board games like tit-tat-toe, go moku, salvo, and many others. 100 pages of detailed mathematical explanations. Appendix of primes, square roots, etc. 135 illustrations. 2nd revised edition. 248pp. 5⅜ x 8. T198 Paperbound **$1.00**

**MATHEMAGIC, MAGIC PUZZLES, AND GAMES WITH NUMBERS, R. V. Heath.** More than 60 new puzzles and stunts based on the properties of numbers. Easy techniques for multiplying large numbers mentally, revealing hidden numbers magically, finding the date of any day in any year, and dozens more. Over 30 pages devoted to magic squares, triangles, cubes, circles, etc. Edited by J. S. Meyer. 76 illustrations. 128pp. 5⅜ x 8. T110 Paperbound **$1.00**

**MATHEMATICAL RECREATIONS, M. Kraitchik.** One of the most thorough compilations of unusual mathematical problems for beginners and advanced mathematicians. Historical problems from Greek, Medieval, Arabic, Hindu sources. 50 pages devoted to pastimes derived from figurate numbers, Mersenne numbers, Fermat numbers, primes and probability. 40 pages of magic, Euler, Latin, panmagic squares. 25 new positional and permutational games of permanent value: fairy chess, latruncles, reversi, jinx, ruma, lasca, tricolor, tetrachrome, etc. Complete rigorous solutions. Revised second edition. 181 illustrations. 333pp. 5⅜ x 8.
T163 Paperbound $1.75

**MATHEMATICAL PUZZLES OF SAM LOYD, selected and edited by M. Gardner.** Choice puzzles by the greatest American puzzle creator and innovator. Selected from his famous collection, "Cyclopedia of Puzzles," they retain the unique style and historical flavor of the originals. There are posers based on arithmetic, algebra, probability, game theory, route tracing, topology, counter, sliding block, operations research, geometrical dissection. Includes the famous "14-15" puzzle which was a national craze, and his "Horse of a Different Color" which sold millions of copies. 117 of his most ingenious puzzles in all, 120 line drawings and diagrams. Solutions. Selected references. xx + 167pp. 5⅜ x 8. T498 Paperbound $1.00

**MATHEMATICAL PUZZLES OF SAM LOYD, Vol. II, selected and edited by Martin Gardner.** The outstanding 2nd selection from the great American innovator's "Cyclopedia of Puzzles": speed and distance problems, clock problems, plane and solid geometry, calculus problems, etc. Analytical table of contents that groups the puzzles according to the type of mathematics necessary to solve them. 166 puzzles, 150 original line drawings and diagrams. Selected references. xiv + 177pp. 5⅜ x 8. T709 Paperbound $1.00

**ARITHMETICAL EXCURSIONS: AN ENRICHMENT OF ELEMENTARY MATHEMATICS, H. Bowers and J. Bowers.** A lively and lighthearted collection of facts and entertainments for anyone who enjoys manipulating numbers or solving arithmetical puzzles: methods of arithmetic never taught in school, little-known facts about the most simple numbers, and clear explanations of more sophisticated topics; mysteries and folklore of numbers, the "Hin-dog-abic" number system, etc. First publication. Index. 529 numbered problems and diversions, all with answers. Bibliography. 60 figures. xiv + 320pp. 5⅜ x 8. T770 Paperbound $1.65

**CRYPTANALYSIS, H. F. Gaines.** Formerly entitled ELEMENTARY CRYPTANALYSIS, this introductory-intermediate level text is the best book in print on cryptograms and their solution. It covers all major techniques of the past, and contains much that is not generally known except to experts. Full details about concealment, substitution, and transposition ciphers; periodic mixed alphabets, multafid, Kasiski and Vigenere methods, Ohaver patterns, Playfair, and scores of other topics. 6 language letter and word frequency appendix. 167 problems, now furnished with solutions. Index. 173 figures. vi + 230pp. 5⅜ x 8.
T97 Paperbound $2.00

**CRYPTOGRAPHY, L. D. Smith.** An excellent introductory work on ciphers and their solution, the history of secret writing, and actual methods and problems in such techniques as transposition and substitution. Appendices describe the enciphering of Japanese, the Baconian biliteral cipher, and contain frequency tables and a bibliography for further study. Over 150 problems with solutions. 160pp. 5⅜ x 8. T247 Paperbound $1.00

**PUZZLE QUIZ AND STUNT FUN, J. Meyer.** The solution to party doldrums. 238 challenging puzzles, stunts and tricks. Mathematical puzzles like The Clever Carpenter, Atom Bomb; mysteries and deductions like The Bridge of Sighs, The Nine Pearls, Dog Logic; observation puzzles like Cigarette Smokers, Telephone Dial; over 200 others including magic squares, tongue twisters, puns, anagrams, and many others. All problems solved fully. 250pp. 5⅜ x 8.
T337 Paperbound $1.00

**101 PUZZLES IN THOUGHT AND LOGIC, C. R. Wylie, Jr.** Brand new problems you need no special knowledge to solve! Take the kinks out of your mental "muscles" and enjoy solving murder problems, the detection of lying fishermen, the logical identification of color by a blindman, and dozens more. Introduction with simplified explanation of general scientific method and puzzle solving. 128pp. 5⅜ x 8. T367 Paperbound $1.00

**MY BEST PROBLEMS IN MATHEMATICS, Hubert Phillips ("Caliban").** Only elementary mathematics needed to solve these 100 witty, catchy problems by a master problem creator. Problems on the odds in cards and dice, problems in geometry, algebra, permutations, even problems that require no math at all—just a logical mind, clear thinking. Solutions completely worked out. If you enjoy mysteries, alerting your perceptive powers and exercising your detective's eye, you'll find these cryptic puzzles a challenging delight. Original 1961 publication. 100 puzzles, solutions. x + 107pp. 5⅝ x 8. T91 Paperbound $1.00

**MY BEST PUZZLES IN LOGIC AND REASONING, Hubert Phillips ("Caliban").** A new collection of 100 inferential and logical puzzles chosen from the best that have appeared in England, available for first time in U.S. By the most endlessly resourceful puzzle creator now living. All data presented are both necessary and sufficient to allow a single unambiguous answer. No special knowledge is required for problems ranging from relatively simple to completely original one-of-a-kinds. Guaranteed to please beginners and experts of all ages. Original publication. 100 puzzles, full solutions. x + 107pp. 5⅜ x 8. T119 Paperbound $1.00

# CATALOGUE OF DOVER BOOKS

**THE BOOK OF MODERN PUZZLES, G. L. Kaufman.** A completely new series of puzzles as fascinating as crossword and deduction puzzles but based upon different principles and techniques. Simple 2-minute teasers, word labyrinths, design and pattern puzzles, logic and observation puzzles — over 150 braincrackers. Answers to all problems. 116 illustrations. 192pp. 5⅜ x 8.
.T143 Paperbound **$1.00**

**NEW WORD PUZZLES, G. L. Kaufman.** 100 ENTIRELY NEW puzzles based on words and their combinations that will delight crossword puzzle, Scrabble and Jotto fans. Chess words, based on the moves of the chess king; design-onyms; symmetrical designs made of synonyms; rhymed double-crostics; syllable sentences; addle letter anagrams; alphagrams; linkograms; and many others all brand new. Full solutions. Space to work problems. 196 figures. vi + 122pp. 5⅜ x 8.
T344 Paperbound **$1.00**

**MAZES AND LABYRINTHS: A BOOK OF PUZZLES, W. Shepherd.** Mazes, formerly associated with mystery and ritual, are still among the most intriguing of intellectual puzzles. This is a novel and different collection of 50 amusements that embody the principle of the maze: mazes in the classical tradition; 3-dimensional, ribbon, and Möbius-strip mazes; hidden messages; spatial arrangements; etc.—almost all built on amusing story situations. 84 illustrations. Essay on maze psychology. Solutions. xv + 122pp. 5⅜ x 8.
T731 Paperbound **$1.00**

**MAGIC TRICKS & CARD TRICKS, W. Jonson.** Two books bound as one. 52 tricks with cards, 37 tricks with coins, bills, eggs, smoke, ribbons, slates, etc. Details on presentation, misdirection, and routining will help you master such famous tricks as the Changing Card, Card in the Pocket, Four Aces, Coin Through the Hand, Bill in the Egg, Afghan Bands, and over 75 others. If you follow the lucid exposition and key diagrams carefully, you will finish these two books with an astonishing mastery of magic. 106 figures. 224pp. 5⅜ x 8. T909 Paperbound **$1.00**

**PANORAMA OF MAGIC, Milbourne Christopher.** A profusely illustrated history of stage magic, a unique selection of prints and engravings from the author's private collection of magic memorabilia, the largest of its kind. Apparatus, stage settings and costumes; ingenious ads distributed by the performers and satiric broadsides passed around in the streets ridiculing pompous showmen; programs; decorative souvenirs. The lively text, by one of America's foremost professional magicians, is full of anecdotes about almost legendary wizards: Dede, the Egyptian; Philadelphia, the wonder-worker; Robert-Houdin, "the father of modern magic;" Harry Houdini; scores more. Altogether a pleasure package for anyone interested in magic, stage setting and design, ethnology, psychology, or simply in unusual people. A Dover original. 295 illustrations; 8 in full color. Index. viii + 216pp. 8⅜ x 11¼.
T774 Paperbound **$2.25**

**HOUDINI ON MAGIC, Harry Houdini.** One of the greatest magicians of modern times explains his most prized secrets. How locks are picked, with illustrated picks and skeleton keys; how a girl is sawed into twins; how to walk through a brick wall — Houdini's explanations of 44 stage tricks with many diagrams. Also included is a fascinating discussion of great magicians of the past and the story of his fight against fraudulent mediums and spiritualists. Edited by W.B. Gibson and M.N. Young. Bibliography. 155 figures, photos. xv + 280pp. 5⅜ x 8.
T384 Paperbound **$1.35**

**MATHEMATICS, MAGIC AND MYSTERY, Martin Gardner.** Why do card tricks work? How do magicians perform astonishing mathematical feats? How is stage mind-reading possible? This is the first book length study explaining the application of probability, set theory, theory of numbers, topology, etc., to achieve many startling tricks. Non-technical, accurate, detailed! 115 sections discuss tricks with cards, dice, coins, knots, geometrical vanishing illusions, how a Curry square "demonstrates" that the sum of the parts may be greater than the whole, and dozens of others. No sleight of hand necessary! 135 illustrations. xii + 174pp. 5⅜ x 8.
T335 Paperbound **$1.00**

**EASY-TO-DO ENTERTAINMENTS AND DIVERSIONS WITH COINS, CARDS, STRING, PAPER AND MATCHES, R. M. Abraham.** Over 300 tricks, games and puzzles will provide young readers with absorbing fun. Sections on card games; paper-folding; tricks with coins, matches and pieces of string; games for the agile; toy-making from common household objects; mathematical recreations; and 50 miscellaneous pastimes. Anyone in charge of groups of youngsters, including hard-pressed parents, and in need of suggestions on how to keep children sensibly amused and quietly content will find this book indispensable. Clear, simple text, copious number of delightful line drawings and illustrative diagrams. Originally titled "Winter Nights Entertainments." Introduction by Lord Baden Powell. 329 illustrations. v + 186pp. 5⅜ x 8½.
T921 Paperbound **$1.00**

**STRING FIGURES AND HOW TO MAKE THEM, Caroline Furness Jayne.** 107 string figures plus variations selected from the best primitive and modern examples developed by Navajo, Apache, pygmies of Africa, Eskimo, in Europe, Australia, China, etc. The most readily understandable, easy-to-follow book in English on perennially popular recreation. Crystal-clear exposition; step-by-step diagrams. Everyone from kindergarten children to adults looking for unusual diversion will be endlessly amused. Index. Bibliography. Introduction by A. C. Haddon. 17 full-page plates. 960 illustrations. xxiii + 401pp. 5⅜ x 8½.
T152 Paperbound **$2.00**

# Psychology

**YOGA: A SCIENTIFIC EVALUATION, Kovoor T. Behanan.** A complete reprinting of the book that for the first time gave Western readers a sane, scientific explanation and analysis of yoga. The author draws on controlled laboratory experiments and personal records of a year as a disciple of a yoga, to investigate yoga psychology, concepts of knowledge, physiology, "supernatural" phenomena, and the ability to tap the deepest human powers. In this study under the auspices of Yale University Institute of Human Relations, the strictest principles of physiological and psychological inquiry are followed throughout. Foreword by W. A. Miles, Yale University. 17 photographs. Glossary. Index. xx + 270pp. 5⅜ x 8. T505 Paperbound **$2.00**

**CONDITIONED REFLEXES: AN INVESTIGATION OF THE PHYSIOLOGICAL ACTIVITIES OF THE CEREBRAL CORTEX, I. P. Pavlov.** Full, authorized translation of Pavlov's own survey of his work in experimental psychology reviews entire course of experiments, summarizes conclusions, outlines psychological system based on famous "conditioned reflex" concept. Details of technical means used in experiments, observations on formation of conditioned reflexes, function of cerebral hemispheres, results of damage, nature of sleep, typology of nervous system, significance of experiments for human psychology. Trans. by Dr. G. V. Anrep, Cambridge Univ. 235-item bibliography. 18 figures. 445pp. 5⅜ x 8.                    S614 Paperbound **$2.35**

**EXPLANATION OF HUMAN BEHAVIOUR, F. V. Smith.** A major intermediate-level introduction to and criticism of 8 complete systems of the psychology of human behavior, with unusual emphasis on theory of investigation and methodology. Part I is an illuminating analysis of the problems involved in the explanation of observed phenomena, and the differing viewpoints on the nature of causality. Parts II and III are a closely detailed survey of the systems of McDougall, Gordon Allport, Lewin, the Gestalt group, Freud, Watson, Hull, and Tolman. Biographical notes. Bibliography of over 800 items. 2 Indexes. 38 figures. xii + 460pp. 5½ x 8¾.
T253 Clothbound **$6.00**

**SEX IN PSYCHO-ANALYSIS (formerly CONTRIBUTIONS TO PSYCHO-ANALYSIS), S. Ferenczi.** Written by an associate of Freud, this volume presents countless insights on such topics as impotence, transference, analysis and children, dreams, symbols, obscene words, masturbation and male homosexuality, paranoia and psycho-analysis, the sense of reality, hypnotism and therapy, and many others. Also includes full text of THE DEVELOPMENT OF PSYCHO-ANALYSIS by Ferenczi and Otto Rank. Two books bound as one. Total of 406pp. 5⅜ x 8.
T324 Paperbound **$1.85**

**BEYOND PSYCHOLOGY, Otto Rank.** One of Rank's most mature contributions, focussing on the irrational basis of human behavior as a basic fact of our lives. The psychoanalytic techniques of myth analysis trace to their source the ultimates of human existence: fear of death, personality, the social organization, the need for love and creativity, etc. Dr. Rank finds them stemming from a common irrational source, man's fear of final destruction. A seminal work in modern psychology, this work sheds light on areas ranging from the concept of immortal soul to the sources of state power. 291pp. 5⅜ x 8.              T485 Paperbound **$2.00**

**ILLUSIONS AND DELUSIONS OF THE SUPERNATURAL AND THE OCCULT, D. H. Rawcliffe.** Holds up to rational examination hundreds of persistent delusions including crystal gazing, automatic writing, table turning, mediumistic trances, mental healing, stigmata, lycanthropy, live burial, the Indian Rope Trick, spiritualism, dowsing, telepathy, clairvoyance, ghosts, ESP, etc. The author explains and exposes the mental and physical deceptions involved, making this not only an exposé of supernatural phenomena, but a valuable exposition of characteristic types of abnormal psychology. Originally titled "The Psychology of the Occult." 14 illustrations. Index. 551pp. 5⅜ x 8.                    T503 Paperbound **$2.00**

**THE PRINCIPLES OF PSYCHOLOGY, William James.** The full long-course, unabridged, of one of the great classics of Western literature and science. Wonderfully lucid descriptions of human mental activity, the stream of thought, consciousness, time perception, memory, imagination, emotions, reason, abnormal phenomena, and similar topics. Original contributions are integrated with the work of such men as Berkeley, Binet, Mills, Darwin, Hume, Kant, Royce, Schopenhauer, Spinoza, Locke, Descartes, Galton, Wundt, Lotze, Herbart, Fechner, and scores of others. All contrasting interpretations of mental phenomena are examined in detail — introspective analysis, philosophical interpretation, and experimental research. "A classic," JOURNAL OF CONSULTING PSYCHOLOGY. "The main lines are as valid as ever," PSYCHO-ANALYTICAL QUARTERLY. "Standard reading . . . a classic of interpretation," PSYCHIATRIC QUARTERLY. 94 illustrations. 1408pp. 2 volumes. 5⅜ x 8.      Vol. 1, T381 Paperbound **$2.50**
Vol. 2, T382 Paperbound **$2.50**

**THE DYNAMICS OF THERAPY IN A CONTROLLED RELATIONSHIP, Jessie Taft.** One of the most important works in literature of child psychology, out of print for 25 years. Outstanding disciple of Rank describes all aspects of relationship or Rankian therapy through concise, simple elucidation of theory underlying her actual contacts with two seven-year olds. Therapists, social caseworkers, psychologists, counselors, and laymen who work with children will all find this important work an invaluable summation of method, theory of child psychology. xix + 296pp. 5⅜ x 8.                    T325 Paperbound **$1.75**

**SELECTED PAPERS ON HUMAN FACTORS IN THE DESIGN AND USE OF CONTROL SYSTEMS, Edited by H. Wallace Sinaiko.** Nine of the most important papers in this area of increasing interest and rapid growth. All design engineers who have encountered problems involving man as a system-component will find this volume indispensable, both for its detailed information about man's unique capacities and defects, and for its comprehensive bibliography of articles and journals in the human-factors field. Contributors include Chapanis, Birmingham, Adams, Fitts and Jones, etc. on such topics as Theory and Methods for Analyzing Errors in Man-Machine Systems, A Design Philosophy for Man-Machine Control Systems, Man's Senses as Informational Channels, The Measurement of Human Performance, Analysis of Factors Contributing to 460 "Pilot Error" Experiences, etc. Name, subject indexes. Bibliographies of over 400 items. 27 figures. 8 tables. ix + 405pp. 6⅛ x 9¼.          S140 Paperbound **$2.75**

**THE ANALYSIS OF SENSATIONS, Ernst Mach.** Great study of physiology, psychology of perception, shows Mach's ability to see material freshly, his "incorruptible skepticism and independence." (Einstein). Relation of problems of psychological perception to classical physics, supposed dualism of physical and mental, principle of continuity, evolution of senses, will as organic manifestation, scores of experiments, observations in optics, acoustics, music, graphics, etc. New introduction by T. S. Szasz, M. D. 58 illus. 300-item bibliography. Index. 404pp. 5⅜ x 8.          S525 Paperbound **$1.75**

**PRINCIPLES OF ANIMAL PSYCHOLOGY, N. R. F. Maier and T. C. Schneirla.** The definitive treatment of the development of animal behavior and the comparative psychology of all animals. This edition, corrected by the authors and with a supplement containing 5 of their most important subsequent articles, is a "must" for biologists, psychologists, zoologists, and others. First part of book includes analyses and comparisons of the behavior of characteristic types of animal life—from simple multicellular animals through the evolutionary scale to reptiles and birds, tracing the development of complexity in adaptation. Two-thirds of the book covers mammalian life, developing further the principles arrived at in Part I. New preface by the authors. 153 illustrations and tables. Extensive bibliographic material. Revised indices. xvi + 683pp. 5⅜ x 8½.          S1120 Paperbound **$3.00** (tentative)

**ERROR AND ECCENTRICITY IN HUMAN BELIEF, Joseph Jastrow.** From 180 A.D. to the 1930's, the surprising record of human credulity: witchcraft, miracle workings, animal magnetism, mind-reading, astral-chemistry, dowsing, numerology, etc. The stories and exposures of the theosophy of Madame Blavatsky and her followers, the spiritism of Helene Smith, the imposture of Kaspar Hauser, the history of the Ouija board, the puppets of Dr. Luy, and dozens of other hoaxers and cranks, past and present. "As a potpourri of strange beliefs and ideas, it makes excellent reading," New York Times. Formerly titled "Wish and Wisdom, Episodes in the Vagaries of Belief." Unabridged publication. 56 illustrations and photos. 22 full-page plates. Index. xv + 394pp. 5⅜ x 8½.          T986 Paperbound **$1.85**

**THE PHYSICAL DIMENSIONS OF CONSCIOUSNESS, Edwin G. Boring.** By one of the ranking psychologists of this century, a major work which reflected the logical outcome of a progressive trend in psychological theory—a movement away from dualism toward physicalism. Boring, in this book, salvaged the most important work of the structuralists and helped direct the mainstream of American psychology into the neo-behavioristic channels of today. Unabridged republication of original (1933) edition. New preface by the author. Indexes. 17 illustrations. xviii + 251pp. 5⅜ x 8.          S1040 Paperbound **$1.75**

**BRAIN MECHANISMS AND INTELLIGENCE: A QUANTITATIVE STUDY OF INJURIES TO THE BRAIN, K. S. Lashley.** A major contemporary psychologist examines the influence of brain injuries upon the capacity to learn, retentiveness, the formation of the maze habit, etc. Also: the relation of reduced learning ability to sensory and motor defects, the nature of the deterioration following cerebral lesions, comparison of the rat with other forms, and related matters. New introduction by Prof. D. O. Hebb. Bibliography. Index. xxii + 200pp. 5⅜ x 8½.          T1038 Paperbound **$1.75**

*Prices subject to change without notice.*

*Dover publishes books on art, music, philosophy, literature, languages, history, social sciences, psychology, handcrafts, orientalia, puzzles and entertainments, chess, pets and gardens, books explaining science, intermediate and higher mathematics, mathematical physics, engineering, biological sciences, earth sciences, classics of science, etc. Write to:*

*Dept. catrr.*
*Dover Publications, Inc.*
*180 Varick Street, N.Y. 14, N.Y.*

## DATE DUE